Obama's America

Obama's America

A Transformative Vision of Our National Identity

IAN REIFOWITZ

FOREWORD BY ELLIS COSE

Potomac Books
Washington, D.C.

Published in the United States by Potomac Books, Inc. All rights reserved. No part of this book may be reproduced in any manner whatsoever without written permission from the publisher, except in the case of brief quotations embodied in critical articles and reviews.

Library of Congress Cataloging-in-Publication Data
Reifowitz, Ian.
  Obama's America : a transformative vision of our national identity / Ian Reifowitz.—1st ed.
    p. cm.
  Includes bibliographical references and index.
  ISBN 978-1-61234-472-0 (hardcover : alk. paper)—ISBN 978-1-61234-473-7 (electronic)
  1. Obama, Barack—Influence. 2. Obama, Barack—Social and political views. 3. National characteristics, American. 4. Multiculturalism—United States. 5. Political culture—United States. 6. United States—Race relations. 7. United States—Ethnic relations. 8. United States—Politics and government—2009- I. Title.
  E908.3.R45 2012
  973.932—dc23

                                                          2012014719

Printed in the United States of America on acid-free paper that meets the American National Standards Institute Z39-48 Standard.

Potomac Books
22841 Quicksilver Drive
Dulles, Virginia 20166

First Edition

10 9 8 7 6 5 4 3 2 1

To my daughters,
Lauren and Kate,
whom I love with all my heart

Contents

Foreword

For centuries, blacks and assorted other so-called minorities in America were defined by their otherness—their options circumscribed by the general assumption that they were too alien, too indigestible, to fully melt into the American pot. In *The Souls of Black Folk*, W. E. B. Du Bois poignantly described the bewilderment and alienation that such beliefs could engender: "[It] dawned upon me . . . that I was different from the others; or like, mayhap, in heart and life and longing, but shut out from their world by a vast veil."

With the election of Barack Obama, many Americans believe, that veil was forever lifted. With one grand gesture, America shook off the prejudices of its past and fully embraced a presidential candidate with visible ancestry from a continent once deemed so savage that its offspring were relegated to the role of slave.

Obama's march to the presidency was America's second beginning; its opportunity, at long last, to exorcise the ghost of Jim Crow. And if public opinion polls are to be believed, a substantial number of Americans thought that their country had finally got things right. Of all the surveys taken in the wake of Obama's victory, the most intriguing came courtesy of CNN. It was an attempt, on the eve of Obama's inauguration, to measure how far we had come since Martin Luther King Jr. challenged America to "live out the true meaning of its creed: 'We hold these truths to be self-evident, that all men are created equal.'"

The question posed by CNN/Opinion Research Corporation in January 2009 was this: "Martin Luther King gave his famous 'I Have a Dream Speech' at a civil rights march in Washington in 1963. In your view, do you think the U.S. has fulfilled the vision King outlined in that speech, or don't you think so?"

Americans were evenly divided in their responses: 49 percent said yes, and 49 percent said no. In January 2011, CNN repeated the question in a new poll, and the results were essentially the same: 48 percent said yes, and 49 percent said no. Among black Americans, the percentage agreeing that King's vision had been fulfilled was substantially higher. When asked the question in 2009, some 69 percent said yes. CNN did not break out the African American responses separately in 2011, presumably owing to the small sample size.

For a nation less than a century removed from the age when blacks could be lynched with impunity, a nation only two generations away from the death of Jim Crow, a nation still wrestling with the reality of highly segregated ghettos in its midst, that was an amazing self-assessment. And it said volumes about the eagerness of Americans—and blacks in particular—to embrace the prospect of change, particularly given that the assessment, only a few months prior to Obama's election, had not been nearly as optimistic. In early 2008 (the poll was conducted between March 26 and April 2) when CNN asked the question regarding King's dream of racial equality, only 34 percent of respondents were ready to say that King's vision had been realized. It's extremely unlikely that the reality on the ground changed so much in a few months.

While researching my book *The End of Anger*, I asked David Thomas, a black Harvard Business School professor, to give his assessment of the CNN survey results. He laughed and replied, "It's irrational exuberance"—a phrase coined by former Federal Reserve Board chairman Alan Greenspan to describe why investors pour money into collapsing financial assets, artificially and temporarily inflating their value.

I'm inclined to agree that there was something irrational about the judgment. There is simply no real evidence that Obama's election was such a game changer, that it substantially altered, in any measurable way, the condition of most blacks or other people of color in America. And certainly, it did not make America a place where all men are created equal—a point the Occupy Wall Street movement drove home.

What it did was show that America was ready to take a step that many, probably most, African Americans had not dared to believe it would take any time soon—if ever. So by the simple act of getting himself elected president of the United States, Barack Obama hacked a huge chunk out of a glacier of black pessimism. And he simultaneously gave whites an opportunity to collectively congratulate themselves for eschewing racial favoritism and elevating a deserving black son.

Not surprisingly, many Americans considered that quite a big deal. Following Obama's election, Gallup's pollsters essentially asked respondents to rank the importance of the event. More than two-thirds said that they considered Obama's election among the top three advances for blacks in the last hundred years.

So why was his election so important? Is it because by making it into the Oval Office, Obama expanded the public's perception of what is possible for a black man in America to become? Or does its importance go far beyond that? Put another way: Is there something special about Obama himself? Does he possess personal qualities that are so remarkable, and leadership skills so potentially transformative, that he will lead America to a state of higher consciousness?

Ian Reifowitz does not pose the question precisely that way. But he makes it clear that he believes that Obama's presidency is incredibly important for reasons other than Obama's race, that, in his opinion, Obama does indeed have particular gifts and preoccupations that make him the right leader for our republic at this particular juncture.

Obama's America is not a book that rehashes the 2008 presidential campaign in an attempt to explain Obama's political breakthrough. Reifowitz is more concerned with Obama's political rhetoric, his uniquely American vision, and the evolution of an identity and a personality uniquely suited, he argues, to bring Americans together.

For a work of political analysis, *Obama's America* is refreshingly free of cynicism. It is, instead, a forthright expression of faith in the United States, and of its potential, under the guidance of a rhetorically and intellectually gifted president, to realize the potential the Founding Fathers said they believed in all along. That ideal is, of course, of an America where people stand together, irrespective of race, religion, or creed—an ideal that has never quite been the American reality.

Given our history of racial divisions and animosity, and our recurring—and still evident—worries about immigrants deemed difficult to integrate, it's hard to see how we will ever become a nation where all its members feel included and where the national sense of identity always triumphs over narrow ethnocentrism. But that, as Reifowitz makes clear, is a vision Obama holds dear; and that, in a sense, is the promise of his presidency.

As I observed in *The End of Anger*, "Obama was not the first black person to run for president. Numerous others came before him, including Shirley Chisholm, Carol Moseley Braun, Alan Keyes, Al Sharpton, and, most famously, Jesse Jackson. But none of them expected to win. Their campaigns were about something else—about making a point, making a name, or collecting delegates with which to bargain."

Precisely because Obama was running to win, he did not have the luxury of tailoring his appeal to a relatively narrow audience—and certainly not to fellow persons of color. He did not have the leeway of a Jesse Jackson or an Al Sharpton. For his message to be taken seriously at all, it had to be an inclusive one. Certainly, no black man preaching anything remotely resembling identity politics would have made it through the Iowa caucuses and the New Hampshire primary—early and essential contests in predominantly white states where a black candidate even hinting at favoring one group over another would have quickly dropped to the bottom of the heap. Obviously, Obama prevailed. He handily won the Iowa caucuses on January 3, 2008, and came in a close second to Hillary Clinton in the New Hampshire primary five days later.

But the fact that Obama had no choice but to hew to a certain line does not diminish the skill or enthusiasm with which he has carried out his self-appointed task, or the sincerity with which he approached it. His presidential rhetoric, and indeed his entire political life, confirms his faith in the American promise.

Obama's approach—which favors race-blind policies that potentially benefit people of all hues as opposed to race-based schemes of remediation—is arguably the only sane way to go in an increasingly multicultural America. It is also, as I have earlier suggested, probably the only way he can go while preserving any share of political viability. And to the extent that a nation can be said to have a psychology, Obama's way is clearly preferable to one that focuses primarily on differences—on those things, in other words, that divide us.

His approach also is something of a necessary corrective to the unthinking assumptions that have led generations to believe that the real America is a very white place, and to the corrosive rhetoric that, in effect, assumes that white racial privilege is a natural right. As Reifowitz puts it, "Obama seeks to help America transcend whiteness, just as it once transcended WASP-ness."

The debate has raged for a while over whether such an approach in policy can conceivably repair the deep race-based inequities that derive from slavery—America's well-acknowledged original sin—and from its lingering successors, which lasted well into the twentieth century. It is not at all clear that it easily can. And Obama's challenge, indeed the challenge of any national politician who aspires to greatness, will be to figure out a way to mobilize public energy behind a real movement for economic and social equity.

I am, by nature and training, a skeptic. It comes with the territory of being a journalist. So I am not as confident as Reifowitz that Obama's presidency will have a transformative impact that approaches that of Abraham Lincoln. But then, Lincoln had an even bigger challenge. He was tasked with uniting a nation that was literally split asunder. For all the incivility and narrow-mindedness rampant in our culture, we are not now on the verge of a civil war.

Like Reifowitz, I have no doubt Obama will give us a big push in the direction of inclusiveness. For whatever so-called birthers and Tea Partiers may say, America's past is not its future. Obama's election, and his rhetoric, is pushing us in a direction where we were inevitably headed—toward a recognition that America, and Americanness, belongs to all of its citizens equally.

There is something very heartening about seeing a dark-skinned president claiming America as his own, asserting, not just by his words but his presence, that he, and others who resemble him, are taking their place in the American family alongside other children of the republic. But despite Obama's election, we, as a nation, have clearly not completed our journey. And Reifowitz is far too clear-eyed to suggest that we have. The United States will continue to struggle with deep divisions, at least some of them having something to do with race. But we can justifiably celebrate our collective awakening, engendered in part by the Obama presidency, to our nation's demographic reality.

But, as I have already noted, embracing the broadening reality is not, in and of itself, a policy to deal with growing inequality. Indeed, in some respects, it may make that inequality more difficult to see, since disadvantage is much less color-coded than it used to be. A great, transformative president would help us to see it anyway, and he would inspire us to make good on the ever-more elusive promise of equal opportunity for all.

It is possible that Obama will become that president. I certainly hope so.

Ellis Cose
former columnist, *Newsweek*
author of *The End of Anger* and *The Rage of a Privileged Class*

Preface

This book is the culmination of almost two decades of work on multiethnic societies, nationalism, and identity. I have a personal interest in the topic. My writing reflects a deep desire to see the success of efforts to strengthen national unity and inculcate an inclusive American national identity.

Having learned from my early explorations of history about the depths to which humanity has sunk—the incomprehensible actions people have taken when motivated by a belief in the superiority of their own tribe, however defined—I decided to devote myself to understanding how a diverse society could develop more inclusionary and unifying concepts of national identity, asking whether it is possible develop a healthy, cohesive nationalism that lacks ethnic or national chauvinism.

I began by studying Austria-Hungary, a classic example of a multiethnic state that failed to do so. My first book, *Imagining an Austrian Nation*, examined the attempt to cultivate a common national identity that could bring together the many peoples of the Austro-Hungarian Empire. Some of the thinkers and politicians I studied—people writing and speaking around the year 1900—accurately predicted the horrors that extreme ethnic nationalism would unleash in central Europe only two generations later. That study taught me how to diagnose and explain both the factors that create national unity and those that tear it apart. And although I was studying Europe, I always maintained an interest in how the United States has dealt with similar questions. In recent years I found myself applying what I learned about the past to the present and future. I wrote a few short articles dealing with pluralism in this country and sought a way to explore these questions in more depth.

Even before I began my academic studies, I had come to believe that America must figure out how to strengthen national unity in a way that would speak to citizens of every background. For me, as an individual, recognizing and embracing my own membership in the American family has given me a coherent way of understanding my relationship with and commitment to the people with whom I share this land.

I came to believe that an American national identity, if properly constructed as a force for inclusion and equality, could serve as a powerful alternative both to a tribalism that seeks to divide us into groups based on ethnicity, culture, and/or religion, as well as to an atomizing and dehumanizing form of hyperindividualism. Furthermore, I came to believe that the way to spread this vision was by teaching the story of America as the journey by which, gradually, and with much suffering and struggle, the idea of equality has largely triumphed over various forms of prejudice, racism, or chauvinism. Those successes, along with the struggles still in progress, are the story of how we, as a country, have broadened the circle of who is an American.

Barack Obama speaks about our national identity and our country's history along exactly these lines. To him, America is fundamentally about the coming together of many peoples into one family, a process—not yet complete—of overcoming deeply ingrained divisions and creating unity. President Obama shines a light on the harsh periods of American history, but also puts the strides made toward progress on center stage. Hearing him speak this way the night he won the Iowa caucuses, January 3, 2008, inspired me to embark on an in-depth study of his bold attempt to transform how we define ourselves as a people. This book is the result of that study.

Acknowledgments

There are many I want to thank and acknowledge for giving me assistance, guidance, and support in the writing of this book. In terms of institutional support, I am grateful to Empire State College of the State University of New York, my professional home since 2002, which awarded me a sabbatical year to research and write the book full-time as well as financial support to help with developmental editing.

The very first person with whom I consulted about this topic—when it was just a few paragraphs for a possible article—was Steven Beller. His encouragement early on was crucial, as were his comments on various chapters. Additionally, Steven's work on pluralism has profoundly influenced my approach to the questions I explore in this book.

Aviel Roshwald not only gave me constructive suggestions on the manuscript, but he also provided a blueprint of how to become a scholar with broad intellectual horizons and how to not be restricted by geography or time period. Daniel Katz, until recently my fellow historian at Empire State College, offered incredibly detailed, helpful feedback on an early version of the book. I am grateful to a number of others who commented on significant sections of it: Joseph McCartin, Jennifer Mercieca, Justin Vaughn, Richard Greenwald, Stirling Newberry, Marcia Dawkins, Alan Mandell, Jeffrey Zalar, and Marsha Rozenblit.

There were many times that I thought this book would never be liberated from my hard drive, and I want to thank my agent, Robert Astle, for believing in my work and for finding a publisher who did so as well. I want to thank Hilary Claggett, my editor at Potomac Books, for her steadfast support for my writing and her incredible expertise in turning a manuscript into a book, as well as Aryana Hendrawan at Potomac, my production editor, for all her work getting the manuscript into its final form. Additionally, I received invaluable editing help from Hillel Black. I want also to give special thanks to Karen Adams, who read through the entire manuscript at two different stages, offering detailed editorial critiques that ranged from line edits to the level of conceptual framework, and also helped me find the person who became my agent. Finally, a heartfelt thank you to Ellis Cose for taking the time to read my work and write the foreword.

My education on American national identity really began when I first picked up Michael Lind's *The Next American Nation*, which put me on an intellectual path that brought me to this book. My uncle Leslie Schuster, a professor of political science, recommended Lind's book to me more than fifteen years ago. Without him, this book may not have happened.

On a more personal note, I could not have written this book without my family. Most importantly, the love and support (both emotional and editorial) of my wife, Jane Kaufman, has sustained me throughout this project, for that I will be eternally grateful. Additionally, having two young children and a spouse who works more than full-time means that I have had a lot of help taking care of the kids. More than just help, I have been blessed to have the peace of mind knowing that my daughters, when I was at work and they weren't in school, were with people who love them: my mother, Helaine Reifowitz, my aunt Genie Schuster, my grandmother (!) Doris Moldovan, and my in-laws, Judy and Bill Kaufman. Finally, I want to acknowledge my father, Jerry Reifowitz, who passed away on February 1, 2010. His and my mother's encouragement and unconditional love over a lifetime helped give me the confidence to pursue this project to completion.

Introduction

Barack Obama is a different kind of president. What Obama brings to the presidency is something far more important than simply being an African American. This book focuses on his particular understanding of what it means to be an American and his commitment to transforming the way we define our national identity by making it fully and equally inclusive of all Americans. From his recognition of the slaves who helped build the White House, to his defense of the right of Muslims to build a mosque in lower Manhattan, to his declaration of support for same-sex marriage, to his acknowledgment of religious nonbelievers in his inaugural address, to his belief that every American deserves access to health care, Obama places inclusiveness at the core of his vision of American national identity. A country's national identity is a living organism, and Obama hopes to change ours in a subtle yet fundamental way.

What does national identity mean? Political scientist Elizabeth Theiss-Morse has explained that the feeling of belonging to a national community—the depth with which Americans think of themselves as part of a "we"—is at the core of what national identity means.[1] According to political theorist David Miller, the content of that national identity includes a "common public culture . . . a set of understandings about how a group of people is to conduct its life together. . . . This will include political principles . . . but it reaches more widely."[2]

True national unity exists in a society where all its members strongly feel that sense of national identity, where all of them feel included in that national community. Political theorist Juliet Hooker characterized the development of this kind of national unity or "political solidarity" as a crucial "challenge" for democratic societies, all of which have some degree of ethnic diversity. She continued, "The task is how to build solidarity among citizens who are strangers to one another."[3] Obama has focused on accomplishing this very task throughout his entire public career.

In Obama's "The America We Love" speech of June 30, 2008, he described the content of our national identity as being not "just loyalty to a place on a map or a certain kind of people. Instead, it is also loyalty to America's ideals—ideals for which anyone can sacrifice, or defend, or give their last full measure of devotion. I believe it is this loyalty that allows a country teeming with different races and ethnicities, religions, and customs, to come together as one."[4] He believes that this kind of national identity can unify America's diverse population because it complements those other forms of belonging.

In his January 24, 2012, State of the Union address, the president spoke of the cohesion that members of a successful military unit feel, bonds that transcend anything that might divide them, and called on us to embrace a similar kind of national unity as Americans:

> "When you put on that uniform, it doesn't matter if you're black or white; Asian, Latino. . . conservative, liberal; rich, poor; gay, straight. When you're marching into battle, you look out for the person next to you, or the mission fails. When you're in the thick of the fight, you rise or fall as one unit, serving one Nation, leaving no one behind. . . . So it is with America . . . our destiny is stitched together like those fifty stars and those thirteen stripes. No one built this country on their own. This Nation is great because we built it together. This Nation is great because we worked as a team."

Obama encourages each of us to feel that all our fellow Americans are united with us in "one American family," a term he used in his speech at the 2004 Democratic National Convention and on many occasions since. His conception of America emphasizes two principles of national unity: First, all Americans regardless of their heritage and cultural traditions can and should identify with America as *their* country. Second, America should embrace all its citizens as participant actors in a common plot.

President Obama's definition of our national identity reflects the core of his intellectual worldview as well as his approach to policy, both of which flow from his belief in the importance of empathy, of people's ability to feel a sense of community with someone different from themselves. He has argued that a strong sense of unity among Americans facilitates a willingness on the part of everyone, from every class and/or ethnicity, to sacrifice narrow group or individual interests for the common good, to share resources, and to prioritize the needs of one's fellow Americans, even those from backgrounds that differ from one's own. As Congresswoman Barbara Jordan noted in her keynote address at the 1976 Democratic National Convention, "Let there be no illusions about the difficulty of forming this kind of a national community."[5] However, we must do exactly that in order for our country to survive and thrive.

The Roots of Obama's America

This study locates Obama's ideas within a broader and often contentious debate, more than two centuries old, over our self-understanding as a country and a people. Exactly who is considered worthy of full and equal membership in the American community has evolved over time; nonwhites, Catholics, non-Christians, women, gays, and others were marginalized for centuries. The civil rights movement helped break down most of the final legal barriers to inclusion for black and other nonwhite Americans, although full equality and integration remained elusive.

Thus in the late 1960s, new movements and thinkers emerged who emphasized multiculturalism, an ideology that criticized the traditional idea of American identity and history as disproportionately focused on white, male, elite culture. Multiculturalism sought to expand our idea of national identity to include the perspectives and accomplishments of ethnic and other minorities. For brevity's sake I use the term "ethnic" to characterize groups and/or identities defined by one or more of the following: skin color, race/descent, country of origin, culture, language, and sometimes religion.[6]

As opposed to this mainstream form of multiculturalism, proponents of a more radical form rejected even the concept of a single American identity, contending instead that because America was so unjust nonwhites should focus their energies and loyalties only on their own ethnic group. According to sociologist Amitai Etzioni, radical multiculturalism "entails giving up the concept of shared values, loyalties, and identity in order to privilege ethnic and religious differences."[7] The radicals drew in part on concepts that reached back to the post-Revolutionary period in American history and were especially prominent in earlier black separatist movements.

Obama's rhetoric gathers together diverse strands of the mainstream multicultural approach to American identity and fuses them with aspects of the more traditional, unity-centered approach to produce a vital, inclusive vision of what America has been and ought to be. He draws on the integrative ideology of Martin Luther King Jr., but differs in two key ways: Obama reflects both the influence of mainstream multicultural thought—just emerging at the time of King's murder—as well as the center-left critiques that began appearing in the early 1990s of the more radical forms of multiculturalism.

These liberal and centrist critics of radical multiculturalism called for a renewed attempt both to strengthen American national identity and create a more inclusive society. They argued that achieving these goals required the crafting and instilling of a singular national story in which Americans of all heritages could recognize their own experiences. The story of America that Obama has told reflects these ideas and has the potential to be such a story. Certainly, his presidency makes an inclusive narrative all the more real. Yet Obama hopes to do far more than simply stand as a symbol of how far America has come. He hopes to redefine what America means and to be a transformational figure in its history.

Strengthening National Unity

In the wake of Obama's election to the presidency, many pundits and thinkers proclaimed a new "postracial" era in American history, but neither Obama's conception of American national identity nor his broader political philosophy is "postracial."[8] Obama has explicitly rejected this view, saying to those who have taken his rhetoric to mean that America has solved the problem of racism: "to say that we are one people is not to suggest that race no longer matters."[9] He also noted that our country's problems relating to bigotry "aren't just solved by electing a black president."[10] Obama recognizes, in other words, that ethnic minorities continue to face widespread discrimination in our society. Rather than having—as one critic accused him of doing—"effortlessly transcend[ed] his own blackness," Obama seeks to help America transcend whiteness, just as it transcended WASP-ness by accepting once-marginalized groups like Jews, Italians, and Slavs as full members of the American national community.[11]

The tremendous increase in the nonwhite population in recent years—seen especially in the 2010 census—has certainly challenged preexisting conceptions of who qualifies as an American, namely that being American means being white.

America will have fully transcended whiteness only when it has completely rejected that definition and constructed a new, ethnically neutral vision of American national identity that is fully inclusive of all citizens. The degree to which Obama advances this process will be one key measure of the impact of his presidency.

"Who are we?" is a question that has bedeviled our society for more than two centuries, and President Obama seeks to answer it in a way that Americans of every background can embrace. Obama is an American nationalist in the tradition of men such as Abraham Lincoln, Frederick Douglass, and Martin Luther King Jr. Each of them approached the problem of exclusion from an essentially reformist position, focusing on existing American traditions, institutions, and documents that were being forgotten, ignored, or misapplied but that could serve as the basis for solutions.[12] They sought, in the words of Lincoln, to appeal to the better angels of our nature and to make progress by making the national identity of the American people more inclusive. Obama and these men are American nationalists precisely because they remained committed to the idea that there must exist a set of strong bonds linking together the members of the American community.

Many contemporary politicians and thinkers, even as they are concerned with advancing equality and fairness, too often depict America solely by listing the groups that make up its population. While such an accounting is certainly an improvement over earlier portrayals of America—which before the emergence of multicultural approaches too often ignored women and members of minority groups—it nevertheless fails to encourage the individuals who make up those groups to identify with the larger American community.

Obama seeks to redress this deficiency. He intends to strengthen the bonds among Americans, emphasizing on July 22, 2007, how "our separate struggles are really one." In his writings, in particular *The Audacity of Hope*, in interviews, and especially in numerous speeches, Obama has chronicled our country's past in a distinctive way. In fact, a central aspect of his enterprise in national integration is a bold redescription of American history. For example, in a speech he delivered in Madison, Wisconsin, on February 12, 2008, he gave the historical fights for equality such as the abolitionist movement, the long campaign for female suffrage and gender equality, and the civil rights movement equal billing alongside such customary historical events as the American Revolution and World War II.[13] Additionally, on July 4, 2010, President Obama spoke of how Americans "celebrate the principles that are timeless—tenets first declared by men of property and wealth, but which gave rise to what Lincoln called a 'new birth of freedom' in America: civil rights and voting rights, workers' rights and women's rights, and the rights of every American."

Through this kind of inclusive and unifying rhetoric, Obama has integrated movements often "ghettoized" as separate discourses into the larger national story, changing the way we define the American community. He has presented our history as the story of one people, rather than a collection of discrete stories of different ethnic groups who merely happen to live among one another. Obama's narrative recharacterizes Americans as a people who have fought and won battles against inequality and oppression both abroad and at home, and have over time extended the equality promised to "all men" in the Declaration of Independence to more and more Americans. This narrative also provides Americans of every ethnicity a way to identify with the story of this country going back to the Revolution, to claim that history as their own, and to embrace their membership in the American people.

Since the early 1990s, many thinkers and scholars have cited the need for a reworking of the American story along similar lines (see chapter 2). In calling for this kind of American narrative, for instance, historian Gary Nash asked, "Can there be any grand narrative more powerful, coherent, democratic, and inspiring?"[14] Obama has contended that bolstering all Americans' commitment to our national community requires, among other things, a unifying narrative of our history to help us connect with the movements for equality and justice that have shaped our past and present.

The narrative of our history Obama has presented clearly emphasizes that America lacked a thoroughly egalitarian and democratic governmental system for a good part of its history. Until the reality of American society finally began to match the rhetoric of American democracy—which did not occur for almost two centuries after the American Revolution—it was essentially unrealistic to expect people who were treated unequally to feel that they were being fully included in the American family.

This is not to suggest that members of any group that faced legal discrimination were unpatriotic until the day they achieved legal equality. There are many examples that show that this was certainly not the case: During World War II, Japanese American soldiers served their country with honor, despite the fact that their own government had imprisoned them and their families simply on the basis of their ancestry. One all Japanese American unit, the 442nd Regimental Combat Team, became, for a unit of its size and length of service, the single most decorated unit in American history. African Americans from Crispus Attucks to the Tuskegee Airmen likewise fought valiantly and bled for the United States long before 1948, when President Harry Truman ordered that all military units be desegregated, let alone before the civil rights movement won its greatest victories. The Navajo Code Talkers are only the most famous of the many Native Americans who have fought alongside their fellow Americans in battle. Gays and lesbians have always served and continue to serve in combat despite not even having the right to do so openly by United States law until very recently. Similar examples abound.

Nevertheless, those Americans whom bigotry consigned to a second-class (or worse) legal status could not help but believe that their government and many of their fellow citizens considered them something less than full Americans. Although virtually all those traditional forms of discrimination are now illegal, we have not yet solved the problem of people feeling less than fully American. Social science research indicates that feeling marginalized or excluded because of one's ethnicity influences the way and the degree to which one identifies as an American.[15] Feeling marginalized can result from discrimination but also when people experience more subtle forms of exclusion, whether intentional or unintentional, such as former Alaska governor Sarah Palin's suggestion (discussed further in chapter 8) of October 16, 2008, that only some of us live in "real America."

This matters because as the non-Hispanic white percentage of our population continues to drop we must ensure that those from non-European backgrounds identify themselves as stakeholders in America's future and as members of a single national community. If half the U.S. population considers the other half of the population to be "them" rather than "us," the long-term stability and vitality of this country is at risk. Such a concern is what gives Obama's push to invigorate our national unity its urgency.

The way Obama depicts America emphasizes to ethnic minorities that the country, represented by him as president, embraces them as fellow Americans, while simultaneously emphasizing to whites that those minorities, also represented by Obama, embrace them as fellow Americans. His goal is to enhance the sense of connectedness among these groups and strengthen their understanding of themselves as comprising one American people.

Achieving the widespread acceptance and adoption of his conception of American national identity is undoubtedly part of Obama's larger political strategy, and will enhance support for his policies, his reelection, and to an extent the fortunes of his political allies. The extent to which Obama succeeds as president in the broadest sense thus depends in part on his success in forging a robust feeling of national community. I will argue, however, that his explorations of this topic over two decades demonstrate a sincere commitment to the project of shaping Americans' understanding of their national identity as well as a belief that doing so can have an effect beyond electoral politics.

According to Obama, bolstering our common bonds as Americans will encourage people to rectify the injustices and heal the racial divisions that continue to plague our country—despite the profound progress we have made in recent decades—and to reject the bigotry that feeds them. He believes that when you recognize someone primarily as a fellow American rather than simply as a member of another ethnic group, you will treat that person as you would want to be treated.

Strengthening Americans' sense that we are one family has occupied Obama for much of his personal and professional life, and he has put doing so at the center of his public rhetoric. In 2004, presidential scholar Mary E. Stuckey noted, "perhaps the central question of presidential leadership is whether any universal vision of the national character can create a collective culture without necessarily enacting the vilest forms of exclusion and scapegoating."[16] She ultimately expressed optimism that such an achievement is possible.

At this writing, approximately three years into his presidency, it is clear that challenges to Obama's inclusive vision have arisen that will occupy us for some time. He is nevertheless particularly well positioned to reshape America's definition of itself over the long term. Certainly, other presidents have sought to change what it means to be American. Franklin Roosevelt emphasized our need to work together in new ways to overcome the Great Depression. Ronald Reagan talked of a return to what he saw as traditional moral values.

President Obama, however, is doing something fundamentally different, even from recent presidents—such as Bill Clinton and George W. Bush—who also spoke of diversity. Obama's deliberate and insistent incorporation of the struggles for equality as central planks in America's common chronicle, as well as his unique focus on including members of groups too often ignored by traditional tellings of our history and definitions of our national identity, stand as meaningful points of departure from even the most inclusive rhetoric used by previous presidents.

Obama is not the first president to talk about nonwhites being Americans or to emphasize that historical events like slavery and the struggle for women's suffrage are important parts of our history. Similarly, Abraham Lincoln was not the first public figure to talk about liberty and equality. However, Lincoln at Gettysburg succeeded in putting the need to achieve liberty and equality for all Americans front and center in our national consciousness. He fundamentally transformed the way we understood our national identity. Obama seeks to do the same. He has put forward a more inclusive national narrative than has ever been suggested by a U.S. president, and has devoted far more attention to strengthening our national identity than his predecessors. I thus argue that he has the potential to have a greater impact on the way we understand our national identity than any president since Lincoln.

1

American National Identity

From the Revolution through the 1960s

Who is an American? The American nation, according to the Declaration of Independence, knew no boundaries at its founding. As written, the Declaration did not differentiate among blacks, whites, or members of any ethnic group when discussing the self-evident truth of human equality. The document cited the "good people of these colonies" as the authority by which it declared freedom and independence from the British Crown, but cited no creed, color, or ethnic definition of who these "good people" were. The apparent inclusivity of the language, however, belied an equally self-evident exclusivity. The right to life, liberty, and the pursuit of happiness belonged more to some than to others, and a good part of the American story over the last two-plus centuries has been the struggle to bring reality in line with our revolutionary rhetoric.

The story of our national identity has thus been one of an ever-changing definition of who counted as an American, both in terms of rights and in terms of something more amorphous but equally important, namely full membership in the American family. While the population of the United States was multiethnic upon its founding, the national community, as it was popularly understood, was not. And while the country's basic institutions were forged primarily by those of Anglo-Saxon ethnicity, the publicly stated terms around which the nation was built were almost wholly civic, based on a commitment to shared political principles. These peculiarities, these contradictions within the American case—fueled by the profound changes of the 1960s—gave rise to an academic and cultural debate in the late 1980s and 90s that became the battle over multiculturalism and how to interpret American history.

Barack Obama, born in 1961, is the first president who was educated in the multicultural era, and his rhetoric evinces a deep understanding of the issues in play. He writes and speaks about American national identity in a way that takes seriously not only multicultural ideas, but the critiques of some of their more radical incarnations as well. Although I will talk in more detail later in this chapter and beyond about the fights over how to define our history, let me here explain briefly how they relate to Obama's conception of American identity and how, in more practical terms, their outcome made his rise possible in the first place.

Beginning in the late 1980s, under the pressure of the battles over multiculturalism, the American center-left seemed increasingly unable to preserve its commitment to its traditional political principles—individual liberty, equal rights, and cross-ethnic integration and cooperation. Many liberals began to see a conflict between supporting these principles and supporting cultural diversity. By this time, supporting diversity had essentially come to mean acceptance of any and all cultural forms or norms, and an implicit endorsement of ethnic-based identity politics, i.e., a politics whereby the interests of one's ethnic group took precedence over either the common good or any broader, universal principles, including the aforementioned liberal ones. The pressure liberals felt to support this understanding of diversity over universalist principles was intensified by "political correctness" and the desire to avoid being tarred as Eurocentric or racist. Universalist liberalism was attacked by radical multiculturalism as a "Western" idea hostile to the perspectives of non-Western (i.e., nonwhite) peoples.

In global terms, the moment was crystallized by the refusal of some Western liberals to condemn the 1989 fatwa issued by Iran's Ayatollah Khomeini against Salman Rushdie for his authorship of *The Satanic Verses,* which allegedly blasphemed the prophet Muhammad. For those liberals, the tenets of multiculturalism prevented them from imposing their "Western" values on another culture.[1]

It appeared possible at the time that the center-left might splinter, perhaps irrevocably, into identity politics–based factions, which would likely have led a significant majority of white Christian America to run screaming to the right on the basis of ethnic and cultural solidarity. Thus, in the early to mid-1990s, many on the center-left began calling for a new approach to issues of national identity. Obama has often spoken about moving the country beyond such battles over identity politics and radical multiculturalism, battles that he sees as leftovers from the 1960s.[2] He has clearly incorporated into his public rhetoric many of the ideas put forth by these center-left thinkers in the 1990s, particularly their call for a new and inclusive American civic nationalism.

We can see a clear statement of this vision in Michael Lind's influential *The Next American Nation*, in which he laid out a new, alternative narrative of American history. He provocatively put forth Frederick Douglass as the single iconic American figure, calling him "perhaps the greatest American, of any race, of any century."[3] Lind and other center-left civic nationalists who emerged in this period attacked radical multiculturalism in part because it was poisoning the public's view of liberalism as a whole, making it seem that liberalism's overriding principle was "tolerance," even of ideas that were in fact intolerant and illiberal. These center-left civic nationalist writers identified the need to inculcate a robust, fully functional understanding of our national identity that was both inclusive and unifying, one that could not only compete with those offered by the far left and hard right (which was far less inclusive of the contributions of nonwhites) but also breathe life into center-left ideology. In the end, this center-left vision helped America "turn the page" on the culture wars of the 1990s.

Ultimately, this was far more than an academic debate among scholars, which is why figures deeply entrenched in the world of political debate such as Michael Lind, Pat Buchanan, Arthur Schlesinger, and Lynne Cheney played central roles. What was at stake was whether America could figure out a way to broaden the definition of who counted as an American while at the same time maintaining and even strengthening the idea that there could be a unitary national identity in light of the raging controversy over how (and whether) to balance unity and diversity. If the radicals on the far left had had their way, the goal of American unity would have been cast aside in favor of ethnic identity politics. Had the hard right vision won out, a good deal of the nonwhite population would likely have felt alienated from any meaningful sense of national community and fellowship with white Americans. Had either of these extreme positions become dominant, there could never have been a President Barack Obama because his candidacy and his personal story would have had no political and cultural context in which to operate.

Walker, Douglass, Du Bois, Obama

The gap between the rhetorical promises of the Declaration of Independence and the reality of racism, both in law and in the hearts of their fellow countrymen, was the central feature of life for black Americans for most of our history. For example,

David Walker (1785–1830), a free-born black American who advocated radical resistance to slavery in his early nineteenth-century pamphlet *Walker's Appeal*, recounted the soaring words of the Declaration of Independence before thundering, "See your Declaration, Americans!!! Do you understand your own language? Hear your language, proclaimed to the world, July 4, 1776."[4]

A generation later, Frederick Douglass was invited to give an Independence Day address in Rochester, New York, the town in which he settled after escaping slavery. On July 4, 1852, he pointedly noted "This Fourth [of] July is yours, not mine."[5] He went on:

> What, to the American slave, is your Fourth of July? I answer: a day that reveals to him, more than all other days in the year, the gross injustice and cruelty to which he is the constant victim. To him, your celebration is a sham; your boasted liberty, an unholy license; your national greatness, swelling vanity; your sounds of rejoicing are empty and heartless; your denunciation of tyrants, brass-fronted impudence; your shouts of liberty and equality, hollow mockery; your prayers and hymns, your sermons and thanksgivings, with all your religious parade and solemnity, are, to him, mere bombast, fraud, deception, impiety, and hypocrisy.

It is worth noting that elsewhere in the speech, Douglass expressed hope for the future of black people in America, as he drew "encouragement from the Declaration of Independence, the great principles it contains, and the genius of American institutions." He concluded: "notwithstanding the dark picture I have this day presented of the state of the nation, I do not despair of this country," and predicted the eventual demise of slavery. But his sense of alienation from America's story at that moment is clear. Over time Douglass grew more positive toward the United States, especially in his discussion of the Founders and the revolutionary period.[6]

Fifty-odd years later, when black Americans were legally free but faced widespread and fully legal discrimination and segregation, W. E. B. Du Bois described the "double consciousness" of black Americans, according to which "one ever feels his twoness—an American, a Negro; two warring souls, two thoughts, two unreconciled strivings; two warring ideals in one dark body, whose dogged strength alone keeps it from being torn asunder."[7] Du Bois's description went beyond merely asserting an ethnic identity along with an American one; for him, and for many other black Americans of his day, the two were literally at war with each other.

There is a poignant contrast between Douglass's refusal to identify with what he labeled "your" Fourth of July, or Du Bois's deeply conflicted double consciousness, and the way President Obama has wholly identified the American story as his own, despite the injustices African Americans and others have faced. In the previously mentioned "The America We Love" speech, he remarked: "For me, as for most Americans, patriotism starts as a gut instinct, a loyalty and love for country rooted in my earliest memories. I'm not just talking about the recitations of the Pledge of Allegiance or the Thanksgiving pageants at school or the fireworks on the Fourth of July, as wonderful as those things may be. Rather, I'm referring to the way the American ideal wove its way throughout the lessons my family taught me as a child." In drawing the comparison between Douglass's speech and Obama's, *Washington Post* columnist Colbert I. King remarked, "While Douglass noted his estrangement from America's experiment with democracy, Obama claimed America as his own and the Fourth of July as a time to rejoice."[8]

Similarly, in his keynote address at the 2004 Democratic Convention in Boston (which I discuss in detail in chapter 6), Obama spoke of how our national greatness derives from the principles of equality and liberty enshrined in the Declaration of Independence. As journalist Scott Malcomson noted, "In citing Thomas Jefferson's opening words on equality from the Declaration of Independence, Mr. Obama also broke the mold; African American politicians have not cited those words without sarcasm and qualification for many years, if ever."[9] While Malcomson might have qualified his assessment to account for the occasional nationally known black conservative politician, someone like Alan Keyes, perhaps, who had spoken this way, the point he made remains a powerful one. Looking back at that speech, we can see the influence that Obama has already had on our public discourse, in that a nonwhite politician speaking similarly today would be relatively unremarkable. The mold was indeed broken.

It would certainly be understandable for any African American to resist embracing Independence Day and the Declaration of Independence, even in the twenty-first century. One could argue that July 4, 1776, did nothing directly to weaken slavery or discrimination, in the moment. Obama took a different approach. By publicly embracing these pieces of American history he accomplishes two equally important things: provide encouragement for other African Americans to do so, and refute the untrue but divisive misconception promulgated by some racial demagogues that black Americans do not really identify with the country as a whole or with people beyond their ethnic community. Such accomplishments increase the bonds of national unity.

While the issues at stake today are quite different from those faced by Douglass, Du Bois, or Martin Luther King Jr., it is fair to say that Obama hopes to have as profound an effect on our understanding of ourselves as a people as these men did. In this era, Obama has a different task. As he said in March 2007, he seeks to "transform the country . . . [and] bring diverse parts of this country together in a way that hasn't been done in some time."[10] Obama hopes to invigorate a broader definition of what it means to be American, one that embraces difference rather than founders upon it, and prioritizes membership in the nation without fueling battles that force one to be either black (or white, or Hispanic, etc.) or American. Rather than "either/or," Obama advocates "both/and," i.e., a multilayered understanding of American identity.

This desire, as later chapters will show, grew partially out of his own struggle with his identity as well as from his reading of American history and the study of the ideas put forth by transformative leaders such as Lincoln, King, and Douglass. Like these men, Obama has reached to the founding documents of this country, its traditions, and the narrative of American history to formulate his view of American national identity. But before we examine his ideas in depth, we turn to a history of our national identity and a discussion of national identity in general.

Conceptions of National Identity and the Challenges Multiethnic Societies Face

A society can define its national identity as either civic or ethnic, although few are truly all one or the other.[11] Briefly, these categories are best understood as ideal types we can use to understand various forms of collective identity. In theory ethnic nations base membership on supposedly objective characteristics, while civic nations define membership primarily by a freely chosen loyalty to the national community and a commitment to shared political principles. The most important difference between these two forms of nationalism is neither the level of assimilation required nor the ability of all types of immigrants to obtain citizenship, but rather whether some people are simply ineligible for membership in the national community because of their religion, ancestry (i.e., "blood"), sexual orientation, and/or cultural heritage(s), and so on.

Along these lines, scholar of national identity Oliver Zimmer employs the term "voluntary" to describe the way civic nations define the borders of the national community, and "organic" (i.e., nonvoluntary) to describe how ethnic nations do so, a useful distinction.[12] As virtually every country has some degree of ethnic diversity—whether it wants to admit it or not—each must decide how to define who is a member of the national community.

Irrespective of a given country's official position, in reality even countries that define their national identity in a fundamentally civic/voluntary way might practice some forms of exclusion. Likewise, a country that sees itself primarily as an ethnic/organic nation might allow for some partial inclusion of people normally excluded from the national community.

Although this was not always so, today a recently arrived legal immigrant to the United States might speak poor English and still be largely unfamiliar with American culture and history and yet, if he is making progress on those fronts, and expresses an American identity as well as a desire to become a citizen, that person will find that many people will accept him as a fellow American. One's heritage is not a bar to becoming an American because American national identity is today fundamentally civic/voluntary rather than ethnic/organic. Obama's goal is to push us even further in that direction.

On the other hand, even some democracies still define the nation in ethnic terms and do not fully embrace pluralism, the idea that a national community can consist of members of diverse backgrounds. Imagine the concept of immigrating to Tokyo and "becoming Japanese." I'm not talking even about gaining Japanese citizenship, but winning acceptance as a member of the Japanese national family. While not impossible, it is a far more difficult hurdle to clear than the one facing a Japanese immigrant looking to win acceptance as an American.[13]

In Germany, it remains exceptionally difficult for those of Turkish ancestry, even those born in Germany, to be truly recognized by their fellow citizens as part of the German national community. We can compare this to the ease with which those citizens of the former Soviet Union who have German "blood" but whose ancestors had left Germany centuries earlier were able to return "home" after 1989 to full citizenship and unquestioned membership in the German people, despite being unable to speak a word of German.

Another instructive example among democracies is Israel, which defines itself as the nation-state of the Jewish people. There is much cultural and ethnic diversity in Israel, both in the population as a whole and even within the Jewish population. Nevertheless, the members of the Jewish people in Israel clearly have a different relationship to the state than do non-Jewish Israelis, irrespective of the question of equal rights before the law. Additionally, non-Israeli Jews have an automatic right to citizenship in Israel based on their membership in the Jewish people. One can convert to Judaism, but even then there are debates in Israel about what kind of conversion the authorities would recognize as legitimate enough to earn Israeli citizenship for a non-Israeli convert. Israel, Japan, and Germany all represent democratic countries that in practice define their national communities in ethnic/organic terms.

Most if not all countries look to foster a sense of national unity. Today, countries with relatively homogeneous populations, such as Japan and Poland for example, have drawn upon common cultural and/or religious traditions as well as a perception of common ancestry in developing strong national bonds among their citizens. By contrast, more multiethnic countries—in particular democracies like the United States—have in recent decades attempted to construct and spread a sense of unity based fundamentally on abstract principles of political practice and an integrative civic nationalism that attempts to expand public participation.

Other multiethnic countries like Canada have de-emphasized integration and the attempt to cultivate a strong national identity among its immigrant and non-Anglo population. The recent and sharp rise in the immigration of non-Europeans—in particular Muslims—to Western European countries have forced them grapple with how exactly to redefine their national identities. France has held to its long-standing ideal that people of any background can win acceptance as Frenchmen, so long as they completely abandon their non-French heritage, adopt French culture, and identify themselves as French and French only. Britain, Holland, and Germany have followed more of the Canadian path, allowing or even encouraging immigrant groups to maintain their own collective identities and institutions without strongly emphasizing national unity. Switzerland, although it has long had an explicitly multiethnic definition of its national identity—those of German, French, and Italian background are included—has been far less willing than other European countries to extend citizenship, let alone membership in the national community, to anyone not born in the country, and especially not to nonwhites.[14]

The study of how different countries are faring in their attempts to develop national unity in an era of unprecedented human mobility is well established in the academic literature, which is keen to investigate this crucial matter. Political scientist Robert Putnam, for example, has found that although increases in ethnic diversity initially reduce social interaction and civic engagement, in the long run, "successful immigrant societies have overcome such fragmentation by creating new, cross-cutting forms of social solidarity and more encompassing identities."[15] Accomplishing this goal has, however, proven elusive for many multiethnic countries throughout history. It is worth noting that from 1997 to 2000 Putnam led a seminar series on civic engagement, the Saguaro Seminars, in which Obama participated.[16]

My own thinking on these issues grows out of my study of Austria-Hungary, a classic historical example of a multiethnic society that never achieved this kind of cross-ethnic unity on a widespread basis (others include the Ottoman Empire and the Soviet Union), and which fell apart in the aftermath of World War I. The Austro-Hungarian population included significant numbers of a dozen ethnic groups. As historian Maureen Healy explained, "Austria had not generated a patriotism that allowed fellow citizens to feel a connectedness among themselves. Supranational Austria had failed as an 'imagined community.'"[17] Due in part to this failure, millions of Central Europeans increasingly came to define themselves—as well as their neighbors—in terms of ethnicity or, to put it bluntly, blood. The prevalence of this definition eased the path toward the mass genocide committed by the Nazis and their collaborators against anyone whose blood they deemed inferior.

The Austro-Hungarian example provides two lessons that relate directly to this book. First, a multiethnic country that wants to ensure its long-term health must create a sense of peoplehood, unifying its population into a single community. Doing so requires government and civic institutions, as well as the broader culture, to encourage its adoption. Second, persuading all sectors of the population to adopt that sense of peoplehood requires a fully democratic and egalitarian political system, which Austria-Hungary lacked. Only such a system can encourage buy-in from every citizen. Citizens of a nation who see that their government denies equality to and withholds access to power from their ethnic group will not buy into the system and will not identify themselves as members of the national community. Many countries in the West now face such challenges. As Kamel Hamza, a highly visible member of the Muslim community in France, remarked: "They can't ask us to sing the *Marseillaise* [the French national anthem] when we're young, then when we're adults shut us out of positions of responsibility."[18]

The Changing Definition of American National Identity: The 1780s through the 1960s

Hector St. John de Crèvecoeur, a naturalized American citizen of French extraction, was perhaps the first to write of the American nation in explicitly multiethnic terms. In 1782 he described Americans as a collection of people from many different lands, including England, France, Holland, and other selected countries in the northwestern corner of the Eurasian landmass.[19] According to Crèvecoeur and those who thought similarly, a commitment to democratic political values trumped the differences of ethnicity among Americans of various origins, at least for those whose origins stemmed from northwest Europe. But for those from any other part of the world, their ethnic background rendered irrelevant their allegiance, however deep and sincere, to American ideals. As such, the self-defined American community excluded many who lived in the United States in 1782 on the basis of their ancestry.[20]

Although the population then may not have included significant numbers from Eastern Europe, Asia, or Latin America, black Americans and American Indians certainly were here in sizable numbers. Crèvecoeur, reflecting the mindset of the era, chose not to include them, however, when describing the groups that made up "that race now called American."[21] The element of ethnic exclusion within our national identity was partly codified in the nation's first law on naturalization, enacted in 1790, which declared that only "free white persons" could obtain naturalized citizenship.[22] That restriction remained in force for almost another two hundred years, until ended as part of the Immigration and Nationality Act of 1952.

The changing nature of nineteenth century immigration gradually led to a broadened definition of the American nation.[23] Initially, however, the arrival of millions of Irish Catholics both before and after the Irish Potato Famine that began in 1845—as well as Catholics from Germany and other lands—provoked a vicious Anglo-Protestant nativism that culminated in rise of the "Know-Nothing" or American Party.[24] The avowed purpose of the party was to severely restrict immigration and naturalization in ways that favored white Protestants. For a moment in the early 1850s, between the demise of the Whigs and the rise of the modern Republican Party, the Know-Nothings were the second most popular political party in the country. We can characterize the battles over whether Irish and German Catholic immigrants and their descendants counted as Americans as a confrontation between ethnic and civic ideas of the nation. The ultimate defeat of the Know-Nothings means the civic idea won out for those groups, though members of other ethnic groups continued to face exclusion.

The belief that only those of Anglo-Saxon "blood" were real Americans retained a strong following among the American Establishment for many years, and continues even today in some forms. Herbert Baxter Adams, a historian and one of the founders of the American Historical Association, advanced an ethno-genetic definition of the nation in "The Germanic Origin of New England Towns," published in 1883. Adams, drawing upon ideas that went back to Jefferson, claimed that democracy and the American people were born in the primeval Saxon forests and, after gestating in medieval England, found their way across the Atlantic to New England in the seventeenth century.[25] Such a view stands in stark contrast to Crèvecoeur's earlier, admittedly limited, notion of a multiethnic America. Nevertheless, by the last decades of the nineteenth century, the memory of the tens of thousands of Irish and German Catholic immigrants who fought and died in the Civil War helped strengthen the mainstream acceptance of those groups' hard-won status as full members of the American nation.[26]

By the mid-nineteenth century, scattered signs began to appear suggesting that even non-Europeans might someday be included in the American community. In 1845, Ralph Waldo Emerson predicted in his diary that the American "race" would include not only all Europeans but also "Africans" and "Polynesians."[27] Herman Melville spoke in 1849 of a not-yet-arrived era when the "blood" of America would consist of "Italians, Indians, and Moors" in addition to then more traditionally accepted groups such as "Frenchmen, Danes, and Scots."[28] In 1853 Wendell Phillips published "The United States of the United Races," which specifically included blacks and excluded no ethnic group from the American nation.[29] Granted, a distinct minority of white Americans shared these highly progressive views. They represented, however, a harbinger of things to come.

The passage of the Thirteenth, Fourteenth, and Fifteenth Amendments to the Constitution after the Civil War ended slavery, enshrined equality before the law for members of all ethnic groups, and recognized the right of black males to vote. However, these achievements proved all too ephemeral as Reconstruction gave way to the institutionalized segregation of Jim Crow. This era of second-class citizenship for blacks posed the next challenge to the expansion of the American national community. Though the country was exhausted by the struggle over racial exclusion it had just endured, and the next period of truly significant progress on that front remained decades away, the stage was set. Abraham Lincoln's words, in particular the stirring prose of the Gettysburg Address, reminded Americans that the Declaration of Independence had indeed promised equality to all. Lincoln at Gettysburg linked the Declaration's radical egalitarianism to the very definition of America in a way that, over time, profoundly transformed it.[30]

The arrival of ever-increasing numbers of immigrants in the post-Reconstruction era, both from northwestern and German-speaking Europe along with, increasingly, those from southern and eastern Europe, coincided with a further broadening of Crèvecoeur's initial definition of the American people. By the turn of the twentieth century, a substantial and gradually increasing number of Americans accepted the idea of expanding the geographic, and thus ethnic, boundaries of who could potentially become members of the nation. Although all immigrants faced significant challenges to inclusion, and some groups faced widespread discrimination and prejudice, Italians, Poles, Jews, and other East Europeans gradually won greater acceptance during the early twentieth century as members of the American community.

Nevertheless, few whites, whatever their ethnic heritage, challenged the predominant belief that the national community included only those of European origin. Most continued to believe in an ethnic idea of the nation, to consider nonwhites to be incapable or unworthy of being successfully integrated. For example, the Chinese Exclusion Act of 1882 (which remained in effect until 1943) explicitly proscribed even allowing any Chinese immigrants into the country, let alone allowing them to become naturalized citizens. Even after repeal, it remained exceptionally difficult for people able to emigrate legally from China until the 1965 enactment of the Immigration and Naturalization Act, which ended discrimination against immigrants based on country of origin.[31]

There was in effect a grand bargain in place in the first half of the twentieth century. Early on, the idea of a "whites only" melting pot combined with so-called 100 percent Americanism to create an atmosphere, particularly during and after World War I, that demanded that immigrants, in addition to displaying loyalty to the United States, also quickly shed their cultural traditions and ethnic identifications.[32] Accordingly, European immigrants "melted" into a new, unified American community that guaranteed legal equality to all white Americans, at least in theory and to a reasonably good degree in reality as the years went on, whether they had sailed across the Atlantic on the *Mayflower* or come through Ellis Island.

It is worth emphasizing that these non-WASP Europeans became not only Americans but white Americans, the two of which were essentially synonymous, according to dominant opinion in the first half (at least) of the twentieth century.[33] Therefore, as much as nonwhite immigrants, native-born black Americans, or American Indians might have wanted to culturally assimilate into the mainstream, they still could not win widespread acceptance into the American community. Entry into the nation required them to pass, in effect, through a funnel of whiteness, a nearly impossible proposition. Detaching the definition of being American from any particular ethnic background, making it thoroughly neutral ethnically speaking, would mean that no longer would people have to qualify as white before they could qualify as American. A wholly civic American nationalism centers on such an ethnically neutral definition of our national identity. When the overwhelming majority of the population accepts this definition, America will have fully transcended whiteness.

Theodore Roosevelt and Woodrow Wilson helped transform the nature of American identity by vociferously supporting 100 percent Americanism. They led the push for a homogenizing form of assimilation that demanded that citizens think of themselves only as Americans, without the so-called hyphens that marked their ancestral ties. Wilson rejected the notion of hyphenated Americans, countering, "A man who thinks of himself as belonging to a particular national group in America has not yet become an American."[34] Theodore Roosevelt similarly added, "There is no room in this country for hyphenated Americans."[35]

The 1920s brought an end to the period of high immigration and a temporary retreat, in terms of the law as well as public opinion, from the notion that southern and eastern Europeans (let alone nonwhites) could truly become Americans by shedding their traditional cultures and loyalties. The Johnson-Reed Act of 1924 all but shut off the flow of immigrants from countries not in northern or western Europe. Albert Johnson, the congressman who lent his name to the law, characterized immigrants from outside that relatively small area as unfit to be Americans because of their "alien blood" and "inherited misconceptions."[36] The decade saw an upswing in racist nativism. The Ku Klux Klan emerged revitalized, due in part to a reaction against the high numbers of non-WASP immigrants in prior decades. Representative Johnson's speech made clear the tenuous status of eastern and southern Europeans, even those already naturalized, as members of the American family.

Nevertheless, those non-WASP Europeans who had managed to make it through Ellis Island and other gateways to the United States before 1924, and even more so their descendants, did ultimately win general acceptance as Americans within a generation or two of Johnson's remarks, thanks in part to the inclusive (of all those of European descent) language of Franklin Roosevelt. Furthermore, unlike previous presidents who specifically denigrated nonwhites as lacking the qualities to become good citizens, FDR largely ignored them in his rhetoric.[37] Comparatively speaking, being ignored thus represented an important step toward their ultimate inclusion.

The Civil Rights Movement

The next era of great change in how we defined what it means to be American occurred in the years after World War II. The history of the civil rights movement cannot be summarized even briefly here, but it suffices to say that the previous era's "whites only" conception of America did not survive the moral and political challenges arrayed against it, the sources of which were both domestic and, due to the Cold War, international in origin. By the 1960s, civil rights leaders and their supporters demanded full equality before the law for Americans of every background and an end to legalized discrimination. They achieved tremendous success toward that end. Historian Eric Foner summarized the result of the movements of this era as follows: "The United States became a more open, more tolerant, in a word—a freer country."[38]

Many theorists and academics who emerged in the wake of these campaigns for equality rejected the clearly inaccurate and triumphalist version of American history that, by the mid-1960s, most textbooks had portrayed for some years, a version of the past that largely ignored oppression based on race, ethnicity, gender, religion, and sexual orientation. That American story, in its most egregious forms, emphasized only our grand ideals of freedom, liberty, and equality without cataloguing in a meaningful way the struggle of those who, thanks to prejudice, were not fortunate enough to receive the fruits of those ideals at the nation's founding and in the decades and even centuries that followed.[39]

According to that mid-twentieth century version of our history, America won its freedom, extended the reach of that freedom across the continent and, thanks to Europeans of various backgrounds coming together as one people, created a unified and democratic nation-state. Blacks and American Indians were presented as being lucky—with as little said as possible about their treatment to that point—to have been blessed with the gifts of civilization and democracy that America ultimately brought to them. Other nonwhites as well as gays barely appear in those American histories, with women largely invisible as well, other than in supporting roles. Likewise, Mary E. Stuckey explained that the rhetoric of President Eisenhower, the dominant political figure of the 1950s, "produced a profoundly nostalgic—and mythologized—view of national identity and national history."[40]

Even this version was no doubt more inclusive and more democratic than the American story put forth by nativists and Klan members, which rejected membership in the American community not only for non-Europeans but also Jews, Catholics, homosexuals, and anyone else who did not fit their narrow definition of who was worthy of being an American. The triumphalist democratic history of America that had coalesced by the mid-twentieth century had thus improved upon the earlier, racialist Anglo-Saxon versions of American history put forth by scholars such as Herbert Baxter Adams, but nevertheless, this "improved" version remained deeply flawed by its lack of complete inclusiveness as well as, in Stuckey's words, its nostalgic and mythologized presentation of the past.

The triumphs of the civil rights movement exposed the flaws in the pre-1960s conception of American history and national identity. Some among the aforementioned late 1960s theorists and academics continued to work with established models and forms in order to bring about greater equality, help America more fully realize its egalitarian ideals, and more accurately represent its past. Nevertheless, a fissure was developing in these fields, mirroring the split in American society that opened due to other developments in this period, such as the growing antiwar and women's rights movements. Thus grew an opposing vision—one that viewed America as permanently poisoned by prejudice and built around an inherently oppressive system that would never evolve. These thinkers and academics formulated a new vision that rejected wholesale even the idea of a unitary American nation and a single, common American history.

2

Since the 1960s

Radical Multiculturalism, Its Critics, and How Obama Fits In

Since its emergence in the 1960s, multiculturalism has come in many varieties—some moderate, others more extreme.[1] Broadly defined, multiculturalism has hovered over the discussion of how to define our national identity for more than four decades. The moderate or "soft" form of multiculturalism celebrates the contributions and identities of nonwhite Americans as part of the narrative of American history, while decrying the earlier presentations of that history for ignoring them. The more radical version of this ideology intertwined with the Black Power movement and similar movements among other nonwhite groups, and drew heavily on the anticolonialist/antiwhite writings of Frantz Fanon (whose words appeared in *Black Power*, a key 1967 tract written by black nationalist leaders Stokely Carmichael and Charles Hamilton).[2]

The radical or "hard" form of multiculturalism offers a vision of America that spurned any substantive common American identity in favor of one that consists of distinct and discrete groups wholly defined by ethnicity and/or culture. This ideology proclaims that ethnic and even cultural boundaries ought to be made impenetrable. Radical multiculturalism is a form of ethnic nationalism because it assigns people a group identity based on the community into which they are born rather than allow them to choose how to identify themselves. One's ethnic affiliation represents the primary if not sole authentic and meaningful element of a person's cultural as well as political group–based identity. Radical multiculturalism ultimately rejects the notion of affiliating or integrating in a truly meaningful way across ethnic or cultural boundaries.

Therefore cultural integration—dismissed as assimilation—is anathema because it dilutes the cultural purity of minority groups who are forced to melt into the dominant mainstream culture. As on other fronts, the "hard" multicultural analysis contains some truth, in that assimilation/integration can take place along such lines when the dominant group imposes homogenization on out-groups. However, in the United States this process has not been so one-sided in reality since the 1960s thanks in part to the influence of multiculturalism itself.

Among these radicals, members of minority groups viewed themselves as "victims of Americanism," while white radicals also rejected anything that smacked of patriotism—such as a call to national unity—as little more than an attempt to suppress dissent and prop up a corrupt, militaristic, and bigoted regime.[3] American history, to the degree such a thing exists according to this radical vision, is merely the histories of the peoples who live here and who have either oppressed or been oppressed.

Radical multiculturalism rejects the goal of teaching all students some form of a common narrative of American history with which they could identify. Instead, its adherents assert that social studies/cultural education ought to work toward the bolstering of ethnic pride and affiliation, a strategy philosopher Kwame Anthony Appiah characterized as "separatism," and continued: "Implicit in much multicultural talk is the thought that the way to deal with our many cultures in public education is to teach each child the culture of 'its' group: in order, say, to define and strengthen her or his self-esteem."[4] He also identified a serious problem with this way of thinking, namely that "it suggests that Western culture belongs to some American children more than others *in virtue of their descent* [emphasis in original]."[5]

According to the mind-set of hard multiculturalism, the United States, as well as its white majority, has shown little but hostility toward its nonwhite citizens throughout its history, giving them little reason either to identify with it as their country or recognize white Americans as fellow members of a unitary national community. This kind of radical multiculturalism gave ideological legitimacy to an oppositional culture whereby being truly authentic required members of minority groups to reject anything associated with white America and/or America itself, the two of which these radicals considered one and the same.

This hard form of multiculturalism presented a one-sided version of the truth that prioritized ethno-cultural difference and reified diversity while rejecting American national unity. Nevertheless, even this radical take on American history was certainly no less accurate than the then dominant triumphalist version it challenged starting in the late 1960s. Moreover, multiculturalism in all its forms served as a potent intellectual and political response to real prejudice, to real discrimination, and to real exclusion. Most importantly, multicultural ideologies served notice that those groups who were not being treated equally were no longer going to accept their place as second-class citizens of a country where a sizable number among its white majority did not consider them to be real Americans anyway, even after the civil rights achievements of the mid-1960s. Those (such as myself) who criticize some of the directions in which radical multiculturalism ultimately sought to take American society must remember these realities regarding its founding.

The Battle over Radical Multiculturalism: Culture Wars of the 1990s

During the late 1980s and early 1990s, the more extreme form of multiculturalism emerged as the most visible and influential segment of the broader multicultural movement, at least in part because of the vociferous debates over social studies/history curricula in high schools and colleges. The polarizing nature of this very public debate resulted in the extreme positions on both ends receiving the most media attention and drowning out, at least for a time, more nuanced approaches within the multicultural spectrum. Hard multiculturalism reflected a variety of viewpoints coming out of the far left wing of academia and politics; while these did not necessarily reflect a unified set of principles, all were connected by their unrelenting condemnation of Western universalist liberalism. As law professor Richard Thompson Ford put it, "Radical multiculturalism would insist that the rights of culturally distinctive groups to retain their distinctive practices and mores should trump the demands of political liberalism."[6]

Afrocentrism served as one key element of this movement and received a disproportionate amount of attention due to the nature of its claims.[7] Thanks to the notoriety he gained, it became personified by Leonard Jeffries, then chair of City College of New York's African-American Studies department, who contended that blacks were genetically superior to whites because the former had a higher concentration of melanin in their skin.[8] Jeffries was dismissed as chair in 1992, but continues as professor at CCNY.

In light of Jeffries's racial bigotry, it is worth contrasting his views to those of Cornel West, who produced a collection of essays in the early 1990s that became the book *Race Matters*. West demonstrated that one can vociferously and unrelentingly condemn white supremacy as well as critically examine the harm it continues to inflict on black Americans without being antiwhite. He rejected Jeffries-style Afrocentrism, as well as the embrace of black separatism or "black supremacy" as a way to resist and overcome white racism.[9] West specifically called for the cultivation of alliances across racial lines to achieve broad progressive goals.[10] Furthermore, he embraced the notion that Americans are, in fact, one people, one nation, with "a common destiny."[11] Jeffries's voice clearly was not the only one among left-of-center black academics speaking about race in this period.

Nevertheless, the radical version of multiculturalism did for a time wield an influence more significant than the number of its actual advocates might have suggested, as it reshaped social studies curricula in a good number of schools and colleges across the country in the late 1980s and early 1990s. For example, we can look at the 1989 and 1991 reports on New York State's social studies curriculum written by state-appointed commissions. Jeffries, a consultant to the Task Force on Minorities, helped write the 1989 report, titled "A Curriculum of Inclusion." He also authored its appendix, where he condemned the then current curriculum—itself the result of a 1987 revision that had sought greater inclusion of nonwhite perspectives and had generally won praise for having done so—as reflecting "deep-seated pathologies of racial hatred."[12] The task force report's executive summary began: "African Americans, Asian Americans, Latinos/Puerto Ricans and Native Americans have all been the victims of an intellectual and educational oppression that has characterized the culture and institutions of the United States and the European American world for centuries."

Certainly, white Americans and American society more broadly have discriminated against and, yes, oppressed nonwhites. Of that there is no question. Nevertheless, opening the report with that sentence reduces the treatment of nonwhites throughout American history and in the present to a simplistic, monolithic, and—most importantly—static generalization: oppression. That is a central part of the story. It is not, however, the whole story. American history includes both horrible crimes and gradual, but nonetheless real, progress. The 1991 report, a rewrite necessitated by the public outcry over the previously cited language, moderated the tone and omitted the inflammatory rhetoric of the 1989 version, but remained largely similar in substance according to historian Arthur Schlesinger, who served as a commission member and dissented from the report.[13]

Liberal Nationalism Pushes Back against Radical Multiculturalism

By the mid-1990s however, radical multiculturalism's influence began to recede and has continued to do so, especially after the attacks of September 11, 2001. It was battered by critics on the conservative right, some of whom, such as Pat Buchanan, hold views that can only be described as nativist (see chapter 8). But there were critiques from the center-left as well. Gary Nash, who led the National History Standards Project in the mid-1990s, lamented that the extreme multiculturalists and the conservative (or even nativist) right had come to dominate the public debate over how to represent American history and, by extension, America itself. According to Nash, the right demanded "history that extols Ozzie and Harriet patriotism and exclusive celebration of the Western tradition. Militant multiculturalists, on the other hand, have romanticized the history of their particular group, and stigmatized Western civilization as the world's oldest evil empire."[14] Those on the center-left sought a middle ground.

According to its liberal opponents, hard multiculturalism rejected the progressive notion of the common good, which calls on citizens to identify in part with the interests of those of a different culture and heritage. These radicals also dismissed broadly universalist ideals, such as equal treatment before the law and the correctness of impartial, objective analysis, as little more than alternative ways to impose "white" Western values on other, equally valid cultures and peoples. Richard Thompson Ford explained that extreme multiculturalists generally considered Enlightenment liberal ideas to be "themselves culturally specific and therefore applicable only to people raised in liberal cultures."[15] Kwame Anthony Appiah warned against emphasizing difference at the expense of equality: "Our moral modernity consists chiefly of extending the principle of equal respect to those who had previously been outside the compass of sympathy; in that sense, it has consisted in the ability to see similarity where our predecessors saw only difference. The wisdom was hard-won; it should not be lightly set aside."[16] Liberals had been espousing such ideals for decades as means to combat economic hardship as well as race-based discrimination and violence.

According to this liberal interpretation of American history, by sanctioning discrimination against many of its citizens for far too long, our country ignored its own founding principles. On the Declaration of Independence, for example, this interpretation would acknowledge the deep hypocrisy of a revolutionary movement stating that all men are created equal while keeping virtually all black Americans in chains and, in the same breath, emphasize that the Declaration provided abolitionists and later civil rights reformers a moral and patriotic cudgel to wield against slavery and bigotry. Proequality reformers from Frederick Douglass to Susan B. Anthony to Abraham Lincoln to Martin Luther King Jr. to Harvey Milk could thus call America out on its hypocrisy, its failure to apply *its own principles* universally.

During the civil rights era, segregationists lacked a similarly effective argument because the proequality forces had already claimed not only the moral high ground, but the "American" ground as well. King in his "Letter from a Birmingham Jail" exemplified this wrapping of the American flag around the civil rights movement, declaring that the movement will succeed because "the goal of America is freedom. Abused and scorned though we may be, our destiny is tied up with America's destiny."[17] Furthermore, in his "I Have a Dream" speech, King proclaimed that his dream was in fact "deeply rooted in the American dream."[18] He called not for America to alter its basic principles, but instead, quoting from the nation's maiden statement to the world, to "rise up and live out the true meaning of its creed: 'We hold these truths to be self-evident, that all men are created equal.'" The segregationists thus had to find a way to justify why the core American principles of equality and freedom only applied to select groups of Americans, an argument that, since the 1960s at least, has found fewer and fewer adherents to a good degree because it simply is un-American.

Its liberal critics contended that the long-term cost of radical multiculturalism's rejection of liberal universal principles far outweighed any gains for members of minority groups that it might win in the moment—and whether it even does so is open to question—because it strengthens the justification for other groups, such as white nationalists/white supremacists for example, to adopt a similar strategy of identity politics. According to sociologist Orlando Patterson, such groups "have not only found comfort in Afro-American chauvinism, but in many cases they have directly modeled themselves on Afro-American brotherhood and consciousness-raising rhetoric."[19] Patterson quoted white racist leader Samuel Francis: "Whites must reassert our identity and our solidarity, and we must do so in explicitly racial terms through the articulation of racial consciousness as whites."[20] Patterson then asked, rhetorically, "Sound familiar?"

These white identity racists are thus able to claim that they are simply embracing the same principles as minority groups. They contend that those who would criticize whites for doing so are the ones denying them equality. Such arguments have worked well enough to convince at least some middle-of-the-road white Americans that white identity politics is no more or less legitimate than the identity politics of minority groups, though of course, hard-core white racists have never needed any such legitimation for their beliefs. In today's America, the results of a clash between an openly declared ideology of bigotry and one of justice and equality are a foregone conclusion. That itself is a sign of the progress our society has made in fighting bigotry. A clash, however, between two groups—each claiming to be simply pursuing their own interests—may well come down to which group has greater numbers. More importantly, a society whose politics consists largely of such clashes cannot sustain itself in the long run without oppression.

In addition to rejecting universal Enlightenment principles, extreme multiculturalists also warned members of minority groups that identifying as an American and/or integrating into the American mainstream represented a betrayal of their culture. Embodying the mirror image of Wilson and Teddy Roosevelt's 100 percent Americanism, radical multiculturalism essentially demanded that nonwhites choose their ethnic heritage over their country 100 percent of the time.

Its liberal critics decried this stance as thwarting the creation of a cross-racial progressive coalition. Perhaps the most eloquent of them was sociologist Todd Gitlin, who asked, "Why insist on difference with such rigidity, rancor, and blindness, to the exclusion of the possibility of common knowledge and common dreams?"[21] Arthur Schlesinger's *The Disuniting of America* arguably had the greatest impact among these critics' writings, as his stature and its relatively early appearance (1992) helped pave the way for those who argued along similar lines in subsequent years.[22] The trend continued later in the decade as well, as seen in the powerful prointegration stance taken by Orlando Patterson.[23]

Same Difference: The Christian Right Adopts the Radical Multicultural Approach

Liberal democratic values do in fact sometimes clash with celebrating diversity. Equal respect for all cultures means exactly that, even those cultures that express values and beliefs that supporters of multiculturalism find distasteful and even undemocratic. Many across the political spectrum recognized this reality when, in the 1990s, the fundamentalist Christian Right started adopting elements of radical multicultural ideology to argue that respect for diversity requires respect for their religious beliefs. They argued, relying on the diversity principle, that they had the right to send their children to public schools where the curriculum did not offend or contradict those beliefs.[24]

In a more recent example, on January 29, 2010, a bus driver employed by the public transportation system serving rural areas near Austin, Texas, refused his assignment to pick up a woman and drive her to a Planned Parenthood facility in Austin because he thought she might seek an abortion, something that conflicted with his religious beliefs. The driver filed a lawsuit on July 14, 2010, on the grounds that, according to one of his attorneys, "Once [he] expressed his religious objection to his employer, his employer had an obligation to attempt to accommodate [him]."[25] The driver essentially claimed that his right to follow his religious beliefs allow him, even while serving as a state employee, to deny a fellow citizen the ability to exercise her rights.

The extreme Christian Right's praise of diversity and talk of respect for religious beliefs was merely a strategy, however, as this movement has sought to create an America in which its religious belief system and those who adhere to it predominate.[26] In fact, the Christian Right and radical multiculturalism share one crucial attribute: both reject the need to build a common national identity with which Americans of different backgrounds and belief systems can identify. The Christian Right is antipluralist; radical multiculturalism is hyperpluralist.[27]

Conservative Christians have also recently organized a more direct assault on the way American history appears in public school social studies curricula, one that mirrors what radical multiculturalists did a generation earlier.[28] The shift in American social studies textbooks away from the traditional, triumphalist, pre-1960s presentation of America's story produced a slow-boiling but ultimately powerful reaction among conservatives who have had significant success in implementing their vision of the national historical narrative, along with other changes in areas such as the teaching of evolution and religion. Such a reaction is not surprising, as the progressive shift was, as journalist Frances FitzGerald wrote in 1979, "the most dramatic rewriting of American history ever to take place in American schoolbooks."[29]

In early 2010, extreme conservatives controlled a majority of votes on the Texas state school board. The state centrally purchases all textbooks used in Texas schools, one of the few large states (other than California) to do so, therefore the board's viewpoint on what is acceptable has a disproportionate influence on what American students read nationwide because of the market share Texas offers to textbook publishers. One industry executive admitted, "Publishers will do whatever it takes to get on the Texas list."[30]

On March 12, 2010, the board passed new social studies guidelines for Texas that largely reflect the agenda of the extreme conservatives. One of their goals is to describe America essentially as a nation founded on Christian theological principles. Hence, one change they approved to the baseline document, which Texas teachers had produced, removed the word "Enlightenment" from the following section: "Explain the impact of Enlightenment ideas from John Locke, Thomas Hobbes, Voltaire, Charles de Montesquieu, Jean Jacques Rousseau, and Thomas Jefferson on political revolutions from 1750 to the present," and replaced Thomas Jefferson, the author of the phrase "wall of separation between church and state" and a known Deist, with Thomas Aquinas, John Calvin, and Sir William Blackstone.[31]

One observer described the aim of these radical conservatives as being to "scrub U.S. history of its inconvenient blemishes—if they get their way, textbooks will paint slavery as a relic of British colonialism that America struggled to cast off from day one and [will] refer to our economic system as 'ethical capitalism.'"[32] On race, these extremists seek to deemphasize civil rights leaders and emphasize the role of the white majority in granting equality to minorities, whereas in the arena of politics they push to portray conservative economic and political movements and figures from Senator Joseph McCarthy to activist Phyllis Schlafly to Ronald Reagan to former U.S. House Speaker Newt Gingrich in an almost uncritically positive light.

Another similar push, if less successful to this point, took place in Tennessee in early 2011. There, a group of Tea Party (see chapter 8) leaders held a press conference where they presented a list of "demands" and subsequently met with state legislators to discuss them. The Tea Party statement declared, "Neglect and outright ill will have distorted the teaching of the history and character of the United States."[33] The group further sought to add the following statement to criteria used to select history textbooks: "No portrayal of minority experience in the history which actually occurred shall obscure the experience or contributions of the Founding Fathers, or the majority of citizens, including those who reached positions of leadership." Hal Rounds, the group's chief spokesperson, spoke of wanting to correct "an awful lot of made-up criticism about, for instance, the Founders intruding on the Indians or having slaves or being hypocrites in one way or another." Clearly, this Tea Party group wishes to undo the shift toward a more inclusive, more accurate history that occurred after the late 1960s.

The Texas conservatives, the Tennessee Tea Party, and like-minded allies in other states want to return as closely as possible to the 1950s presentation of American history in terms of its predominantly white focus, and, at least in the case of Texas, to go back perhaps to the turn of the twentieth century or earlier in highlighting Christian theology's centrality in terms of the development of the United States. Irrespective of the matter of its partisanship or its inaccuracies, such a narrative of our country's history stands clearly opposed to that presented by Obama, which itself represents the balanced approach that in the early to mid-1990s grew out of the largely centrist/center-left critiques of the extreme left and right's view of America.

Radical Multiculturalism's Decline

Looking back, we can see that radical multiculturalism was clearly weakened by its excesses—exemplified by the virulent anti-Westernism of the 1990 Stanford students chanting "Hey hey, ho ho, Western culture's got to go!" when protesting the school's Western Civilization curriculum.[34] However, multiculturalism also achieved great successes, in that most Americans by the end of the century came to recognize that the traditional, pre-1960s conception of our national identity had in significant ways excluded or at least devalued groups other than white, straight, male Protestants. Mainstream multiculturalism won in that it exposed and deconstructed that concept of America, while its radical form withered as a result of overexposure and over-reaching.

The alternative concept of America the more extreme multiculturalists offered—namely a society consisting of tribes who shared little other than proximity and mutual suspicion—struck many as too focused on diversity and difference, and not enough on unity and commonality, to offer hope for an improved future. Furthermore, its attempt to simply and totally discredit the entire Western tradition as centered on oppression—to deny the disproportionate influence of the Western Enlightenment and, in particular, English notions of political liberty on American society, and to replace the old history with an approach that disproportionately emphasized the contributions of non-WASP males in order to build those groups' self-esteem—simply did not ring true for most Americans. Multiculturalism killed the king but could not hold the crown.

The 1960s left a dual legacy in the eyes of many observers. As Obama put it: "The victories that the sixties generation brought about—the admission of minorities and women into full citizenship, the strengthening of individual liberties and the healthy willingness to question authority—have made America a far better place for all its citizens. But what has been lost in the process, and has yet to be replaced, are those shared assumptions—that quality of trust and fellow feeling—that bring us together as Americans."[35] His push to invigorate our sense of unity seeks to redress that loss. It is perhaps ironic that the vision Obama put forth starting in the mid-1990s developed to a significant degree as a reaction against the excesses of extreme multi-culturalism and related forms of identity politics on the far left; yet it now faces a far stronger challenge in 2012 and beyond from the identity politics of the hard right.

"Benign Multiculturalism" and Liberal Nationalism

By the mid-1990s, Americans had begun to come together around a compromise position on multiculturalism, something sociologist Alan Wolfe referred to as "benign multiculturalism."[36] After surveying middle-class Americans across the country during those years, he concluded: "Most Americans . . . support the principle that groups within the United States ought to be allowed to retain their distinctiveness, but only so long as they do so within an official culture that insists on the priority of the national community over subnational ethnic groups."[37] Wolfe also found support for a brand of multiculturalism "tailored to be compatible with the more universal values of America."[38] His respondents believed that ethnic groups ought to be allowed to preserve their own identities; however, they must do this "under the broad umbrella of Americanism." In other words, diversity is a good we should support, but unity is a greater good we must prioritize.

An array of scholars, political commentators, and policymakers began offering prescriptions for revitalizing American national identity along these lines in the mid-1990s.[39] Political scientist Noah Pickus found that these figures—whose broader politics spanned the left-right spectrum—generally agreed that "a robust national identity is required to bind Americans," one that "combines . . . inclusiveness and nationalism."[40]

One of the most prominent was the aforementioned Michael Lind, who had urged America to leave behind what he called the multicultural era and embrace a fully inclusive yet unitary national identity. Unlike some others who made similar statements about American identity, Lind also forcefully emphasized the economic costs of our society being so ethnically divided, explaining that such divisions had blurred lines of class and prevented the development of a multiethnic coalition that could work on behalf of progressive economic policies favoring the working and middle classes. Although one can talk about strengthening ties across ethnic lines without mentioning the economic hardships faced by too many Americans, those who wish to achieve that goal would do well to remember Lind's broader socioeconomic argument.

Lind further recognized that strengthening a sense of American national unity would be difficult because such a vision of America "so far lacks not only a self-conscious communal identity as something other than a mere citizenry and more than an aggregate of people of different colors, it also lacks its own national story, its own understanding of its origins and its possible future." [41] He further explained that any national community needs "believable myths."

Tamar Jacoby, a center-right thinker/activist, framed the issue put forth by Lind particularly well in her analysis of immigrants and American identity, explaining that they—and, by extension, all of us—need:

> A national story about America that they can identify with. The old story from the 50s…plainly doesn't work for them. But it's not clear that the story of the 1980s and 1990s—a story built around the idea of diversity—does the job either. Much as they may appreciate their own and others' ethnic backgrounds, [immigrants] seem increasingly to be hungering for something else, too—a larger, shared story that allows them to escape their narrow origins and provides an understanding of what holds us all together as Americans….We need a beacon: not just a rationale but a shared narrative, a common vocabulary, symbols, songs and holidays that we can all buy into together. [42]

Along similar lines, historian David Hollinger in 1995 called for us to move beyond multiculturalism—while recognizing the legitimate reasons why it emerged—and into "postethnic America." [43] Hollinger and Lind both recognized important commonalities between their views on American national identity. [44]

In a later essay, Hollinger called for a balanced American history narrative based on "a national solidarity committed—but often failing—to incorporate individuals from a great variety of communities of descent." [45] Such a narrative would, he hoped, "reinforce the liberal and cosmopolitan elements of the national self-image without denying the parts of American history that are not liberal and not cosmopolitan."

The story of America that Obama has offered, one mindful of the centrality of past injustices while simultaneously celebrating the progress made in overcoming them, centers on this very same balance. His understanding of the relationship between ethnic identity and American national identity—first explored in 1995's *Dreams from My Father*—shares much with the basic framework put forth by the center-left civic nationalists from this period.

Dreams appeared in print in the same year as the key books by Lind, Hollinger, and Gitlin, and only three years after Schlesinger's. Their approaches were certainly not identical. Perhaps because Obama had temporarily embraced some radical ideas in his youth (see chapter 3), he certainly displayed more patience toward the separatist excesses of the radicals than did Schlesinger. Nevertheless, these center-left thinkers all sought a way to broaden the definition of American national identity in a way that addressed the accurate criticisms raised by mainstream multiculturalism while recognizing that the country nevertheless needs the vibrant sense of national unity that hard multiculturalists rejected. In that sense, *Dreams from My Father* and indeed Obama's conception of American national identity in its entirety represents a "postradical multicultural" approach.

Multiculturalism, in particular its more extreme version, gave some nonwhites an intellectually coherent structure through which to vent their anger at the mistreatment American society has inflicted on them and to articulate their alienation from that society. Obama's conception of American national identity, one whose underlying optimism about egalitarianism in her future is buttressed by the fact of his own election, offers an alternative structure through which minorities can, as he has, wholeheartedly embrace America and their fellow Americans.

Pessimism about Liberal Nationalism

Other recent scholars have presented more critical views of the prospects of developing a thoroughly inclusive sense of American national identity. Political scientist Desmond King characterized "postmulticultural" America as a society trying simultaneously to acknowledge our division into ethnic groups while enacting policies that do not exacerbate those divisions. He emphasized the degree to which group identities will continue to exist in America despite our desire to cultivate a unitary national identity.[46] King warned against pursuing the goal of unity too zealously, citing historian Gary Gerstle's work on the "coercive" nature of the history of Americanization as well as political scientist Rogers Smith's analysis of how America has historically suppressed its "multiple traditions."[47] To be clear, King remained more optimistic than Gerstle about America's ability to achieve an all-encompassing unity while avoiding homogenization.[48]

These critics' arguments can be summarized in Gerstle's own rhetorical question: "If the past has been so coercive, why should we expect the future to be so different?"[49] He endorsed the strengthening of a civic national identity for Americans, having clearly supported the idea in his book *American Crucible*, where he noted: "A vigorous civic nation that is both tolerant of difference and generative of social solidarity would be a wonderful place in which to live."[50] Gerstle acknowledged that Hollinger's civic nationalist blueprint, because it embraced rather than sought to stamp out diversity, differed in theory from earlier Americanization attempts that centered around the Woodrow Wilson–Teddy Roosevelt concept of 100 percent Americanism. Nevertheless, Gerstle suggested that these differences might well disappear if Hollinger-style civic nationalism were actually put in practice, noting that theorists in the time of Wilson and Teddy Roosevelt developed similarly "liberal and humane" ideas about integration only to see their liberal and humane aspects disappear after becoming the basis of government policies.[51]

To me, this is circular logic: because it was once so, it will likely be so if tried again. History can play a vital role in strengthening the sense of peoplehood among all Americans. It can also confine us in chains of our own making, with the sins our country committed against some of our people in the past preventing us from imagining, and thus creating, a different and more just future. Certainly Gerstle recognizes this as well, and his pessimism is not unreasonable. My concern is that pessimism can become a self-fulfilling prophecy.

In reality, the views of Hollinger, Lind, Jacoby, and other neo-integrationists (whether right-of-center like Peter Salins or on the left like Todd Gitlin) are not incompatible with those of Desmond King et al., in that they accept King's assessment that group identities will continue to exist and that American unity will not center on an Americanism that, as demanded by Wilson and Teddy Roosevelt, completely denies ethnocultural ties. Furthermore, King approvingly cited Rogers Smith's acceptance that "a common culture" does indeed exist in the United States, a key contention of the neo-integrationists.[52] The neo-integrationists call for a de-emphasis, encouraged by American society but ultimately voluntarily adopted by Americans of all backgrounds, on one's ethnicity and cultural heritage in favor of a renewed emphasis on our commonality as one people and what Hollinger referred to as "the civic character of the American nation-state."[53] The voluntary aspect is crucially important. As Tamar Jacoby noted, "We won't get there through exhortation—by scolding ethnic activists or denouncing multiculturalism or trying to force-feed anyone an American identity."[54]

So, the question becomes how do we create, in Lind's words, the "self-conscious communal identity" that America so sorely needs? How do we inculcate the associated "believable myths"? Certainly we can and must do so through education. Political scientist Stephen Macedo rightly emphasized the need for real civic education in public schools and described in detail the content thereof.[55] On June 30, 2008, Obama also bemoaned "the loss of quality civic education" from America's class-rooms. I would argue that, in addition to his rhetoric, another way the president can strengthen Americans' national identity would be to convince states and localities to improve the civic education in their curricula.

But Lind and Jacoby are right that we need something more as well. We need history makers who understand the civic nationalist vision and can facilitate its widespread adoption both by telling the story—spreading the myths—and making those myths real by demonstrating that America is today becoming the pluralistic, inclusive, yet strongly unified nation toward which its history has been building. The election of Barack Obama, as well as the ground-breaking electoral success in 2008 of his most prominent competitor for the Democratic presidential nomina-tion, Senator Hillary Clinton, for that matter, demonstrates that race and gender in and of themselves no longer prevent any citizen from achieving the highest positions of leadership in the American political system. It was more than just a cliché when Obama said, just after the South Carolina primary, "We're going to write a new chapter in American history."[56]

Obama Compared to Other Recent Presidents on National Identity

Not all the presidents who followed Theodore Roosevelt and Woodrow Wilson were similarly hostile to the idea that Americans might choose to maintain some identi-fication with their heritage and still consider themselves to be fully American.[57] Bill Clinton, however, was the first president who expressed an understanding of American peoplehood that incorporated ideas in a significant way from the mul-ticultural era. In 1997, in his second inaugural address, he proclaimed, "Our rich texture of racial, religious and political diversity will be a godsend in the twenty-first century."[58] George W. Bush likewise noted in 2002, "America's experience as a great multiethnic democracy affirms our conviction that people of many heritages and faiths can live and prosper in peace."[59]

Bush and, more so, Clinton devoted time and energy as president to the cause of racial reconciliation—as evidenced by the latter's Initiative on Race, which pro-moted dialogues on racial issues across the country and produced a report titled "One America in the 21st Century."[60] Nevertheless, even Bush and Clinton did not decisively break the connection between American national identity and whiteness, according to scholar of presidential rhetoric Vanessa Beasley. She explained that when discussing issues such as immigration and race relations, presidents from 1885 through 2000 had frequently linked what she called "the civil religious 'idea of America'" to white Americans.[61] Beasley concluded: "As a result, this idea has been rhetorically racialized."

Some African Americans have expressed similar feelings. In 1993, author Toni Morrison declared that "American means white,"[62] and in 1994 stated, "I know that I've never felt like an American."[63] Such feelings result from a perception on the part of black Americans that they are not accepted as part of the American community. In surveys conducted between May 29 and July 21, 2002, Elizabeth Theiss-Morse found that African Americans identified as Americans less strongly than members of other groups, whereas American identity registered equally among nonblack Americans regardless of ethnicity.[64]

In addition to the effect of his election itself, President Obama constantly invoking the idea of America in an ethnically inclusive, unifying manner helps neutralize the equation of America with whiteness by claiming that idea for citizens of any hue. It seems likely that such a transformation would strengthen the identification of nonwhite minorities with America and with their fellow Americans. As political scientist Melissa Harris-Perry (formerly Harris-Lacewell), said of Obama, "A president is not a country, but he embodies the national identity."[65]

Even more explicit was the comment made by professor of psychiatry Carl Bell to journalist Ellis Cose: "Malcolm [X] made the point of saying 'the nation' instead of 'our nation.' When Barack got elected, I started saying 'our nation,' because it's a huge step closer to actualizing the ideal."[66] Thus, Obama is poised to have a qualitatively different impact on our national identity because he is doing something previous presidents have been unable to do, namely help our national identity transcend whiteness by making it finally and unequivocally clear that a white person is no more or less American than a nonwhite person.

Obama is the first president educated from early adolescence during the multicultural era. His intellectual worldview has been profoundly influenced by the intellectual debates that have roiled American academia since the 1960s.[67] When he was a teenager in the 1970s at the elite, private Punahou School in Honolulu, his history teachers assigned books, for example, on the settling of the American West written from an Indian perspective, and on the World War II–era internment of

Japanese Americans.[68] Additionally, his education exposed him to the idea that our identities—ethnoracial, national, etc.—did not develop organically, but rather are to a good degree constructs that individuals and groups fashioned in response to circumstances.[69] This helps explain why Obama has focused so much on strengthening American national identity and making it more inclusive, because his education taught him that people shape their own identities.

Moreover, having a white mother and African father in a time when that act truly broke taboos and challenged long-held prejudices, as well as growing up in highly diverse Hawaii and Indonesia, forced him to think consciously in ways few of us have about one's ethnic and national identities. Going through that process has given him a unique perspective on these issues among leading politicians—let alone presidents. He learned that our society must actively inculcate a strong sense of national belonging that all Americans can embrace.

Democratic Pluralism and Obama's Vision of America

The concept of democratic pluralism informs Obama's rhetoric. A society that embraces democratic pluralism recognizes that some of its citizens will identify as members of groups based on shared heritage, cultural traditions, religious beliefs, sexual orientation, etc., and that these affinities may even cross the borders of countries. Such a society acknowledges this diversity and the choices it offers citizens in expressing their identity. However, a robust and successful democratic pluralism, in the case of the United States, calls on its citizens to identify with America as their country and, equally importantly, to identify as members of the community of all Americans. Such a community evinces a commitment to democratic ideals and the common good as well as a shared history, and is one where citizens communicate with one another by means of a common language and culture. On the idea of a common history, Michael Lind said it best, "Even if our genetic grandparents came from Finland or Indonesia, as Americans, we are all descendants of George Washington—*and* his slaves"[70] (emphasis in original). Obama's American history narrative embraces exactly this idea.

Furthermore, because Obama is the president, his version of our national story stands a good chance of being adopted by a significant percentage of its target audience, the American people. His election has had a profound impact on black Americans specifically.[71] Furthermore, Obama's notion of American identity has the potential to move the country as a whole further away from the divisions caused by the legacies of both white supremacy and the oppositional culture among blacks that arose in response. According to Orlando Patterson, these intertwined legacies led a generation of black leaders in the post–civil rights era to embrace "separate but truly equal, though glossed over with multicultural rhetoric."[72] He deeply lamented what he characterized as the "betrayal and abandonment of the once cherished goal of integration."[73]

Patterson, however, declared in 2009 that Obama's election and his prointegration rhetoric could potentially weaken these neo-separatist views among blacks. "[Obama's] own life and spectacular achievements are, after all, a living demonstration of what integration promises: not so much the transcendence of race as the mainstreaming power of cultural fusion."[74] As Manning Marable, the late African American studies scholar, told Ellis Cose, "[Obama's election] blows away the nationalist argument that the system is white and racist and won't ever change."[75] The journalist Touré wrote: "[Obama's] election told me I didn't know my country as well as I thought I did….[It] forced me to reevaluate America."[76]

Obama's message of unity also encourages whites to reach out to members of minority groups, whom some whites perceive as rejecting integration and a common American identity. Real success on this front, however, requires that the ethnic prejudices of all Americans but in particular those expressed by some whites continue to decrease. Blaming either multiculturalism alone or some people of color for not strongly identifying with America while ignoring white racism's role in creating that alienation would be inaccurate as well as unhelpful.

One can hope that Obama's election, his unity-centered rhetoric and, presumably, his actions as president will push that ever-shrinking segment of the population who either views black people as somehow inferior or who believes that black leaders only want to help other blacks to rethink that assessment. Undoubtedly, some will continue to demand that African Americans stop pointing out the continued existence of racism now that Obama is president, as if his election completely ended racial discrimination and eliminated the effects of past discrimination.

This attitude was expressed in Sarah Palin's Facebook post of July 13, 2010. She had thought that Obama's election meant that "our country had become a new 'postracial' society," but then explained that the NAACP's charge that the Tea Party harbored racist elements (discussed in chapter 8) made her "sad for those who choose to divide" us along racial lines.[77] She further criticized the NAACP by declaring: "It is time to end the divisive politics." Despite what Palin may claim, noticing racism is not the same thing as practicing it.

Although some people's prejudices may just be too deeply embedded to be changed, we can be optimistic that some among such people can be convinced to at least soften their prejudices. Furthermore, we are talking about gradual shifts in attitudes over time. It is possible that different groups of Americans reaching out across lines of ethnicity will set off a virtuous cycle that feeds on itself, with reconciliation and unity giving rise to more reconciliation and unity.

Invigorating the sense that Americans are one people rather than merely a collection of ethnic groups will help ensure that when we disagree it does not divide us irreconcilably along ethnic lines. A stronger sense of community encourages Americans of every background to examine potential policy solutions based on how each would impact the society as a whole, rather than simply how it would affect either themselves and their families or their own narrow group. More citizens thinking this way will both improve the quality of public debate and make it easier to reach compromises that may ask some to sacrifice their own group interests, to a reasonable degree, for the greater good.

Furthermore, Obama's American civic nationalism could potentially undermine the hyperindividualistic ideology of laissez-faire economic conservatives. His rhetoric on what it means to be an American cannot by itself knock down the systemic barriers to success that the underprivileged face. Nevertheless, inculcating these ideas can enhance social solidarity and thus improve the prospects of enacting policies that can weaken those barriers.

In the end, President Obama has offered an understanding of our national identity that should satisfy—at least in theory—most of those who currently identify themselves as multiculturalists as well as most of those who see that concept as a threat to American unity. Some small number who continue to hold to a more extreme form of multiculturalism may remain reluctant to embrace a push for national unity, even coming from Obama, because they see such a project as inherently oppressive. Such a push does mean cultivating American nationalism, but a civic rather than an ethnic form of nationalism.

A truly civic form of nationalism must allow people to have a "both/and" form of identity, one that can contain more than one layer, rather than force them to make an "either/or" choice between their ancestral background and their nation. Obama's civic nationalism incorporates the need for this; he noted on July 11, 2009, "We all have many identities—of tribe and ethnicity; of religion and nationality." He stated in his December 10, 2009, Nobel Peace Prize acceptance speech: "Given the dizzying pace of globalization, the cultural leveling of modernity, it perhaps comes as no surprise that people fear the loss of what they cherish in their particular identities—their race, their tribe, and perhaps most powerfully their religion." Here and throughout his career, Obama echoes the philosopher of nationalism Isaiah Berlin, whose take on pluralism stakes out a middle ground between more strident forms of ethnic nationalism and a kind of rootless cosmopolitanism that rejects ethnic identity completely.[78]

Obama's definition of American national identity exists alongside, rather than in lieu of, other traditional forms of belonging. He does not believe that one must feel less Jewish, black, or Chinese in order to feel more American. Asking people to reject their ancestral identities and adopt an all-encompassing, totalizing national identity—as Teddy Roosevelt did in his version of 100 percent Americanism—would almost certainly fail because it would provoke the fears Obama described above and would discourage the kind of empathy needed for real integration.

The civic nationalism Obama has advocated promotes support for the common good, shared sacrifice, and ties across ethnic lines among Americans, while rejecting antipathy toward those outside our borders. Todd Gitlin declared shortly after September 11, "It's a time for patriotism of mutual aid. . . . It's time to diminish the gap between the nation we love and the justice we also love. It's time for the real America to stand up."[79] Obama intends for his vision of the country to do exactly these things.

In 1998, philosopher Richard Rorty issued a clarion call for the cultivation of a progressive version of national pride. He rightly emphasized that such a feeling is "to countries what self-respect is to individuals. A necessary condition for self-improvement."[80] Rorty went on to encourage left-of-center figures to take up the task. "Those who hope to persuade a nation to exert itself need to remind their country of what it can take pride in as well as what it should be ashamed of. They must tell inspiring stories about episodes and figures in the nation's past . . . to which the country should remain true. . . . Competition for political leadership is in part a competition between differing stories about a nation's self-identity, and between differing symbols of its greatness."

Nationalism must not be only a tool of the nativist right wing, nor must that right wing be allowed to define American nationalism. Nationalism need not be xenophobic; it can be inclusionary, cross-ethnic, and progressive, which is how Obama has defined it. He hopes that his concept of American unity and community will push us to see one another as brothers and sisters who, because we share a history together, also share a future together as one people.

3

Obama's Search for His Own Identity

A s many observers have noted, Obama's autobiography, *Dreams from My Father: A Story of Race and Inheritance*, is strikingly literary and not typical for its genre.[1] The work falls somewhere between two well-established categories. It is clearly within a long tradition of identity narratives written by African Americans and in its approach to race and identity draws on the writings of Frederick Douglass, W. E. B. Du Bois, Richard Wright, and "especially" Ralph Ellison.[2] Additionally, because of the arc of Obama's career, it has become something of a political autobiography as well.

Dreams was first published in 1995, shortly after Obama graduated law school and was beginning his work as a civil rights lawyer and law professor. Obama had initially drawn media attention in 1990, when he was named the first black president of the *Harvard Law Review*. He was then offered a publishing contract, and he initially intended to write a book on race relations. But as he noted in the introduction, as he settled down to write, having thoroughly outlined a race relations book in his mind, the writing quickly neared "rockier shores" and became personal.[3] The result is a personal memoir that traces Obama's life through the early 1990s, describing how a young man found a multilayered identity that fit with his experiences and views of American history and society as well as the larger world. His discussion of these views therefore gives the book a wider scope than might be suggested by memoir.

The work shows the process by which Obama knit together the various strands of his identity through an exploration of his ethnic and historical inheritance as well as the influences of the communities in which he lived. As Obama noted in an interview with journalist Joe Klein for *Time*, "I had to reconcile a lot of different threads growing up—race, class."[4] Thus, said Klein, "Obama believes his inability to fit neatly into any group or category explains his relentless efforts to understand and reconcile opposing views." *Dreams* is the story of this reconciliation. In it Obama described the crafting of an identity that united the disparate elements of his background. His explorations of these elements necessitated a parallel foray into American history and national identity more broadly, thus crystallizing his views on those topics as well. These explorations thus played a central role in Obama's political development and shaped the rhetoric he has employed as a public figure. His personal identity—what being black, Christian, and American means to him—bears directly on his broader political views, especially the emphasis he places on service to and empathy for others.

In the introduction to the first edition of *Dreams,* Obama described the book as a depiction of his search for "a workable meaning for his life as a black American."[5] In the book itself he added, "I was trying to raise myself as a black man in America, and beyond the given of my appearance, no one around me seemed to know exactly what that meant."[6] In the preface to the second edition (published in 2004, as he was running for the U.S. Senate), he stated that he had sought to "speak in some way to the fissures of race that have characterized the American experience, as well as the fluid state of identity—the leaps through time, the collision of cultures—that mark our modern life."[7] In a November 23, 2004, interview on CBS's *Early Show,* then senator Obama pointed out that in contemporary America, many of us struggle to define the various elements of our identity, to figure out to which groups or communities we belong and how to characterize as well as prioritize those memberships. He also relayed his hope that the book would draw attention to the confusion that many young, talented black men in America face regarding their identities, emphasizing that many of them "may not have the same margins of error that I did." Thus, these are at once collective and personal issues.

Discovering the Question of Identity

The forty-fourth president was born on August 4, 1961, in Honolulu, Hawaii. He had one black parent, Barack Obama Sr., who was born and raised in Kenya, and one white parent, Stanley Ann Dunham (as an adult she went by "Ann"), who was born in Kansas and lived there as well as in Oklahoma, Texas, Washington, and Hawaii. They met as students at the University of Hawaii and married February 2, 1961. In the fall of 1962, the senior Obama left his wife and son to attend graduate school in economics at Harvard. The couple divorced in January 1964. The young Obama spent his early years mostly in Hawaii with his mother, other than a few months in Seattle in the spring of 1962.[8] At the age of six, he and his mother moved to Indonesia to live with his Indonesian stepfather, Lolo Soetoro, who had met and married his mother in 1965 while both were studying at the University of Hawaii.

Starting as an adolescent, Obama began asking questions about his ethnic identity and he wrestled with them constantly through early adulthood. During his first six years of life, however, he had not yet discovered that he "needed a race."[9] In terms of his own family's racial makeup, he said: "That my father looked nothing like the people around me—that he was black as pitch, my mother as white as milk—barely registered in my mind."[10] As Obama noted, Hawaii was extraordinarily ethnically diverse—a mix of Filipinos, Portuguese, Japanese, Hawaiians, whites, and blacks—and cultivated a certain kind of inclusive ethos. Being a young child in such a place helped keep him sheltered from the need to confront questions of ethnicity.

This circumstance continued for a time after the family's move to Indonesia. But his pre-racial Eden did not last long. Obama described the moment that it changed for him: At the age of nine, while waiting for his mother as she engaged in business at the U.S. embassy in Jakarta, he came across an issue of *Life* magazine. It contained a story about a black man who had undergone a chemical treatment to his lighten his skin in an attempt to pass as white. The man was instead left with a "strange unnatural pallor, as if blood had been drawn from the flesh."[11] The photographs provoked a visceral reaction in the young child. He wanted, needed, to get some explanation from his mother about why a person would do such a thing. But Obama restrained himself from bringing the matter up and forced a smile for her when she returned to the embassy library to retrieve him.[12]

This was a watershed moment for Obama, when he became critically engaged in exploring ethnicity, racism, and his own identity. The *Life* article, he said, "was violent for me, an ambush attack. . . . That photograph had told me something else: that there was a hidden enemy out there, one that could reach me without anyone's knowledge, not even my own."[13] Until then, Obama's ideas about blackness had come primarily from his mother, who had told him nothing but positive things about his father and black people generally. Ann Dunham described the elder Obama as a brilliant and principled man. In discussion with her son, she focused on the heroism of civil rights leaders and courageous blacks of all walks of life who fought for justice and equality. To the young Obama, in his mother's presentations "every black man was Thurgood Marshall or Sidney Poitier; every black woman Fannie Lou Hamer or Lena Horne. To be black was to be the beneficiary of a great inheritance, a special destiny, glorious burdens that only we were strong enough to bear."[14]

But the *Life* article "permanently altered" Obama's understanding of the way blacks saw themselves and were perceived by other Americans. It revealed a pathological bigotry that deeply affected the psyche of many black Americans. His mother's optimistic presentation of the way things were regarding race in America no longer fit with the reality he had discovered.[15] This event left Obama deeply shaken. He "wondered if something was wrong with me. The alternative seemed no less frightening—that the adults around me lived in the midst of madness."[16]

Another critical development in this period was Obama's developing sense of himself as an American. The family could not afford an international school in Indonesia, so he attended local schools—two years in a Muslim school, two years in a Catholic school. Obama had Indonesian friends and classmates, and from their stories—and his observations of the community in which he lived—he became aware of the hardships that poverty, disease, and brutality caused for many Indonesians. His mother was likewise acutely aware of the realities of Indonesian life, and she determined not only to make certain that her son would have the opportunities that being an American offered, but that he would have a firm grounding in American values as well. Obama noted that she spoke of "the virtues of her midwestern past and offer[ed] them up in distilled form."[17] She made clear, Obama said, that "I was an American…and my true life lay elsewhere."[18] She taught him an English correspondence course from an American curriculum, waking him at 4 a.m. Monday through Friday for his lessons. When he complained about the loss of sleep, his mother replied, "This is no picnic for me either, buster."[19]

In 1971, his mother decided to send the ten-year-old Obama back to Hawaii when he received a scholarship to attend the Punahou School. He lived with his mother's parents, Madelyn (known as "Toot," a derivative of the Hawaiian word for grandmother) and Stanley Dunham ("Gramps") in Honolulu. Obama's mother remained in Indonesia for another year before returning to Hawaii herself to begin her PhD studies in anthropology (completed in 1992), and ultimately divorced Soetoro in 1980.

Race became an issue for Obama on his very first day at school. There was only one other black child in his class and roughly half a dozen in the entire student body. By way of introductory conversation, Obama's grandfather had informed the teacher

that the elder Obama was Kenyan. She had visited the country, and while taking at-
tendance asked the young Obama if he knew the tribe to which his father belonged.
Surprised, he hesitated, then finally answered "Luo," then another boy "repeated the
word in a loud hoot, like the sound of a monkey," provoking gales of laughter from
his classmates.[20] It was another crucial moment in Obama's confrontation with the
pathologies of race that he initially discovered in *Life* magazine, and prompted him
to begin the exploration of his ethnic identity in earnest.

Stages of Ethnic Identity Development for African Americans

In her seminal article, "Talking about Race, Learning about Racism," scholar of
race and psychology Beverly Daniel Tatum described the five stages of identity development: pre-encounter, encounter, immersion, internalization, internalization–
commitment.[21] In the first stage, pre-encounter, African Americans absorb negative
stereotypes about black people and black culture from the larger society, "including
the notion that 'White is Right' and 'Black is Wrong.'" In this stage, they seek to "act
white" and to separate themselves from things associated with blackness.[22]

While one can question whether Obama had been "acting white" in his early
childhood, his discovery of the idea that blacks might want to change their skin
color is precisely the kind of event Daniel Tatum cited as precipitating the move
from the pre-encounter into the encounter stage. Likewise, Obama referred to it as
a "revelation" similar to that experienced at some point by most African American
children, although his experience differed in that, unlike many of them, he had had
"a stretch of childhood free from self-doubt" because he had been relatively sheltered
from American society's negativity toward blackness to that point.[23] This is the most
significant way that Obama's path of identity development differs from the typical
path that, according to Daniel Tatum, most black kids follow.

The encounter stage typically begins with an event—like the one Obama
described—that reveals the impossibility of the individual "becoming white" and/or
avoiding the effects of racism. During the encounter stage, the individual comes to
accept the reality of racial prejudice and is "forced to focus on his or her identity as
a member of a group targeted by racism."[24] Encounter leads into immersion, during
which the individual typically pushes away white people and nonblacks in general,
begins immersing him or herself in black culture and history, and typically forms a
worldview that focuses almost exclusively on black people. Often, this stage witnesses the individual expressing a wholly negative view of whites and an exaggeratedly

positive view of blacks. Moving deeper into this process of exploration of blackness, however, often lessens hostility towards whites, because "so much of the person's energy is directed toward his or her own group—and self-exploration. The result of this exploration is an emerging security in a newly defined and affirmed sense of self."[25]

The exit from immersion leads to internalization, in which the individual becomes confident in and comfortable with his or her blackness and is ready to reengage in a healthy way with those of other backgrounds, white and nonwhite, who are interested in being similarly engaged. The final stage, internalization–commitment, sees the individual finding a path toward bringing about greater racial equality. Daniel Tatum further noted: "The process of internalization allows the individual, anchored in a positive sense of racial identity, both to proactively perceive and transcend race."[26]

In *Dreams*, Obama rendered the construction of his personal identity in terms that largely resemble Daniel Tatum's schema. Additionally, his struggle with race in the broadest context, i.e., society and politics, influenced many of the policies he later proposed. In this personal exploration of identity, Obama became vitally interested in examining contemporary society and culture, as well as the larger narrative of the history of America. These examinations shaped his views on American national identity.

Identity Development During His Adolescence in Hawaii

According to Obama, in the early 1960s Hawaii was a place where the racial progressivism expressed by his mother and her parents fit into the mainstream. Across the country, the successes of the civil rights movement pointed toward what he characterized as "the seeming triumph of universalism over parochialism and narrow-mindedness, a bright new world where differences of race or culture would instruct and amuse and perhaps even ennoble."[27] Looking back from the perspective of the early 1990s, Obama referred to this optimism as both a "useful fiction" and a "lost Eden" that had a crucial impact on the way his family and, ultimately, he came to understand race in America.[28] According to historian James Kloppenberg, Obama "shares the skepticism" toward this mid-twentieth century universalism of those who criticized it, but "he nevertheless understands its power and appeal."[29]

Growing up in Hawaii played a profound role in shaping Obama's views on race and the American national community. In 1999, he wrote in the *Punahou Bulletin*,

"The opportunity that Hawaii offered—to experience a variety of cultures in a climate of mutual respect—became an integral part of my world view, and a basis for the values that I hold most dear."[30] Additionally, in a February 11, 2007, interview on *60 Minutes*, he credited living in Hawaii (as well as Indonesia) with exposing him to many cultures and to people of diverse backgrounds, exposure that he believes has helped him be able to "bring people together in ways that may be useful to the country." On November 13, 2011, Obama further explained that in Hawaii, "we're a single 'ohana'—one family. We remember that beneath the surface, behind all the different languages and some very long names, we all share the same hopes, the same struggles and the same aspirations. And we've learned that we're more likely to realize our aspirations when we pursue them together. That's the spirit of Hawaii. It's what made me who I am." In the 2008 presidential campaign, Obama presented this personal experience of having lived in various cultural environments as a major asset because it helps him understand American society.

Despite Hawaii's relative racial harmony, when Obama began middle school there he was not only engaged in normal adolescent struggles, but he also grappled with his ethnic identity. When he was younger, in a culture in which focusing too much on skin color was somehow seen to be boorish, many questions could be elided or ignored. Obama's grandfather, for instance, secretly mocked tourists who inquired after the ethnicity of the child playing on the beach, by telling them he was a young Hawaiian prince, next in line for the throne. At Punahou, Obama dealt with his classmates asking if he came from a tribe of cannibals.[31] In response, he spun tales of his father as chief of the tribe. All of this coincided with the only visit Obama ever had with his father, when the elder Obama came to Honolulu for a month in December 1971. The younger Obama also began his first forays into studying Kenya at this point, but found himself abandoning a book, still open on the table where he had been reading it, and walking out of the library when he found that, among other things, the Luo's "traditional costume was a leather thong across the crotch."[32]

When Obama was twelve or thirteen, another development occurred that indicated an important change to the way he approached his identity. Up to then, he had, upon meeting whites, often "advertise[d]" the fact that his mother was white.[33] He decided to stop because he had started to think he was doing so in order to encourage white people to like him. This suggests that Obama had come to harbor at least some of the negativity about blackness that he had managed to avoid in earlier years. It can also be seen as his pragmatic recognition that whites responded positively to hearing that he had a white mother, so he had sought to take advantage of that fact. Either way, the significance lay not in the fact that he had told whites about his mother or the reason he did so, but rather in the fact that he ceased this practice and the reason he did so.

As a sophomore in high school, Obama began to draw what he described as some preliminary conclusions about the broader society's view of black people. What he saw was "suffocating in its implications. We were always playing . . . by the white man's rules. . . . Because of that fundamental power he held over you . . . any distinction between good and bad whites held negligible meaning. . . . Following this maddening logic . . . being black meant only the knowledge of your own powerlessness."[34]

At the same time, however, Obama's bond with his mother and maternal grandparents acted as a check on his anger at whites, which is not to say that he never felt it. His confusion about how to square what he was learning and experiencing about racism with the fact that he loved and respected his mother and grandparents only grew as he moved deeper into adolescence. He related, "Sometimes I would find myself talking . . . about *white folks* this or *white folks* that, and I would suddenly remember my mother's smile, and the words that I spoke would seem awkward and false."[35] Nevertheless, the teenage Obama's anger toward white society and racism was powerful and deep. He needed to find a constructive way to channel that anger.

The search for answers brought Obama back to the library. He began reading black authors: James Baldwin, Ralph Ellison, Langston Hughes, Richard Wright, W. E. B. Du Bois, and Malcolm X, with the latter resonating most strongly for him, specifically because of Malcolm's emphasis on self-respect.[36] Here we see Obama taking active steps toward developing the content of a specifically black identity as a response to the racism that confronted him. As part of his immersion into black American culture, the teenage Obama leaned politically toward what he referred to as black nationalism. He acted, at least in circumstances where doing so would not have severely negative consequences, in ways that he thought would prove his "authentic" blackness and mask the insecurity he felt about that status. What Obama sought was "to reconcile the world as I'd found it with the terms of my birth."[37] To be more specific, he was trying to reconcile the racism that he had encountered with the "lost Eden" of racial harmony that he had once believed in as a child, as well as the universalistic, integrationist ideals with which his grandparents and especially his mother had imbued him.

Another incident occurred a few weeks later (presumably still his sophomore year or perhaps early in his junior year of high school) that affected Obama profoundly. One day, a particularly persistent panhandler had scared his grandmother. Panhandlers had asked her for money before, and some of them had been aggressive, yet this was the first time she had been truly frightened, too frightened to take the bus to work by herself as she had normally done. His grandfather told him that this time the panhandler had been black and that was the reason for her heightened reaction. From the text it is not clear whether Toot herself admitted this or whether it was Gramps's interpretation, although Obama's reaction implies that his grandmother had in fact admitted it to his grandfather. In either case, Obama described hearing this information as "a fist in my stomach."[38] He knew that his grandparents loved him, had sacrificed for him, and had themselves both shown an admirable progressivism on race, not just in the abstract but also with real human beings among whom they lived and worked. Nevertheless, at that time Obama took from this incident that "men who might have easily been my brothers could still inspire their rawest fears."[39]

Afterward, Obama went to speak to a friend of his grandfather's, a black man of Gramps's generation named Frank who, coincidentally, had also grown up in Wichita, Kansas, in roughly the same era that his grandparents had lived there. Frank told Obama of an unbridgeable chasm between blacks and whites, explaining that Toot was "right to be scared. . . . She understands that black people have a reason to hate."[40] After that conversation, Obama lamented that he "knew for the first time that I was utterly alone."[41] In addition to whatever he thought this assessment meant for his own family, if Frank was right—if all whites should fear blacks because racism gave them reason to hate—then the vision of an integrated America his mother had instilled in him was even more unrealistic than he had previously thought.

During the 2008 presidential campaign, Obama revisited some of these questions. On one occasion, he put himself in his mother's position and talked about "the sadness and the sense of pain and hurt that my mother would feel from a sense that blacks were painting whites with a broad brush."[42] By the early 1970s, the optimistic hope that real integration was right around the corner had largely vanished. Obama described the racial climate then as having grown tense and noted that "the view of the civil rights movement got much more complicated. Both the views of blacks and whites."[43] Here we can see just how being raised by the Dunhams rather than by black relatives gave him a different perspective on race than that of most people.

Obama demonstrated an understanding of those racial tensions both from his own viewpoint as a black person and, in a real and palpable way, that of his mother, as a stand-in for racially progressive whites. In 2004, he made a similar point about his ability to understand the perspective of working- and middle-class whites in general. Speaking about white Illinoisans he had met at a rally in central Illinois, Obama explained, "I know these people. Those are my grandparents. . . .Their manners, their sensibility, their sense of right and wrong—it's all totally familiar to me."[44]

The dashiki-wearing black nationalist Frank and the integrationist liberal Ann Dunham represented ideologically polar opposites in Obama's life at that time. He saw both, to some degree, as living in a "sixties time warp."[45] One day early in his senior year of high school, Obama had tried (but failed) to tell Ann that her "faith in justice and rationality was misplaced, that we couldn't overcome after all, that all the education and good intentions in the world couldn't help."[46] Frank, at least for a time, seemed to speak more of the truth in Obama's eyes. Toward the end of the school year, Frank told him that college and upward mobility would demand the price of "leaving your race at the door . . . leaving your people behind."[47] Frank further warned that the goal of college was nothing other than to get blacks to believe in "equal opportunity and the American way. They'll give you a corner office...and tell you you're a credit to your race. Until you want to actually start running things, and then they'll yank on your chain and let you know that you may be a well-trained, well-paid nigger, but you're a nigger just the same."

In the long run, however, Obama rejected Frank and Black Power, and his rhetoric ultimately came to embody much of his mother's approach to race. He commented during the 2008 presidential campaign that "there's an idealism that my mother passed on. And I'm glad for it. . . . If we can't aspire to something better, then why get into politics?"[48] More broadly, Obama acknowledged, "The values [my mother] taught me continue to be my touchstone when it comes to how I go about the world of politics."[49]

College Years: From Black Nationalism to American Civic Nationalism

In 1979, however, Obama had not yet come to see things that way. In that year he graduated from Punahou and enrolled at Occidental College in Los Angeles. Obama wrote of the tight-knit community he formed there with other black students, and as a group many of them "chose to function like a tribe."[50] He still felt unsure of his identity, however. Even though Obama had his crowd of fellow black students, he did not have the same kind of unselfconscious black identity that he thought some-one from Compton or Watts (his examples) had, what he called "the certainty of the tribe."[51] He felt "more like the black students who had grown up in the suburbs, kids whose parents had already paid the price of escape. . . . They weren't defined by the color of the skin. . . . They were individuals."[52]

Another student, Joyce, typified this kind of person for Obama. She identified herself as multiracial rather than black and complained that blacks rather than whites were forcing her to choose among the various elements of her heritage. Obama wrote about how, as a freshman, he had responded to these ideas with withering criticism, that he was critical of Joyce for talking about the "richness of [her] multiracial heri-tage" but in reality simply avoiding blacks.[53] Even at the same time he was being critical of her, however, he realized that he was being "too hard on poor Joyce."[54]

In the attitudes of Joyce and those like her, Obama recognized many of his own, including some that he was trying to suppress because they frightened him. He fur-ther explained that these students' ambivalence and uncertainty led him to "question my own racial credentials all over again. . . . I needed to . . . convince myself that I wasn't compromised—that I was indeed still awake. To avoid being mistaken for a sellout, I chose my friends carefully. The more politically active black students . . . we discussed neocolonialism, Franz (sic) Fanon, Eurocentrism, and patriarchy."[55] This is an almost iconic image of one type of college experience for African American students, according to which they adopt black nationalist and radical multicultural political stances.

As Obama described it, in order to reconfirm (for himself more than others) his racial credentials, he reacted against black students who behaved in ways that didn't live up to his own definition of "black enough." On one occasion he was involved in a dorm room conversation with two other black students, one of whom was Marcus, who at that time exemplified for Obama the "authentic black experi-ence."[56] A fourth student, Tim, entered the room, asking Obama, "Do you have that assignment for econ?" Obama described him as acting and talking white: "Tim wore argyle sweaters and pressed jeans and talked like Beaver Cleaver." After Tim left the room, Obama suggested to the others that he should "change his name from Tim to Tom." Immediately, Marcus chastised him, suggesting that he focus on himself rather than judge others. Obama "burned with . . . resentment" for an entire year be-fore he realized that Marcus had been right. Obama spent his freshman year, which he characterized as "one long lie," inwardly grappling with his insecurity about the authenticity of his blackness while outwardly trying to be blacker-than-thou.

One important positive thing occurred. Obama forged a deep connection to Regina, a classmate from Chicago's South Side. He spoke to her about a goal that drove his academic studies and on which, psychologically speaking, his very life depended. Obama sought "to understand how people learn to hate."[57] Obama was thus determined not only to understand who he was and why he acted the way he did, but also why others were who they were and acted the way they did. As for Regina, he envied her as she talked about her family and the black community in which she was raised. "Her voice evoked a vision of black life in all its possibility, a vision that filled me with longing—a longing for place, and a fixed and definite history."[58]

About this time, Obama began to go by his given name, Barack, rather than Barry, which he had always used. He did not write much about this change, other than to mention that during the next few years he sometimes corrected those who called him Barry. In a conversation with Regina he related that his father had called himself Barry upon arriving in Hawaii because "it was easier to pronounce. You know—helped him fit in. Then it got passed to me. So I could fit in."[59] He was, however, pleased when Regina offered to call him Barack.

During his sophomore year of college, Obama had another epiphany, also thanks to Regina. He had spoken one afternoon at an antiapartheid rally, publicly displaying his passion about the issue of South Africa, and then ran into her at a party that evening. When Regina praised what he'd done that day, Obama cynically dismissed the value of that kind of activism as simply feeding the ego of the activist. In response, she called him out on his narcissism, "Well, let me tell you something, Mr. Obama. It's not just about you. It's never just about you."[60]

This reprimand and Regina's carefully chosen words that followed, along with the words of Marcus, the student who had chastised him for putting down Tim as a "Tom," opened Obama's eyes to a fundamental truth about race and values. After reflection, he realized that what he had begun to think of as "white" values—honesty, thoughtfulness, diligence, humility, responsibility, and accountability—the values he had heard praised by his mother and grandparents, read about in philosophy texts, and heard from some parts of broader mainstream American culture, were shared by these black students he had come to deeply respect.

At some point in his teenage years, he had begun to think of these values as tainted because they came from a world that, because of racial bigotry, had devalued men like himself and his father. Obama had rejected those values because he was "so eager . . . to escape the imagined traps that white authority had set for me. To that white world, I had been willing to cede the values of my childhood, as if those values were somehow irreversibly soiled by the endless falsehoods that white spoke about black."[61] Obama had been engaged in a profound struggle, having rejected anything white, even the lessons he learned from his own family. Now, however, we see him beginning to integrate the parts of his identity into a coherent whole and move forward. In a July 25, 2004, interview on *Meet the Press*, Obama credited his ultimate success in overcoming his confusion about identity—and in leaving behind some of the self-destructive behavior he had engaged in while dealing with it—to the "very much midwestern values" his mother and maternal grandparents had instilled in him.

After Regina's reprimand, Obama began to consider his own actions more critically. How had he become all about himself? He recognized, he said, that this self-absorption grew out of his fear and insecurity about who he was, and where and whether he belonged. His real fear was that he would not find acceptance from either whites or blacks, that he would "forever remain an outsider."[62] Obama realized that he could no longer operate so selfishly. He would have to focus not only on himself, but also on those around him and the world in which they lived. Obama would find a place for himself in that world by engaging with it, by standing up for other people in order to change it for the better. For whom would he stand up?

I imagined Regina's grandmother somewhere, her back bent, the flesh of her arms shaking as she scrubbed an endless floor. . . . The old woman's face dissolved from my mind, only to be replaced by a series of others. The copper-skinned face of the Mexican maid [a reference to the woman who cleaned up after Obama and other careless students in his dorm], straining as she carries out the garbage. The face of Lolo's mother drawn with grief as she watches the Dutch burn down her house. The tight-lipped, chalk-colored face of Toot as she boards the 6:30 a.m. bus that will take her to work. Only a lack of imagination, a failure of nerve, had made me think that I had to choose between them. They all asked the same thing of me, these grandmothers of mine. My identity might begin with the fact of my race, but it didn't, couldn't, end there. At least that's what I would choose to believe.[63]

This realization is the key moment on Obama's journey toward self-discovery. After exploring both sides of his heritage, he has integrated them into a single yet multilayered identity. He now recognized the commonalities shared by the white family members he loved and the black peers he admired, as well as Americans and beyond that human beings of all ethnicities. Obama was coming to a fully formed understanding of his sense of belonging. He had advanced beyond a self-absorbed identity—one focused solely on assuaging insecurities about his blackness—toward empathy and the embrace of a broader sense of community that began with his black identity but no longer ended there. In political terms, he moved from identity politics and radical multiculturalism toward an inclusive, liberal nationalism of the kind described in chapter 2.

Obama echoed these sentiments in more recent comments as well. In the February 11, 2007, *60 Minutes* interview he noted: "I am rooted in the African American community, but I'm not defined by it. I am comfortable in my racial identity and recognize that I'm part of a very specific set of experiences in this country, but that's not the core of who I am. Another way of saying [sic] is that's not all I am." These remarks echo what Obama said in a March 2004 interview, just after winning the Democratic primary for the U.S. Senate seat from Illinois: "I'm rooted in the African American community, but I'm not limited by it."[64] In an October 2004 interview, he remarked, "I never saw being black as something that carried negative connotations," and continued, "I'd describe myself as coming from several cultures and feel I belong to all of them."[65] Similarly, in his second book, *The Audacity of Hope*, published in 2006, he explained that, thanks to the multiracial nature of his family, "I've never had the option of restricting my loyalties on the basis of race, or measuring my worth on the basis of tribe."[66]

Some critics, in particular during the scandal around his former pastor's sermons (see chapter 5), have dismissed these relatively recent remarks, accusing Obama of downplaying for political gain the depth of his black identity and his exploration of black nationalism. Such criticism ignores his expression of a multilayered identity going back to *Dreams*. As for the book itself, it also includes frank admissions of his drug use, including cocaine. This suggests that he was not writing a campaign biography designed to win future votes, especially considering that he wrote it in an era when even youthful marijuana use was controversial among candidates for high office (i.e., Bill Clinton in 1992 having had to claim that he had tried marijuana but "didn't inhale").

For African Americans, the process of reconciling the different elements of their identity is particularly complex. Du Bois famously termed it "double-consciousness." Martin Luther King Jr. said that being African American meant having a dual-layered identity, and that a black American must "accept his ambivalence. . . . The Negro is the child of two cultures—Africa and America. The problem is that in the search for wholeness all too many Negroes seek to embrace only one side of their natures."[67] He asserted that blacks should be proud of their black heritage and never be ashamed of their oppression as slaves in America. Unfortunately, King said, some rejected anything black and "end up frustrated and without cultural roots" while others "seek to reject everything American and to identify totally with Africa. . . . This approach also leads to frustration because the American Negro is not an African. . . . He is Afro-American, a true hybrid, a combination of two cultures." This notion of hybridity, of having more than one layer to one's identity, is one that Obama adopted for himself and brought to his definition of American national identity.

In *Dreams*, Obama also examined his maternal inheritance. His grandparents grew up in Wichita, Kansas. His grandmother, Toot, came from Scottish and English stock. A distant ancestor was rumored to be full-blooded Cherokee, which was a source of shame to Toot's mother, though Toot herself proudly showed off her "beaked nose, which, along with a pair of jet black eyes, was offered as proof of Cherokee blood."[68] On May 23, 2011, President Obama spoke about his Irish ancestry (on his maternal grandfather's side) in some detail during his visit to Ireland. There he noted that the American dream had drawn both his grandfather's grandfather from Ireland and his own father from Kenya to cross the Atlantic and come to this country.

At the end of his sophomore year, Obama transferred from Occidental to Columbia University, in New York City. He was demoralized by the contrast in Manhattan between the Wall Street–led boom and the poverty he saw in other communities on the island. Now, more sure of his own identity, he still wasn't quite sure where he fit in the world in which he lived. Of this period, he wrote: "I was seeing the steady fracturing of the world taking place. I had seen worse poverty in Indonesia and glimpsed the violent mood of inner-city kids in L.A.; I had grown accustomed, everywhere, to suspicion between the races. But . . . it was only now that I began to grasp the almost mathematical precision with which America's race and class problems joined; the depth, the ferocity, of resulting tribal wars."[69] This was his general frame of mind when his mother and sister came to visit, and Obama found himself irritated, particularly with his mother's reaction to an old film and what he saw as her naiveté in matters of race. He was becoming disheartened, thinking that "emotions between the races could never be pure. . . . The other race would always remain just that: menacing, alien, and apart."[70]

But a few days later his mother, apparently unaware of what Obama was feeling, retold the story of how his parents had met, their relationship, and the details of his father's life, the man he had seen only once since infancy. His mother had always tried to help her son to know his father, but the love with which Ann spoke about the elder Obama on this day taught the son something else that proved vitally important, "something that I suspect most Americans will never hear from the lips of those of another race, and so cannot be expected to believe might exist between black and white: the love of someone who knows your life in the round, a love that will survive disappointment."[71] This conversation with his mother about his father opened, or perhaps more accurately, re-opened his eyes to a possibility he had once believed as a child but had somehow lost touch with over the years. The conversation later took on a special poignancy because a few months later, on November 24, 1982, Obama's father died at the age of 46 in a car crash in Nairobi, Kenya.

In 1983, just before graduating from Columbia, Obama decided that he would become a community organizer. He was drawn to the chance to engage directly in helping African Americans in a constructive way. He put it a bit more bluntly in an August 1995 interview, "Through this work [as a community organizer], I could be angry about the plight of African Americans without being angry at all white folks."[72]

In describing what inspired him to pursue this calling, Obama reflected back on the stories his mother told him as a child about the civil rights movement. He came to believe that community organizing would allow him to truly earn membership in the African American community through service, and to find his place in the multiethnic American community as well. Obama expressed his hope that "because this community I imagined was still in the making, built on the promise that the larger American community, black, white, and brown, could somehow redefine itself—I believed that it might, over time, admit the uniqueness of my own life."[73] Here we see him, in his very early twenties, identifying himself in a meaningful way as both part of a particular ethnic group (black) and a multiethnic, civic nation (American). Additionally, Obama revealed his optimism that the generally accepted definition of the American national community would grow more inclusive over time.

Community Organizing: Cementing His Identity as Black and American
Two years after graduating from Columbia, Obama got a job as a community organizer in Chicago on a project devoted to bringing together blacks from the city and
whites from the suburbs to preserve manufacturing jobs in the area. Obama's job
was to organize the urban blacks while the man who hired him, "Marty," organized
the suburban, mostly white communities.[74] Obama was excited by the potential
of bringing together working-class people of different races around their common
economic interests: "Seeing all these black and white faces together in one place,
I, too found myself feeling cheered, recognizing in myself the same vision driving
Marty, his confidence in the populist impulse and working-class solidarity."[75] He saw
the need to invigorate cross-ethnic unity in order to help ameliorate the debilitating
economic problems faced by all disadvantaged Americans. Doing so also happened
to be the best way to help the black community. This lesson, which paralleled the
thinking of Martin Luther King Jr., proved central to Obama's rhetorical and political approach to socioeconomic inequality (see chapter 4).

His work with Chicago's black community gave Obama "the sense of place and
purpose" for which he'd been searching.[76] He had not yet, however, answered all
his questions about black identity, in particular about what kind of black identity
would be the most productive from the perspective of the black community as a
whole. Obama had initially been concerned that a collective focus on self-esteem
and racial pride could easily slip into "vague exhortation."[77] Perhaps it would be
better, he thought, to focus on education for children and job skills for adults, and
let that foundation serve as a basis for self-esteem. But Obama came to reconsider
that judgment, as he learned just how widespread were negative feelings about blackness in the black community itself. He decided that positive change would require
a transformation in the way black individuals viewed themselves and one another.
The question was: what was the right way to go about achieving that transformation?
Despite having rejected such notions as a younger man, Obama admitted to at least
asking himself once again whether it might be necessary to turn black self-hatred
outward toward white society, which was, after all, the original source of those negative stereotypes.[78]

As part of Obama's work, he began meeting fairly regularly with Rafiq, a black
nationalist activist who considered anyone not black to be an enemy. "His was a
Hobbesian world where . . . loyalties extended from family to mosque to the black

race—whereupon notions of loyalty ceased to apply."[79] Obama had rejected any ideology that required hating whites in order to lift blacks up; however, he saw how nationalists like Rafiq were able to successfully utilize that hatred in their attempts to do so. The kind of black nationalism professed by Rafiq presented "an unambiguous morality tale that was easily communicated and easily grasped. . . . Whites are responsible for your sorry state, not any inherent flaws in you. In fact, whites are so heartless and devious that we can no longer expect anything from them."[80] Obama recognized the appeal of such an approach, in a world with such deep and destructive black self-hatred. In fact, he wondered whether Rafiq might not be right, whether an approach "that failed to elevate race loyalty above all else was a politics inadequate to the task."[81]

Rafiq prompted Obama to at least reconsider the possibilities of black nationalism. Obama now saw firsthand the grinding problems faced every day by Chicago's black community. Nevertheless, the idea that Rafiq even might be right was painful for Obama. As had Frank, Rafiq contradicted the values Obama had learned from his mother, namely that he should judge each person as an individual based on how that person treated him as well as others. Although he had explored adopting other moral frameworks earlier in his life, ones that more closely resembled the solely race-based thinking of Frank and Rafiq, he found ultimately that he believed, needed to believe, much the same things as Ann Dunham did.

However, even if Obama knew that black nationalism was wrong for him personally, Rafiq's seeming effectiveness led him to ask whether, at least temporarily, it might be the right path for black Americans as a community to follow. Perhaps his own experiences truly were so different from those of other blacks that the stance Obama needed to take for his own sake was one that African Americans could not afford as a community. Ultimately, it came down to this: "If [black] nationalism could create a strong and effective insularity, deliver on its promise of self-respect, then the hurt it might cause well-meaning whites, or the inner turmoil it caused people like me, would be of little consequence."[82]

Examining the question pragmatically, however, Obama came to believe that black nationalism could not bring about fundamental change and progress either for black Americans or for the American community. Watching how Rafiq operated, over time, convinced Obama of this. He noted that "[Rafiq] was less interested in changing the rules of power than in the color of those who had it."[83] In other words, a simple strategy calling for replacing whites at the top of an oppressive system with blacks was not a feasible strategy for solving the problems of the black community. Obama acknowledged that stoking black anger through race-baiting could prove, unfortunately, to be a good strategy for an individual black politician looking to move up. In the end, however, Obama condemned this kind of race-baiting, conspiracy-mongering, and prejudice towards whites, Jews, Asians, or anyone else because it did tremendous damage.

Such slander not only insulted those targeted as well as sabotaged the creation of a multiethnic coalition, but it created in the black community a gap between "our talk and our action. . . . It eventually eroded our ability to hold either ourselves or each other accountable. And while none of this was unique to black politicians or to black nationalists . . . it was blacks who could least afford such make-believe."[84] In his final mention of Rafiq, which took place approximately a year after their initial contact, Obama told of how the erstwhile black nationalist was encouraging him to help raise funds from "white" nonprofit foundations.[85]

Being grounded in reality and creating a plan to deal productively with that reality creates real self-esteem, Obama said. It was this fundamental truth that led him "to conclude, perhaps for the final time, that notions of purity—of race or of culture—could no more serve as the basis for the typical black American's self-esteem than it could for mine."[86] Black self-esteem "would have to arise from something more fine than the bloodlines we inherited. It would have to find root . . . in all the messy, contradictory details of our experience." Here Obama has put to rest the temptations of black nationalism, both for himself and the community. He instead embraced integration, both for himself and the community.

On Obama's ethnic identity development in Chicago there is one other salient anecdote. He described meeting Asante Moran, a public high school teacher whose curriculum leaned heavily on African culture and history. Commenting on the African posters he saw in the teacher's office, Obama asked himself what effect they might have on the black students who came there. He decided that the answer was: "Probably not as much as Asante himself. . . . A man willing to listen. A hand placed on a young man's shoulders."[87] For Obama, meaningful, sustained contact with an adult whom a young person could admire as a role model was the real key, whether that adult wore kente cloth or an Oxford blazer.

The Development of Obama's Religious Identity

The one remaining major piece in Obama's identity development was his religious identity, something he solidified during his time in Chicago. As his ties to the black community grew deeper, he found himself drawn to the Christian faith that most of its members expressed, and specifically the faith he found in the black church. Obama was raised a nominal Christian in the Dunham household but had virtually no experience with a church community and considered himself to that point mostly a skeptic about organized religion. He referred to his mother's parents as "'non-practicing' Christians."[88] Obama described his mother as "secular," but added: "She was in many ways the most spiritually awakened person that I've ever known."[89] In remarks at the National Prayer Breakfast on February 3, 2011, Obama expanded on the influence of his mother's spirituality: "She was somebody who was instinctively guided by the Golden Rule. . . . And it's because of her that I came to understand the equal worth of all men and all women." The elder Obama, although raised Muslim, had become "a confirmed atheist" by the time he met Ann Dunham, according to their son.[90]

Upon his move to Chicago, however, Obama remained independent of any particular congregation or faith institution at first. Eventually he chose Trinity United Church of Christ in Chicago, where the pastor was Reverend Jeremiah A. Wright Jr. Obama described the congregation's core principles, what it called a "black value system."[91] The members were to become "black Christian activists, soldiers for black freedom and the dignity of all humankind." Other principles included "a commitment to the black community and black family, education, the work ethic, discipline, and self-respect." One other principle stood out for Obama: the value system called for blacks to avoid the divisive temptation to use one's material success to look down on other, less successful blacks, an attitude it called "middleclassness." The principles offered a combination of old-fashioned values, ethnic consciousness, and black unity, as well as a more universal commitment to humanity. Obama found these ideals compatible with his worldview, referring to the list as "powerful."[92]

Obama found himself deeply moved listening to a sermon titled "The Audacity of Hope," in which Reverend Wright talked about both the hard, brutal conditions black people had faced due to racism, as well as the hope that their Christian faith gave them to move forward. Obama began to embrace a new understanding of what this faith could mean to him and—most crucially for the purposes of this book—of his understanding of his ethnic identity and his relationship to other Americans who were not black:

> I imagined the stories of ordinary black people merging with the stories of David and Goliath, Moses and Pharaoh, the Christians in the lion's den, Ezekiel's field of dry bones. Those stories—of survival, and freedom, and hope—became our story, my story; the blood that had spilled was our blood, the tears our tears; until this black church, on this bright day, seemed once more a vessel carrying the story of a people into future generations and into a larger world. Our trials and triumphs became at once unique and universal, black and more than black; in chronicling our journey, the stories and songs gave us a means to reclaim memories that we didn't need to feel shame about . . . memories that all people might study and cherish—and with which we could start to rebuild. . . . I also felt for the first time how that spirit carried within it, nascent, incomplete, the possibility of moving beyond our narrow dreams.[93]

Christianity and the black church became a central part of Obama's identity in two ways. First, it gave him a spiritual foundation for his commitment to helping others and the faith in humanity he inherited from his secular mother. Second, his faith influenced his blackness as well, because the black church and its role in fighting for equality for African Americans became central to his understanding of what it meant to be a black American. Moreover, finding this religious/cultural community also strengthened his commitment to another, more universal sense of belonging that stood alongside his black identity, one that complemented rather than superseded blackness. The trials of black people paralleled the trials of peoples from all traditions and faiths. The black church helped Obama to marry more completely the two fundamental categories of his identity: the particularistic and the universal, the ethnic and the cross-ethnic, the black and the American/human.

The similarities between that quotation and the earlier one in which he described Toot, Lolo's mother, Regina's grandmother, and the Mexican maid as "these grandmothers of mine" are striking. In each quotation, the commonalities of the struggles that members of all ethnic groups face outweigh the boundaries that separate them, allowing someone from any background to identify with the struggles a person from any other group has experienced. In each quotation, Obama described an integration process by which he, to paraphrase Daniel Tatum, proactively perceives and transcends race, a process that both respects difference and appeals to universality and unity.

"What Binds Us Together": Obama's America in Dreams

The rest of *Dreams* detailed Obama's visit to his father's family in Kenya in the middle of 1988, which further helped him understand his relationship to his father and to his African relatives. After his return from Kenya, Obama began attending Harvard Law School in the fall of 1988. After graduation in the spring of 1991, he returned to Chicago to practice law. In the book's epilogue, written six years after the Kenya trip, Obama reflected back on what he had learned about himself. He also offered his view on the meaning of the American community and of American history. "*We hold these truths to be self-evident.* In those words, I hear the spirit of Douglass and Delany, as well as Jefferson and Lincoln; the struggles of Martin and Malcolm and unheralded marchers to bring these words to life (emphasis in original)."[94]

Obama went on to describe other members of the American community, both past and present, to whom the truths of the Declaration belong: "Japanese families interned behind barbed wire; young Russian Jews cutting patterns in Lower East Side sweatshops; dust-bowl farmers loading up their trucks with the remains of shattered lives . . . the people in Altgeld Gardens [the housing project in Chicago whose residents he worked with closely], and . . . those who stand outside this country's borders, the weary, hungry bands crossing the Rio Grande."[95] Looking forward, he found himself "modestly encouraged" about the prospect that "what binds us together might somehow, ultimately, prevail."[96] It is worth contrasting Obama's cautious optimism on this question with the harsh pessimism offered by many black political thinkers in the same period, perhaps typified by law professor Derrick Bell, who bluntly declared at the outset of his 1992 book: "Racism is an integral, permanent, and indestructible component of this society."[97]

The national narrative Obama offered in *Dreams* includes "outsider" groups, people typically excluded from the traditional, pre-1960s chronicle of American history. Obama depicts them all—interestingly, even the undocumented immigrants crossing the Rio Grande—as legatees of the Declaration's proclamation of equality. This is not, however, a radical multicultural depiction of America. The people in Obama's version all embrace their roles in a single, common story. The groups he lists do not reject America, despite the hardships and severe mistreatment they have faced here; nor are they separate nationalities defined solely by ethnicity or culture or religion. They are Americans, unified around the central principle of equality proclaimed in 1776; they constitute a single people who will remain bound together. In these words we see Obama's America.

During the 2008 presidential campaign, Obama remarked that his purpose in writing *Dreams* had been "to try and locate my own experiences, that on their face seem pretty odd and atypical, within the larger American story."[98] What is so important about his memoir, for the purposes of my book, is that it shows not only the construction of his black identity, but also the self-conscious construction of his American identity. Obama was writing the book in the early 1990s, when debates about multiculturalism, ethnic identity, and American national identity were perhaps at their most fierce. In *Dreams* we see the core of how Obama would describe American national identity when he reached the national stage a decade later.

In the 2004 preface to the work, Obama noted that he intended to address the political and cultural struggle "between those who embrace our teeming, colliding, irksome diversity, while insisting on a set of values that binds us together, and those who would seek, under whatever flag or slogan or sacred text, a certainty and simplification that justifies cruelty toward those not like us."[99] In this statement, Obama laid out a vision of balance: a nation that "embraces" ethnic and cultural diversity in a realistic way, although it may indeed be "irksome" at times, while simultaneously cultivating a unity based on democratic values. He added in a 2008 interview that a key goal of *Dreams* as well as his campaign for the presidency was to demonstrate "what America is about: people from diverse backgrounds and unlikely places finding a common culture and a common set of values and ideals that make them American."[100]

This vision of our country captures the essence of democratic pluralism. Obama has long sought to influence the way Americans understood their ethnic and national identity. Specifically, Obama hoped that the story laid out in *Dreams* would encourage us to resist the pull of adopting a narrow, particularistic sense of belonging and instead find empathy for and commonality with Americans of other backgrounds. Toward that end he proclaimed, "The hardening of lines, the embrace of fundamentalism and tribe dooms us all."[101] Here, he juxtaposed his conception of American national identity to the identity politics of the far left and of the hard right. Obama has said that spreading this lesson, which he identifies as the core of what America represents, stands at the center not only of this first book, but his entire political career.[102]

In the final pages of *Dreams*, Obama described his work as a lawyer fighting discrimination cases, the kind, he noted, "we like to tell ourselves should no longer exist."[103] In doing so, he sought to help bring about the vision of America he described above. Obama explained that these cases succeed when the black plaintiff who experienced the discrimination and the white coworkers who testify as witnesses decide to take a stand, despite the various reasons all of them have to be reluctant to come forward. These people all realize that "a principle is at stake, that despite everything that has happened, those words put to paper over two hundred years ago must mean something after all. Black and white, they make their claim on this community we call America. They choose our better history."[104]

In his inaugural address on January 20, 2009, Obama deftly tied his own life story and family history to the historic discrimination faced by black Americans. He talked about how amazing it was that "a man whose father less than sixty years ago might not have been served in a local restaurant [in then segregated Washington, D.C.] can now stand before you to take a most sacred oath." This was a neat rhetorical trick, considering that his father never did have such an experience, at least Obama never wrote or spoke publicly about it, but this hypothetical anecdote served an important purpose nonetheless, namely to situate his own family's story within the collective experiences of black Americans and that of the American nation more broadly.

4

Obama on Racial Discrimination

Causes, Effects, and Policies to Combat It

Melissa Harris-Perry has identified four basic, broad ideologies that encompass much of contemporary African American political thought: black nationalism, black conservatism, black feminism, and liberal integrationism.[1] There certainly are significant divergences—particularly in rhetorical style and points of emphasis—among liberal integrationists. Nevertheless, Obama's approach to combating racial prejudice and overcoming the harm it has caused clearly fits within this category.

Harris-Perry summarized liberal integrationism as seeking an America where blacks possess the same rights and can exercise the same freedoms as all other citizens. In her view, liberal integrationists "locate the source of black inequality in corrupt institutions but believe that individuals can have good intentions and that cross-racial alliances are both possible and necessary. . . . [They] accept that the American system works in theory, the problem is that, in practice, it only works for privileged members of society."[2] Ultimately, integrationists believe that "the most effective way to pursue the interests of blacks is to link black interests to those of the larger American society." This philosophy bears strong similarities to broader American liberalism, albeit with a "greater emphasis on equality, the notion of collective rather than individual rights, and the reliance on a strong central state."

Liberal Integrationism: Obama and Martin Luther King Jr.

The liberal integrationism of Obama reflects most strongly the influence of the twentieth century's most important liberal integrationist thinker: Martin Luther King Jr. Thinkers and politicians on just about all sides—both liberals and conservatives—

of any issue relating to racism and equality in America find themselves looking to King's words for ideological support, a testament to his iconic status.[3] Right-wing media personality Glenn Beck, at his "Restoring Honor" rally of August 28, 2010 (held forty-seven years to the day, and at the same location where Reverend King delivered his "I Have A Dream" speech), listed a number of heroic figures, including Moses, George Washington, Abraham Lincoln, and King. Beck then claimed that of them, "I can relate to Martin Luther King probably the most."

Obama looks to King, however, not just for rhetorical flourish or in support of an isolated policy position, but in terms of King's very specific and coherent ideology. Reverend King considered integration to be fundamental to solving the problems African Americans confronted. He envisioned it not simply as a by-product of achieving civil rights, but rather as the core element of the process by which black Americans would achieve equality in the first place.

In terms of ethnic identity, Obama also paralleled the approach of King. Reverend King believed it was important to strengthen the "group consciousness" of blacks, but distinguished this from what he described as black nationalism's push for a self-imposed isolation or exclusivity.[4] He summarized black nationalism as "a nihilistic philosophy born out of the conviction that the Negro can't win . . . that America is so hopelessly corrupt and enmeshed in evil that there is no possibility of salvation from within."[5] Obama's approach bears a striking similarity.

Having achieved tremendous legislative victories in the mid-1960s, King argued that economics, rather than race, should be the focus of black politics in the years moving forward. In *Where Do We Go from Here*, written in 1967, he said: "One unfortunate thing about Black Power is that it gives priority to race precisely at a time when the impact of automation and other forces have made the economic question fundamental for blacks and whites alike. In this context, the slogan 'Power for Poor People' would be much more appropriate than the slogan 'Black Power.'"[6] He called for a shift in the movement's priorities.

Now that black Americans had won legal equality and had triumphed in matters relating to their "personal dignity," the time had come to push for changes that would "go beyond race and deal with economic inequality, wherever it exists. In the pursuit of these goals, the white poor become involved, and the potentiality emerges for a powerful new alliance."[7] In addition to the severe poverty among blacks, King noted, "We must not overlook the fact that millions of Puerto Ricans, Mexican Americans, Indians, and Appalachian whites are also poverty stricken. Any serious war against poverty must of necessity include them."[8] He appealed for an alliance of liberals, working-class whites, and blacks to achieve real reform on these issues.[9] King had, in 1964's *Why We Can't Wait*, lamented the fact that thus far, unfortunately, poor Southern whites "saw the color that separated them from Negroes more clearly than they saw the circumstances that bound them together in mutual interest."[10]

Obama has adopted the same approach. Like King, he has cast his calls for greater economic equality in universal, nonracial terms going back to his time as a community organizer in Chicago, where he worked for three years on an effort to unite urban blacks and suburban whites in an attempt to save manufacturing jobs in Chicago, among other goals.[11] In the view of liberal integrationists, the disproportionate nature of black economic inequality means that the successes won by a broad, multiethnic coalition would ultimately bring significant benefits to African Americans.

For example, in a December 1995 interview done just after he announced for the Illinois Senate, Obama spoke about the Million Man March of that October and black politics in general. He acknowledged the legitimacy of expressing a strong racial identity, and argued, as had King, that black nationalist sentiments grew in direct proportion to the feeling that "white Americans couldn't care less about the profound problems African Americans are facing."[12] Obama further noted: "Cursing out white folks is not going to get the job done. Anti-Semitic and anti-Asian statements are not going to lift us up." He rejected an approach based on black economic self-sufficiency and the contention that racism alone held African Americans back. Instead, Obama called for transforming "the larger economic forces that are creating economic insecurity for all workers—whites, Latinos, and Asians."

During his failed 2000 bid for the U.S. House of Representatives, Obama similarly said: "We have more in common with the Latino community, the white community, than we have differences, and you have to work with them, just from a practical political perspective."[13] The parallels are striking between his rhetoric and that of King on the issue of how economic insecurity affects members of all ethnic groups as well as the need for a cross-ethnic approach to tackling that problem.

Throughout his career, Obama has called attention to specific issues or policies that disproportionately affect African Americans without approaching them solely as issues of race. During his years in the Illinois Senate (1997–2004), Obama wrote a semiregular column in the *Hyde Park Herald*. One article contained a section called "consumer issues" in which he stated, "Since taxpayers are often overpowered by large financial interests in Springfield, I am working to help consumers in financial transactions. I am specifically interested in protecting consumers from 'redlining,' which is when certain financial institutions discriminate against people because of income, race, or where they live."[14] Redlining is typically associated with discrimination in the area of housing and mortgages. The goal of redlining is to segregate neighborhoods by race. In that same section, Obama mentioned his sponsorship of legislation to protect consumers who write checks at department stores and groceries, and to investigate so-called payday loans that often carried egregiously high interest rates.

Combating redlining is a major civil rights issue, one that black leaders in particular have emphasized for decades. Notice how Obama framed the issue for his own constituents. He talked about how redlining discriminates on the basis of race, but also income and location. Obama did not mention blacks or African Americans specifically, and presented the issue in terms of consumer protection rather black grievance. This is a textbook example of how he chooses a nonracially specific way to discuss an issue that disproportionately affects the black community. Obama instead drew on universal principles and linked the issue to broader questions of economic power and justice while nevertheless making clear to anyone familiar with the issue that he understood that racial discrimination stood at the core of the matter.

Certainly Obama did also address, on a number of occasions, the specific problems that urban blacks face. One of his *Hyde Park Herald* columns, for instance, contrasted two race-related incidents. Lenard Clark, a black teen, entered a white neighborhood and was subsequently severely beaten by white teens "apparently motivated solely by racial hatred."[15] The other incident involved a march, attended by over one thousand young black men, protesting the drug and conspiracy trial of Larry Hoover, whom Obama described as "a convicted felon and acknowledged head of one of the country's largest street gangs." Both stories, he argued, should be "just as troubling to those of us concerned with the state of race relations, and the state of the nation."

While the first story laid bare the harm African Americans experienced due to racist violence, the second reflected the alienation of large numbers of black youth. Obama rejected the idea that poverty and lack of opportunity served as excuses for criminal behavior and he acknowledged the need for punishment. However, he argued that Illinois could reduce juvenile crime by spending more on various forms of prevention-oriented programs and less on juvenile correctional facilities. Over the years Obama often reiterated the message that it made little sense to jail young, nonviolent offenders, and criticized legislatively mandated minimum sentences that required locking them up.[16]

Obama spoke this way throughout his service in the state legislature—sometimes mentioning race, but more often raising the issues that concerned his urban constituents in a race-neutral way. For instance, his *Hyde Park Herald* columns during his first three years in Springfield included discussions of: tax fairness (a common theme for the duration of his time in office), genetic testing, campaign finance reform, health care coverage, and child support payments. Obama wrote a column that brought attention to the problem of excessive lead levels in the blood of Chicago's young children.[17] He noted persistent questions about whether the enforcement of gun laws was disproportionately vigorous in minority communities, and talked about his plan to introduce a bill that would measure racial profiling by mandating that police keep racial statistics of those citizens stopped by officers.[18]

From 2000 to 2004, the state senator wrote about the death penalty (he ultimately led a successful push to enact legislation that required police to videotape all interrogations in cases where capital crimes were committed), the earned income tax credit, public school funding, financial assistance for home heating, job training for laid off workers, treatment rather than incarceration for nonviolent female and juvenile offenders, funding for homeless shelters and homeless programs, budget priorities during a recession, prescription drugs for the elderly, health insurance coverage, the Iraq war, minimum wage, the expansion of Chicago's airport capacity, and reform for retirees' corporate pensions, among other issues. He lamented the poor service and facilities available on the public transportation system, particularly the one rail line out of eleven that served a predominantly black clientele.[19] Obama emphasized the need for government to do more to help reintegrate ex-felons into society by helping them to find gainful employment as well as receive necessary services. In keeping with his career-long rhetorical approach, he described these policies in a relatively race-neutral fashion, but noted that they would disproportionately aid minority communities.[20] Obama criticized then governor George Ryan's veto of $2.2 million for AIDS prevention outreach and treatment in minority communities, but did so without accusing anyone of bigotry.[21]

Here, Obama was speaking generally to the benefits of such policies to the communities that he represented and Illinois in general, presaging the rhetoric he would employ on the national stage. Obama's liberal nationalism holds that such programs and policies are not only a matter of justice but that they also benefit the country by maximizing the productive potential of too often ignored segments of the population. In this he draws on King as well.

Obama's depiction of America's core values also strongly parallels that offered by Reverend King. In his "Letter from a Birmingham Jail," for example, King said of civil rights protestors: "They were in reality standing up for what is best in the American dream and for the most sacred values in our Judaeo Christian heritage, thereby bringing our nation back to those great wells of democracy which were dug deep by the Founding Fathers."[22] Obama echoed these sentiments when, at the 2004 Democratic National Convention, he spoke of "the greatness of our nation. . . . Our pride is based on a very simple premise, summed up in a declaration made over two hundred years ago, 'We hold these truths to be self-evident, that all men are created equal. That they are endowed by their Creator with certain inalienable rights. That among these are life, liberty, and the pursuit of happiness.'"

In terms of the broader story of race in this country's past, present, and future, King rejected hopelessness in favor of a more nuanced yet ultimately optimistic vision, one that contains strong parallels to the vision Obama would present two generations later. Reverend King identified the "schizophrenic duality of conduct" in an America founded on ideals of equality but that had subsequently committed great acts of violence and oppression based on white supremacy.[23] If America would merely apply its own core principles, "return to her true home . . . she would give the democratic creed a new authentic ring."[24] King summarized: "The racism of today is real, but the democratic spirit that has always faced it is equally real. . . . A people who began a national life inspired by a vision of a society of brotherhood can redeem itself. But redemption can come only through a humble acknowledgment of guilt and an honest knowledge of self."[25] As for the future, he emphasized hope, citing the diversity of the crowd at the March on Washington of August 28, 1963, as well as statistical surveys indicating significant white support for equal rights and even integrated schools as well.[26]

Martin Luther King Jr. aimed to transform American society, with integration and unity at the core of that transformation. He offered the following vision in December of 1961: "I look forward confidently to the day when all who work for a living will be one with no thought to their separateness as Negroes, Jews, Italians, or any other distinctions. This will be the day when we bring into full realization the American dream—a dream yet unfulfilled."[27] This statement exemplifies liberal integrationism and clearly contrasts with radical multiculturalism's commitment to preserve the very distinctions that King hoped will someday be replaced by an interethnic American unity built around progressive ideas. The themes Obama has employed in his rhetoric make clear that he shares King's dream, updated to reflect the progress that America has made on this front while taking into account the challenges that remain.

Obama on Race and Change: "Better Isn't Good Enough"

One of Obama's very earliest public statements encapsulated his essential take on America's progress regarding racism and black inequality. In February 1990, he said that his selection as the first black president of the *Harvard Law Review* "shows a lot of progress. . . . It's encouraging but it's important that stories like mine aren't used to say that everything is okay for blacks. You have to remember that for every one of me, there are hundreds or thousands of black students with at least equal talent who don't get a chance."[28] Obama offered almost exactly the same sentiments during the presidential campaign almost two decades later, declaring that problems caused by discrimination against blacks "aren't just solved by electing a black president."[29]

Perhaps the most comprehensive statement of Obama's views on this topic is his 2006 book, *The Audacity of Hope*. He allowed that America had not yet solved the problems caused by racism, yet he urged his audience to remember how much had been achieved, how much had improved: "When I hear some in the black community deny those changes, I think it not only dishonors those who struggled on our behalf but also robs us of our agency to complete the work began."[30] Nevertheless, Obama tempered his optimism with an admonition to keep pushing for progress: "But as much as I insist that things have gotten better, I am mindful of this truth as well: Better isn't good enough."

Obama reflected on a campaign visit to Cairo, in southern Illinois, particularly on how much a town that had witnessed terrible racial strife in the 1970s had changed. He had initially been unsure what to expect there, but found himself greeted by a crowd of supporters that included three whites for every black resident. They discussed bread and butter economic issues. At the end of the day in Cairo, Obama recalled the impact as being "nothing transformative, but perhaps enough to weaken some of our biases and reinforce some of our better impulses....Such moments...can wear down, in slow, steady waves, the hatred and suspicion that isolation breeds."[31]

This anecdote encapsulates Obama's approach to race and change. He has argued that such change comes one person at a time, as shifts of individual attitudes increase support among people of all ethnicities for policies that tackle the structural causes of poverty and inequality. Strengthening our sense of American national identity goes hand in hand with strengthening support for the common good, but neither can occur without invigorating a sense of connectedness tying together Americans of all ethnicities.

Regarding blacks and whites specifically, Obama proclaimed that "a profound shift in race relations" had occurred since the early 1960s.[32] He recognized that prejudice still affects the "snap decisions of who's hired and who's promoted, on who's arrested and who's prosecuted."[33] For this reason, Obama emphasized integration and, specifically, the kinds of one-on-one interactions between whites and blacks that he experienced on that day in Cairo, Illinois. Those types of interactions help build "a quotient of trust" across the ethnic divide.[34]

Experiences with white Illinoisans from all over the state had convinced Obama that "the overwhelming majority of [whites] . . . are able—if given the time—to look beyond race in making their judgments of people."[35] Whites who did continue to hold racial prejudices nevertheless held them "far more loosely" than they had prior to the 1960s, and thus these prejudices had become "subject to refutation."[36] Likewise, in 2006, Obama told Ellis Cose that although prejudice still exists, now "stereotypes can be overcome in a way they could not before."[37] In fact, Orlando Patterson—whose views on this Obama's most resemble—cited research demonstrating that white attitudes toward race are pliable. Most whites can be "induced" to change seemingly deeply held prejudices and "can be easily talked out of nearly all their negative positions."[38]

Obama acknowledged, however, that doing so "can be a wearying business [for minorities]."[39] It takes a tremendous amount of effort to keep proving stereotypes wrong, to keep showing whites that one is, in fact, not what they may have been brought up to believe. He recognized that many members of minority groups are at times tempted to stop trying and simply get by with as little contact with whites as possible, however difficult that may be in a majority-white society. Obama related that a number of African Americans have asked why they should have to expend so much energy "to disabuse whites of their ignorance about us"? His reply: "The alternative is surrender—to what has been instead of what might be."

Combating Inequality: Policies, Economic Growth, and Personal Responsibility

In his section on race in *The Audacity of Hope*, Obama addressed the question of what kinds of programs those who wish to improve the situation of African Americans should pursue. He began by citing both economic progress made by blacks and Latinos in the past thirty years, as well as the gaps in wages and net worth that remain stubbornly wide. Presaging many of the themes of his presidential campaign, Obama advocated for much stronger enforcement of nondiscrimination laws, in particular in employment, housing, and education. He criticized recent Republican presidents, in particular George W. Bush, for the lack of federal enforcement of these laws, and lamented that the cases pursued have typically been misguided attempts to target affirmative action programs as "reverse discrimination."[40]

On health care reform and race, Obama endorsed targeted programs to shrink the health care gap between whites and members of minority groups, but pointed out that comprehensive health care reform that would guarantee access for all would do far more on that front. It is worth noting that in the long debate over health care reform in 2009 and early 2010, President Obama rarely discussed the matter directly in terms of ethnic disparities.

On education, Obama defended affirmative action as a "useful, if limited, tool to expand opportunity to underrepresented minorities."[41] He supplemented his defense of affirmative action with a demand that progressives push for increased education funding across the board. In a debate on April 16, 2008, Obama qualified his position, arguing that perhaps wealthy minority children—he cited his own daughters as examples—ought not benefit from affirmative action when applying to schools and that poor whites ought to receive some special consideration.

In terms of economic matters more broadly, Obama declared in *The Audacity of Hope* that "the most important tool to close the gap between minority and white workers may have little to do with race."[42] Rather, workers of all ethnicities would benefit from the same things: job opportunities, tax fairness, stronger labor protections, and reliable systems that offered health care, child care, and economic security in retirement. He noted that in 1999 African American incomes reached a new high, while black unemployment reached a new low, largely because of two universal factors: a strong economy and progressive economic policies like the Earned Income Tax Credit.[43]

Alongside this universal approach to problem solving, Obama identified two specific areas relating to interethnic relations—namely the problems faced by inner-city African Americans and the issue of illegal immigration and immigration overall (which I discuss in chapter 6)—that require "special attention."[44] In discussing the former, he reiterated his desire to focus on universal solutions for most problems and not argue that racism is the sole cause of every woe in the black community. Nevertheless, the legacy of racism had resulted in some specific, complex problems that continue to profoundly afflict the inner city. Strong measures targeted at those communities were necessary to solve them. Universal measures alone would not suffice.

The level of deprivation seen in some of these neighborhoods once shocked America, Obama contended. The country responded with the war on poverty of the 1960s. The "real and perceived" failures of that set of policies allowed opponents of progressive economic ideas to convince much of America that government could do little to combat poverty.[45] Obama argued that conservatives emphasized only the values of and choices made by poor blacks, ignoring the powerful effect discrimination had had on African Americans' opportunities, as well as the reality that many had actually made good choices and had strong values yet remained poor. Some liberals and civil rights leaders, he asserted, took the opposite approach and denied that behavior did in fact exacerbate this poverty to some degree. "This willingness to dismiss the role that values played in shaping the economic success of a community strained credulity and alienated working-class whites."[46]

Obama had also publicly addressed this point two years earlier. On July 25, 2004, two days before his keynote address in Boston, Obama was asked on *Meet the Press* how to deal with the fact that more than three-quarters of black children in Illinois are born to unmarried mothers. He talked about the lack of jobs for black men—how the decline in manufacturing had devastated the state's economy, disproportionately affecting blacks—but he also spoke of the need for an increased focus on "individual responsibility."

During the keynote address, Obama spoke in similar terms. He emphasized the need for parents to do a better job emphasizing education, "to turn off the television sets and eradicate the slander that says a black youth with a book is acting white." His own experiences had taught Obama that the cultural values that engender success did not belong to whites alone. However, he added that more progressive government policies were also necessary to fix what ailed the inner city.

Obama reiterated this same two-part message in *The Audacity of Hope* and on many other occasions as well. Obama did so both when addressing predominantly black audiences—such as at an NAACP dinner on May 1, 2005, a Selma voting rights march commemoration on March 4, 2007, a ministers' conference at Hampton University on June 5, 2007, and a black church on Father's Day, June 15, 2008—and when he addressed a national television audience on *Meet the Press* on July 27, 2008. On a related note, in his January, 17, 2010, speech honoring Martin Luther King Jr. Day, Obama corrected those who assumed that his call for people to work hard and embrace individual responsibility was aimed predominantly at black people: "No, no, no, no. I'm talking to the American community."

Generally, Obama has tried to carve out a political space for himself by rejecting both conservative arguments and those of the 1960s-style black and liberal leadership. To some degree, he has built a straw man with his description of what traditional civil rights leaders believed, as few still resembled that one-sided caricature by the mid-1990s. Nevertheless, Obama has sought to position his own take as one that combines the best of both extremes. It is a persuasive rhetorical tool. Despite any exaggerations, there is indeed a gap between assigning most of the blame for the plight of urban blacks to racism, thus downplaying the impact of self-destructive behavior, and taking the opposite approach.

Obama noted that many blacks as well—at least "in private"—bemoaned the aforementioned decline in values "with a fervor that would make the Heritage Foundation proud."[47] The difference between them and conservatives is that they "know the back story to the inner city's dysfunction."[48] After the great black migration northward in the early twentieth century, discrimination in housing created poor ghettoes that then received substandard services, education, and police protection. These African Americans also had unequal access to the jobs that previous, largely white migrants to the cities had gotten in prior decades. According to Obama, the majority of blacks believe that cultural values mean a great deal, but also that "culture is shaped by circumstance. We know that many in the inner city are trapped by their own self-destructive behaviors but that those behaviors are not innate."[49]

Based on this recognition, Obama argued that changing the material circumstances confronting the urban poor would lead them to change their behavior and alter their values, which was necessary in order to achieve long-lasting improvement. As for specific steps to reduce poverty in the inner cities, in *The Audacity of Hope* Obama talked about the need to encourage girls to get a high school diploma and not become single mothers. Increasing funding for programs that have proven to be successful can help, but individual leaders and parents need to speak out as well. He also applauded changes to the traditional welfare system, which discouraged family stability by denying benefits to families where a man lived with his children, and by "detaching income from work."[50] Obama went on: "Any strategy to reduce intergenerational poverty has to be centered on work, not welfare—not only because work provides independence and income but also because work provides order, structure, dignity, and opportunities for growth in people's lives."

Focusing on work was important, Obama continued, but would not be enough. He endorsed expanding the Earned Income Tax Credit, as well as stronger police protection, better health care (including nutritional and reproductive counseling), drug treatment, better schools, access to affordable child care, and other government programs that the urban poor need in order to succeed. For men, too many of whom have a criminal record, Obama suggested programs that would employ ex-convicts to do necessary work in their neighborhoods. Steady employment would lead to reduced recidivism, and thus the programs would pay for themselves and improve the neighborhood's physical infrastructure at the same time. Furthermore, improving employment prospects and reducing crime would set off a virtuous cycle that would help alleviate many other problems by improving family stability, leading to more success in school, etc. Obama had spoken about the need for these policies as a state senator. As a U.S. senator he cosponsored the Second Chance Act, a law aimed at improving the health, education, and job prospects of released prisoners, which President George W. Bush signed on April 9, 2008.

During 2008, Obama declared that "simply shouting racism and trying to guilt people into getting things done" was not an effective way to win broad support for reforming, for example, aspects of the criminal justice system.[51] Too many black political leaders did operate that way, he contended, relying on a "narrative . . . still shaped by the sixties and black power."[52] Obama argued that his experience in the Illinois Senate had taught him that he could win white support for progressive programs by appealing to American values and simple effectiveness. The key, he declared, was to make an attempt to "see the world through the eyes of people who don't agree with you. If I can imagine myself in their shoes, it means I can answer their objections."[53]

Obama on Race and Inequality in the U.S. Senate and Beyond

During his first six months in the U.S. Senate, Obama kept relatively quiet, including on matters of race. Reports began to appear of a rift between Obama and other members of the Congressional Black Caucus who were disappointed he said little about what they characterized as "black issues."[54] In July 2005, however, Obama grilled Henrietta Holsman Fore, the Bush administration's nominee for a high-ranking position in the State Department that requires Senate confirmation, specifically asking her to explain public comments from 1987 that stereotyped blacks as drug pushers and Hispanics as lazy.[55] Obama aides denied any connection between his actions on the nomination and the reports of grumbling from the Congressional Black Caucus, and the senator further commented: "I'm not somebody who uses race to score political points—quite the opposite. . . . I would hope that it wouldn't just be something that I would do because I'm black, I would hope that any senator in my position would do the same thing."[56] Here we see Obama holding a public official accountable for bigotry, yet arguing that doing so is not a "black issue" but in fact a universal one.

Throughout his time as a U.S. senator, Obama spoke out about and/or introduced legislation to address various issues on which African Americans and members of other minority groups were being left behind or mistreated. He called for action on: ethnic disparities in environmental health (November 17, 2005); the unequal quality of education that largely hurts poor children of all ethnicities and parts of the country (March 16, 2006, July 18, 2007, January 26, 2008), and specifically highlighted inequalities in the area of early childhood education (May 5, 2007); on funding for predominantly black colleges not recognized as historically black (May 24, 2007); as well as the gap between the performance in learning between black and Hispanic students and the rest of the population (July 24, 2009). Obama pointed out ethnic disparities in health insurance coverage and health care results, as well as in the percentage of medical professionals who are black, Latino, or Native American (September 29, 2006), as well as discrimination against black farmers (November 16, 2007). In a speech to the National Council of La Raza on July 22, 2007, he demanded that we do more to shrink these kinds of gaps and disparities, "because that's what's really going to solve the race problem in this country."

On a related aspect of discrimination, in his January 27, 2010, State of the Union address, Obama urged Congress to "repeal the law that denies gay Americans the right to serve the country they love because of who they are." On December 22, 2010, the president signed a law establishing a process for doing away with that law, "Don't Ask, Don't Tell," and explained his take on that accomplishment in terms of his definition of our national identity: "We are not a nation that says, 'Don't ask, don't tell.' We are a nation that says, 'Out of many, we are one.'" Again we see him connecting the struggle to right historic wrongs by implementing equality with the strengthening of an inclusive national unity. The law officially came off the books on September 20, 2011.

The rhetoric then senator Obama used on two specific instances illustrates his general approach. On March 8, 2007, he declared, "The crisis of the black male is our crisis whether we are black or white, male or female," and called for specific policies to address that crisis if we are going "to make the American dream, and the American ideals of opportunity and equality, real." Obama's hope is that his years of rhetoric in which he unreservedly embraced America has given him more credibility to talk this way about the problems African American men face and, presumably, enhanced his ability to win support for policies aimed at addressing inequality.

On April 25, 2007, when talking about the underrepresentation of women and members of some ethnic groups in the fields of science and technology, Obama framed the problem in terms of national productivity rather than emphasize prejudice as a cause. He declared, "If we do not tap the diversity of our nation as a competitive strength, we will diminish our capacity to innovate. Full participation by all segments of our populace would do more than just increase the number of workers in high technology fields; full participation would bring fresh perspectives and inventive solutions."

The government's response to Hurricane Katrina offered Obama a particularly trenchant opportunity to explore the intersection of race and inequality. Eight days after Katrina touched ground in New Orleans, he took to the Senate floor. In previous days, some commentators and political leaders had argued that naked racial bigotry was why majority-black New Orleans had been allowed to suffer so, and why in particular its poor black residents had been disproportionately left behind in the rescue efforts.

Although not a political figure, rapper Kanye West perhaps best summed up these sentiments when, during a live September 3, 2005, network broadcast of a fundraiser for Katrina's victims, he thundered, "George Bush doesn't care about black people!"[57] Obama rejected this analysis, contending instead on September 6: "The ineptitude was colorblind." He went on to accuse those in charge of assuming that every resident of the area had the means to be able to escape in their own vehicles, with government providing little more than a request to leave. Obama summarized his view as follows: "I see no evidence of active malice, but I see a continuation of passive indifference on the part of our government toward the least of us." Finally, he returned to his theme of national unity, calling on all of us to remember our "mutual responsibilities to our fellow Americans," responsibilities that require government to play an active role in carrying them out. This latter part is key, as Obama's understanding of national unity demands not just feelings, but concrete, collective action.

A few days later, Obama talked about how Katrina had left him "outraged and heartbroken . . . anxious."[58] He returned to Katrina a number of times in subsequent months. In *The Audacity of Hope* he wrote about his wish that Katrina would arouse the conscience of the American people and encourage them to make a renewed comprehensive effort to address poverty. Obama also expressed his disappointment that the country had not done so. In January 2007, he called attention to the lack of a "sense of urgency" in the federal effort to rebuild New Orleans, characterizing it as "shameful."[59] In his March 4, 2007, speech in Selma, then Senator Obama noted that after 9/11 the federal government had waived a rule that would have forced New York City to contribute 10 percent of the amount it received in federal aid toward rebuilding, a waiver that had also been granted to communities hit by Hurricane Andrew in Florida in 1992. Why, he asked, was this not done for New Orleans? Many others asked the same question, and Congress ultimately passed a provision, signed by President Bush, to waive the requirement. In his rhetoric on Katrina, Obama called attention to the disproportionality of the storm's impact on the poor in general and African Americans specifically, but framed his criticism in a nonracial call for a more aggressive government effort to aid the victims.

Targeted Universalism

We can see the direct influence of Martin Luther King Jr. on Obama in the latter's use of rhetoric that john powell of the Kirwan Institute for the Study of Race and Ethnicity characterized as "targeted universalism."[60] On January 17, 2010, Obama explained that King won so much support because of his "commitment to universal ideals—of freedom, of justice, of equality—that spoke to all people, not just some people." Obama praised Reverend King for embracing the concerns not only of blacks but of "the white auto worker in Detroit . . . the Mexican farm worker in California," and for having "united people of all colors in the noble quest for freedom." Obama's words have hewed to these principles as well. Essentially, he has offered an updated version of King's preference for "Power for Poor People" over "Black Power." On April 4, 2008, the fortieth anniversary of King's assassination, Obama praised him specifically for understanding that "the struggle for economic justice and the struggle for racial justice were really one."

In *The Audacity of Hope* Obama declared that "an emphasis on universal, as opposed to race-specific, programs isn't just good policy; it's also good politics."[61] He presented another example from Illinois that helped him understand this reality. A black Senate colleague (Obama called him "John Doe") who represented an urban, largely low-income constituency offered a detailed, emotional condemnation of a particular legislative action on the grounds that it was nakedly racist. A liberal white senator sitting next to Obama commented, "You know what the problem is with John? Whenever I hear him, he makes me feel more white." Obama could have responded with indignation and another lecture. Ever the pragmatist, he showed a greater interest in achieving concrete results than in feeling the satisfaction that comes with expressing an ideologically pure position. Obama drew the conclusion that even among racially progressive whites, "rightly or wrongly, white guilt has largely exhausted itself in America."

There were two primary causes of this development according to Obama. First, conservatives had successfully played to white frustration by exaggerating the degree to which racial preferences in hiring and education had harmed the prospects of white applicants. Even more importantly, a growing percentage of whites who rejected discrimination against nonwhites, and who were themselves struggling to get by, refused to support programs aimed exclusively at nonwhites. Obama contended that such programs ultimately left Americans more divided along ethnic lines. Thus, while they might bring some immediate benefits, in the long run they weakened the prospects for building the kinds of multiethnic alliances that fundamental change requires. Obama instead asserted that "universal appeals around strategies that help all Americans . . . along with measures that ensure our laws apply equally to everyone and hence uphold broadly held American ideals (like better enforcement of existing civil rights laws) can serve as the basis for such coalitions—even if such strategies disproportionately help minorities."[62]

A significant portion of the resentment on these matters among conservative whites, including Tea Party members, emanates from the notion that the government is redistributing resources from those who are "hard-working" to those who are "undeserving." This notion extends into a belief that such policies breed dependency among those who receive the benefits. Sometimes these beliefs are clearly tinged with an element of racial animus, as many among the resentful whites envision that the government is largely taking from whites and giving to blacks, about whom they harbor bigoted stereotypes fed by the aforementioned conservative exaggerations.[63]

In chapter 8 I discuss the way some on the right have spoken about Obama, however, at this point I want to mention a few examples that speak exactly to this point. Former Massachusetts governor Mitt Romney, the presumptive Republican nominee for president as of late spring 2012, attacked Obama in terms that echoed these stereotypes in Iowa on January 2, 2012, on the eve of that state's caucuses. Romney stated: "I think President Obama wants to make us a European-style welfare state, where instead of being a merit society we're an entitlement society, where government's role is to take from some and give to others."[64] If this effort succeeds, Romney continued, Obama would "poison the very spirit of America and keep us from being one nation under God." Here we see Romney placing Obama clearly outside the boundaries of the American community, albeit on ideological rather than ethnic or cultural grounds. Nevertheless, *New York Times* columnist Maureen Dowd chided Romney for speaking in such racially loaded terms, accusing him of "raising the specter of welfare lines in inner cities."[65]

Other major presidential candidates, including Newt Gingrich and former U.S. senator Rick Santorum of Pennsylvania, made comments around the same time about black Americans and entitlements that were, if anything, even more racially loaded.[66] On January 1, 2012, Santorum appeared to tell an Iowa audience, "I don't want to make black people's lives better by giving them somebody else's money. I want to give them the opportunity to go out and earn the money." He later said that he did not actually say the word "black," and told CNN's John King on January 4, "In fact, I'm pretty confident I didn't say black. What I think . . . I started to say a word and then sort of changed and it sort of—blah—mumbled it and sort of changed my thought." Having watched the video myself, he clearly began to say a word that began with "bl" and a vowel sound that became "ah" but then stopped himself mid-word.[67] *New York Times* columnist Charles Blow found the denial "incredulous," as did many others in the media.[68]

As for Gingrich, on January 5, he proclaimed: "I'm prepared, if the NAACP invites me, I'll go to their convention and talk about why the African American community should demand paychecks and not be satisfied with food stamps." This statement—in particular his assertion that the African American community is currently "satisfied" with food stamps—is a prime example of that kind of racially loaded language.

Of Obama specifically, in Gingrich's January 21, 2012, victory speech following the South Carolina primary, he declared: "President Obama has been historically the most effective food stamp president in American history."[69] Gingrich continued, "If you want your children to have a life of dependency and food stamps, you have a candidate: that's Barack Obama." Gingrich has used virtually identical words to describe the President regularly throughout the campaign, beginning with a speech given in Macon, Georgia on May 13, 2011, two days after he announced his candidacy for the White House; in Iowa; New Hampshire; and—in the examples that received the most media coverage to that point—in the two South Carolina debates that immediately preceded that state's primary.[70] A *New York Times* editorial condemned Gingrich's "exploitation of racial resentment" in South Carolina, in particular at the debates where he "lectured a black questioner . . . about the amount of federal handouts to blacks, suggesting their work ethic was questionable."[71] The editorial argued that such rhetoric helped fuel his victory there.

The aforementioned resentful whites may not believe that the negative characteristics they attribute to impoverished African Americans are inborn or biological in nature; rather, in keeping with conservative ideology, they are seen as the products of a dysfunctional culture and poorly designed government policies. Nevertheless, this prejudice at least partially motivates some of the conservative white distaste for policies aimed at helping the disadvantaged. It would be exceedingly difficult to reach these whites with an argument based on remedying past racial wrongs because they believe that the remedies for past harms are now causing greater harm to those who receive them. Obama has expressed a belief, however, that he can reach at least some of these erstwhile opponents with nonethnic or universal appeals. His election is evidence of at least temporary, potential success on that front.

In condemning discrimination more broadly, Obama also relied on universalistic rhetoric. He began one section of *The Audacity of Hope* by emphasizing the importance of liberty, by which he meant not only negative liberty, i.e. freedoms that cannot be abrogated by government but also, in a positive sense, the opportunities offered to people in a free society. Success in such a free society, Obama contended, depends on values such as thrift and personal responsibility, and requires a system that offers rewards based on merit. Therefore, "the legitimacy of our government and our economy depend on the degree to which these values are rewarded, which is why the values of equal opportunity and nondiscrimination complement rather than impinge on our liberty."[72] Discrimination and the lack of equal opportunities, because they conflict with the founding belief that America should be a meritocracy, are themselves incompatible with America's core values.

5

Candidate and President Obama's Broader Rhetoric on Race

The way Barack Obama has approached race in America drew harsh criticism from some black commentators as early as late 2006, when it became apparent that he was seriously considering a run for the White House.[1] Some accused him of downplaying black issues or the importance of racism, of somehow being "not black enough" in his politics. For example, Stanley Crouch at the *New York Daily News* and Debra Dickerson at Salon.com both categorically rejected the notion that Obama is black, at least in the way each one understands the term.[2] On February 11, 2007, Al Sharpton criticized Obama for not announcing his candidacy for the White House in front of a majority black audience and urged him to explain "what's his embrace of our agenda."[3] In fact, *Miami Herald* columnist Leonard Pitts Jr. found that as of August 2007, the words "black enough" appeared in reference to Obama 464 times in print.[4] Such talk combined with the fact that throughout 2007 Obama was winning a lower percentage of black support than did Hillary Clinton in most national polls led Obama to address the issue of his approach to race on a number of occasions during that campaign's first twelve months.

In the February 11, 2007, *60 Minutes* interview—which took place the day after the announcement of Obama's candidacy for the presidency—the journalist Steve Kroft stated that Obama "grew up white" and that "at some point" had "decided" that he was black. Then senator Obama disagreed with this simplification, replying: "If you look African American in this society, you're treated as an African American." In Obama's view, he had no choice about whether to be seen as black, but could decide how he would understand his blackness and incorporate it into his overall identity. African Americans, he continued, are by definition "a hybrid community.

It's African. It's European. It's Native American. So it's much more difficult to define what the essential African American experience is, at least more difficult than what popular culture would allow."

Obama rejected the kind of narrow definition of blackness that would have excluded him, with his atypical ancestry and experiences, from being considered an "authentic" black American. He then linked the hybridity within the black community to the broader American national community, which he presented as, "by definition, a hybrid experience. . . . We have these people coming from . . . all four corners of the globe converging . . . and over time coming together to create this tapestry that is incredibly strong. . . . I feel that my background ironically, because it's unusual, is quintessentially American." Furthermore, his definition of America as "hybrid" mirrors his definition of himself. As journalist David Remnick put it, "Obama proposed to be the first president who represented the variousness of American life."[5]

Addressing the matter of black identity at a forum of the National Association of Black Journalists (NABJ) on August 10, 2007, Obama said that he sought to expand "our sense of mutual responsibility toward one another. . . . I am not just my black sister's keeper, I am everybody's keeper."[6] On a related note, he lamented that too many in the black community were "still locked into the notion that somehow if you appeal to white folks then there must be something wrong."

Obama had made a similar comment in a 2005 interview: "We have a certain script . . . for black politicians. . . . For them to be authentically black they have to somehow offend white people. And then if he puts a multiracial coalition together, he must somehow be compromising the efforts of the African American community."[7] Here he rejected the idea that "authentic blackness" requires one to reject whites specifically and America more broadly—the two of which are indelibly linked by those who follow that "script" in any case.

Further distancing himself from the identity politics often associated with radical multiculturalism, in *The Audacity of Hope* Obama declared, "I reject a politics that is based solely on racial identity, gender identity, sexual orientation, or victimhood generally."[8] In an October 2004 interview, he likewise said, "I don't have a lot of patience with identity politics, whether it's coming from the right or the left."[9] Along comparable lines, Obama told Chris Matthews of MSNBC on April 4, 2008, "We're at our worst when we're divided and when our politics is based along tribal and ethnic lines instead of based on who we are as Americans." Although employing this kind of rhetoric on identity was arguably a prerequisite to winning statewide and national office, Obama has employed it consistently going back to the early 1990s.

To return to the NABJ forum, Obama was asked how he would "advance or perhaps resume a discussion on race and racial equality in America, and should it begin with an apology for slavery?" Obama did not want to have a conversation about race just to have one; he would rather focus on specific issues. For example, are blacks and whites being treated equally and fairly in the criminal justice system? Or, what can be done about the educational achievement gap between the races?

Similarly, in an NPR interview on February 28, 2007, the interviewer asked for a response to the comment of Congressman Bobby Rush, who had contrasted himself with Obama by saying: "I'm a race politician and he is not. I don't compromise. I don't step back. I don't try to deny I'm proud to be an African American."[10] After pointing out that Rush had endorsed his candidacy for president, Obama pointed out that there had always been disagreement among black politicians about whether to talk in "universal" or in "race-specific" language regarding the community's challenges. He simply stated that "by virtue of my background . . . I am more likely to speak in universal terms."

Over the course of his run for the White House, Obama employed rhetoric that can be characterized as targeted universalism. Although he spoke most often in universal terms, the senator also called attention to specific injustices and/or inequalities that disproportionately affected blacks and other nonwhites, albeit more so during the primary campaign when African American voters were more up for grabs than during the general election season.

For example, in a September 13, 2007, statement, Obama called attention to the treatment of the "Jena Six," a group of black teenagers who faced serious charges after beating a white student. The beating took place not long after the hanging of nooses on school property and other violent incidents had exacerbated racial tension in Jena, Louisiana. He returned to the topic on September 28, 2007, at a Howard University convocation, condemning the "outrageous charges; the unreasonable and excessive sentences," and cited them as evidence of the "glaring inequalities" that continue to permeate the justice system. Obama railed against disparities in sentencing based on "what you look like and where you come from." He again criticized the Bush Justice Department, "whose idea of prosecuting civil rights violations is trying to roll back affirmative action . . . whose idea of prosecuting voting rights violations is to look for voting fraud in black and Latino communities where it doesn't exist."

On a number of occasions in 2007, Obama also strongly criticized the outcome of the case of Genarlow Wilson, citing it as evidence of the unfair treatment African Americans received in the justice system.[11] As a seventeen-year-old boy, Wilson had engaged in consensual oral sex with a fifteen-year-old girl in Douglasville, Georgia. He was charged with statutory rape and received a ten-year prison sentence. He ultimately served two years before the Georgia State Supreme Court ruled in a 4–3 decision on October 26, 2007, that his sentence was cruel and unusual and ordered him released.[12] During the time Wilson was imprisoned, the law was changed to reclassify what he did as a misdemeanor. Obama consistently discussed discrimination in a nuanced way, both emphasizing progress and pointing out where America needed to improve.

On Martin Luther King Jr.'s birthday, January 20, 2008, Obama addressed a largely black audience at King's home church, Ebenezer Baptist, in Atlanta, Georgia. Obama highlighted the structural forces that hinder the disadvantaged of all backgrounds and talked about how African Americans had suffered greatly from prejudice. He called for unity among Americans and reconciliation across ethnic lines, but warned that attaining those goals would require more than simply an end to white prejudice. Americans of all backgrounds needed to change some of their attitudes and challenge their own prejudices. Amplifying the condemnation of black prejudice he had made on previous occasions, Obama continued that blacks must "acknowledge that our own community has not always been true to King's vision of a beloved community." He demanded that black Americans confront and defeat the bigotry toward gays and Jews and the hostility toward immigrants that too many continued to express in the black community. Living up to King's vision required blacks to "erase the empathy deficit that exists in our hearts."

Obama consistently spoke along similar lines, proclaiming that all Americans must confront discrimination and bigotry. At a debate among Democratic candidates in South Carolina on January 21, 2008, for instance, he expressed his expectation that a president of any gender or ethnicity should pursue similar goals on matters of race and discrimination, because "the pursuit of racial equality and the perfection of this union is not just a particular special-interest issue of the African American community; that is how all of us are going to move forward."

Five days later, in an appearance on NBC's *Today*, he rejected the notion that he was running as "a black candidate" for president. Instead, he claimed to bring "a different perspective" to issues such as racial discrimination, one that contends that

America "continue[s] to carry the historical legacy of Jim Crow and slavery." That legacy, Obama asserted, "manifests itself in much higher rates of poverty and violence and lack of educational achievement in minority communities." He also stated, "I know in my heart that there is a core decency to the American people," praised the progress that we have achieved on race, but concluded: "Better is not good enough. And we've still got a long way to go."

That evening Obama won the Democratic primary in South Carolina. In his victory speech he expanded on the *Today* remarks, decrying "a politics that tells us that we have to think, act, and even vote within the confines of the categories that supposedly define us. . . . The assumption that African Americans can't support the white candidate; whites can't support the African American candidate; blacks and Latinos can't come together." The alternative he presented to this kind of ethnic identity politics is a country where "men and women of every color and creed . . . serve together, and fight together, and bleed together under the same proud flag." Obama then declared that one of his primary goals was to "help the entire nation embrace this vision." Doing so would require "a battle in our own hearts and minds about what kind of country we want."

From "Not Black Enough" to "Too Black"

After spending the first twelve months of his presidential campaign answering questions about why he was not talking about race and American society the way a traditional black candidate would, March 2008 found Obama facing a different question: Was he in fact running on his blackness? It started with a remark made by Geraldine Ferraro, Walter Mondale's running mate in 1984 and the first woman nominated by a major party for vice president. Ferraro, then serving on Hillary Clinton's finance committee, offered the following observation in an interview published March 7, 2008: "If Obama was a white man, he would not be in this position."[13] She continued, "And if he was a woman (of any color) he would not be in this position. He happens to be very lucky to be who he is. And the country is caught up in the concept."

The ensuing media frenzy meant that Obama could not avoid responding. He declined to call Ferraro or her comments racist, but criticized them as being "divisive," something that—as Obama made clear in his Philadelphia race speech—earns particular scorn from him because of his emphasis on invigorating American unity across ethnic lines. Furthermore, he declared, "anybody who understands the history of this country knows [the comments] are patently absurd."[14]

After a few days of withering criticism from Obama supporters and many center-left commentators, some of whom did accuse Ferraro of racism, she replied in a follow-up interview on March 11, "I really think they're attacking me because I'm white. How's that?"[15] The following day Obama rejected that accusation out of hand. Additionally, he linked Ferraro's remarks to "identity politics," something he criticized as harmful to the Democratic Party. Then he pivoted back to his more universalist message, about the economic anxieties people of all ethnicities shared. Obama noted that the Ferraro affair had become "an enormous distraction. When we are in these conversations, it means that people are not recognizing their common concerns."[16]

Only a few days later, Obama confronted a challenge that threatened his entire campaign, but which ultimately led him to deliver one of the most important speeches on racism and America in our country's history. On March 13, ABC News ran a story about some of the sermons delivered by Obama's pastor, Reverend Jeremiah A. Wright Jr., at the Trinity United Church of Christ, where Obama and his wife Michelle had been members for two decades. Other media outlets began showing Wright's most radical pronouncements on what seemed like an endless loop. In one sermon, he declared, "No, no, no, not God bless America. God damn America—that's in the Bible—for killing innocent people. God damn America, for treating our citizens as less than human."[17]

The clip that arguably caused the most outrage was from a sermon he delivered only five days after the attacks of September 11, 2001. He said, in part: "We bombed Hiroshima, we bombed Nagasaki, and we nuked far more than the thousands in New York and the Pentagon, and we never batted an eye." Wright continued, "We have supported state terrorism against the Palestinians and black South Africans, and now we are indignant because the stuff we have done overseas is now brought right back to our own front yards. America's chickens are coming home to roost."

Less than a month before the ABC News story ran, another relatively minor dust-up had occurred involving Obama and Reverend Wright when Louis Farrakhan, whom Wright had previously praised, expressed support for Obama's candidacy on February 24, 2008. When asked about Farrakhan's support for him on February 26, at a debate in Cleveland, Obama referred back to his condemnation of anti-Semitism at the Martin Luther King Jr. birthday speech, and denounced and rejected Farrakhan. Nevertheless, Wright's radical speeches and his support of Farrakhan began to raise questions in the minds of some Americans about whether Obama was a radical, or anti-Semitic or even anti-American, based on his connection to Wright and, indirectly, to Farrakhan.

Two overwhelmingly divisive stories about race—the back and forth around Ferraro's remarks and the firestorm over Reverend Wright's sermons—dominated the American news media for more than two weeks during perhaps the most highly competitive phase of the campaign for the Democratic presidential nomination, a contest between two ground-breaking candidates. Most importantly, the Wright controversy—because it called into question Obama's patriotism and his identification with America, two essential prerequisites for any presidential candidate—created a do-or-die moment for Obama.

"A More Perfect Union": The Philadelphia Race Speech

After the ABC News story ran, Obama gave a couple of interviews in which he condemned the sermons, but the story continued to grow until there remained no room to discuss anything else. Finally, on March 18, in Philadelphia, Obama spoke about Wright's sermons as part of a larger address on race in America, titled "A More Perfect Union: Race, Politics, and Unifying Our Country." He described the sermons as expressing "a profoundly distorted view of this country—a view that sees white racism as endemic, and that elevates what is wrong with America above all that we know is right with America. . . . As such, Reverend Wright's comments were not only wrong but divisive, divisive at a time when we need unity; racially charged at a time when we need to come together to solve a set of monumental problems . . . that confront us all." Obama further offered that "the profound mistake of Reverend Wright's sermons is not that he spoke about racism in our society. It's that he spoke as if our society was static; as if no progress has been made."

These two brief comments encapsulate Obama's entire viewpoint on the way America has treated its black citizens. He acknowledged that there are both things "right" and "wrong" in that history. In Obama's view, Wright was not incorrect to talk about the wrongs, but rather was incorrect to focus on them exclusively, ignoring the positives and ignoring the capacity for further change toward which that progress itself points. This, it is worth pointing out, is exactly how the liberal civic nationalists in the early to mid-1990s characterized the radical multicultural approach to talking about bigotry and discrimination in America over time.

Obama also lamented the fact that Reverend Wright's sentiments would further divide Americans along racial lines and thus make it harder to overcome the continuing impact of those very wrongs against which Wright railed. The reverend—echoing Derrick Bell in the early 1990s—assumed that white racism is permanent and that American society is static. Wright would not have worried about whether his remarks could worsen race relations because in his view, nothing could make them better. Obama, on the other hand, like King before him and Orlando Patterson more recently, expressed optimism about the future and thus condemned actions or statements that threatened further progress.

The next section of the speech detailed Obama's relationship with Wright and with Trinity United Church of Christ over the years. Obama talked about why, even after now seeing and hearing these most offensive sermons, he could not sever his ties to his pastor because he believed that the good things Reverend Wright had done outweighed the bad things. As a comparison, Obama repeated the aforementioned story from *Dreams from My Father*, about his own grandmother's fear of a black panhandler. He explained that his grandmother and Reverend Wright were a part of his life, and that the contradictions on matters of race contained in both of them reflected those of America itself. Obama referred to "the complexities of race in this country that we've never really worked through—a part of our union that we have yet to perfect." In his view, understanding race in America required nuance and balance.

As on previous occasions, Obama in Philadelphia declared that racial oppression had stained America's past and present. He detailed some of the gravest offenses and discussed how they continued to affect us. Obama described the inferior schools black children attended during segregation and that too many still attend today, and how this injustice helps explain the gap in educational achievement. He spoke of how discrimination in areas like housing and employment created a wealth and income gap that we can continue to see in the disproportionate numbers of black poor, but also in the precarious financial status even of blacks with decent incomes but comparatively low net worth.

In addition to these structural inequalities, Obama also acknowledged the effect of welfare policies. All of these combined to help "create a cycle of violence, blight, and neglect that continue to haunt us." Many of his critics have accused Obama of not openly discussing racism or its contemporary impact on America and its black citizens, or perhaps not doing so in front of mainstream audiences. In this speech, about which 54 percent of Americans had heard "a lot" when surveyed by Pew nine days after its delivery, Obama clearly did so.[18]

Reverend Wright's generation came of age, Obama pointed out, during segregation, and many of its members simply could not overcome the barriers that racism placed before them. The senator continued, "Even for those blacks who did make it, questions of race, and racism, continue to define their worldview in fundamental ways. For the men and women of Reverend Wright's generation, the memories of humiliation and doubt and fear have not gone away; nor has the anger and the bitterness of those years." Obama sympathetically acknowledged the reality of their feelings, calling their sentiments "real" and "powerful." He noted, however, that these feelings were "not always productive." Additionally, Obama lamented that "at times, that anger is exploited by politicians, to gin up votes along racial lines, or to make up for a politician's own failings." He urged those who have not shared the experiences of African Americans of that generation to resist simply condemning their perspective without understanding its source. Only by doing so can America avoid worsening race relations.

In the next section, Obama did something notably different from what most other prominent black politicians have done when discussing race. He began by proposing that "a similar anger exists within segments of the white community." Obama described the point of view, as he understood it, of many whites on questions of race: "Most working- and middle-class white Americans don't feel that they have been particularly privileged by their race." They believe they have earned their achievements, and many of them face their own economic anxieties. This leads them to reject the notion that they have received active advantages from being white—something that would clash with their own belief in treating people equally irrespective of ethnicity—and to resent what they interpret as a demand that they sacrifice some of their own less-than-bountiful opportunities to compensate others simply because they are not white, even those nonwhites who may in some cases have more wealth than they do.

In *The Audacity of Hope*, Obama likewise reflected on "the white Southerner who growing up heard his dad talk about niggers this and niggers that but who has struck up a friendship with the black guys at the office and is trying to teach his own son different, who thinks discrimination is wrong but also doesn't see why the son of a black doctor should get admitted to law school ahead of his own son."[19] Obama recognized the importance of the progress this represents and offered a warning against assuming that all opponents of affirmative action are racist by definition.

To return to Philadelphia, Obama declared, "Black leaders need to appreciate the legitimate fears that may cause some whites to resist affirmative action." This call was part of a larger discussion of how Americans from all backgrounds, political perspectives, and economic situations must try to understand the perspectives of those whom they oppose in terms of the positions they take, a call he has made throughout his career. It was not an isolated haranguing of black leaders on the matter of affirmative action, but a call for approaching one's opponents with empathy and nuance. Obama concluded his section on white resentment by lamenting that for too many whites, "opportunity comes to be seen as a zero-sum game, in which your dreams come at my expense."

This white resentment has had a tremendous effect on American politics over the past generation. Obama described how "anger over welfare and affirmative action helped forge the Reagan coalition. Politicians routinely exploited fears of crime for their own electoral ends. Talk show hosts and conservative commentators built entire careers unmasking bogus claims of racism while dismissing legitimate discussions of racial injustice and inequality as mere political correctness or reverse racism." He then drew some parallels, in terms of their effect, between these white resentments and those of black Americans: "Just as black anger often proved counterproductive, so have these white resentments distracted attention from the real culprits of the middle-class squeeze." Nevertheless, Obama said, just as with the resentment of African Americans like Reverend Wright, "to wish away the resentments of white Americans, to label them as misguided or even racist, without recognizing they are grounded in legitimate concerns—this too widens the racial divide and blocks the path to understanding."

Did Obama Pander to White Resentment?

Some critics on the left have cited the above sections as evidence that Obama equated legitimate black anger about racism with the white backlash against affirmative action and other remedies for discrimination and its legacies. Antiracist activist Tim Wise, to whom I will return in chapter 8, condemned Obama for having "pandered to the lie . . . wherein he mentioned, as though it were perfectly valid, white anger over losing out on a position because of a preference given to a minority."[20] Wise also claimed that Obama "mentioned, within the same paragraph, black anger over racism with white anger over affirmative action—as if these two were remotely equivalent in terms of their legitimacy."[21] He claimed that, while Obama noted the negative consequences of black anger, "one could even read his comments as doing more than equating black and white anger; in some respects he was even more doting on white fears and insecurities. . . . These remarks were nowhere balanced by the notion that white fears too, and white anger too, might be just as counterproductive or misdirected."[22]

The aforementioned quotations from the Philadelphia speech offer evidence to the contrary. By accusing Obama of pandering, Wise seems to want the senator to have told whites that the perception that affirmative action damaged them is, in Wise's words, an "irrational and nonsensical delusion."[23] He thundered that Obama did not "speak this fundamental truth."[24] However, Obama clearly called out those who had lied and exploited white resentment over affirmative action and other remediation measures—those talk show hosts and conservative commentators to which he referred. By mentioning these categories of media figures, people whom all but their most devoted followers would likely associate with political extremism of the right and a tendency to twist facts beyond recognition, Obama made clear his belief that white resentments about affirmative action and racial preferences are not 100 percent grounded in fact. Although he did so as politely as a candidate seeking the votes of those same resentful whites can, he clearly did so. Obama essentially said that those white resentments resulted at least in part from the manipulations and misleadings of right-wing hucksters.

Rather than blame them for their resentment, however, Obama demonstrated real empathy for people who, whatever amount of white privilege they may enjoy, nevertheless live below the median income line and can ill afford to lose out on any job opportunity. The fact that prejudice against nonwhites remains all too powerful does mean that being white offers some advantages in America. But, he explained, those whites who are poor or in an economically vulnerable position do not necessarily feel particularly advantaged.

Furthermore, when taken to an extreme, the concept of white privilege can be applied so broadly as to suggest that anything a white person has accomplished is largely due to him or her being white. Without debating the reality of that argument, it is reasonable to suggest that it might put some politically middle-of-the-road whites on the defensive. Rather than focus on an argument that could alienate these potential white allies, Obama instead acknowledged their feelings and perspective, hoping to convince them to support measures that would improve the socioeconomic circumstances of the disadvantaged of all races and increase economic security for all Americans. His balanced rhetoric seeks to build cross-racial coalitions with universal appeals; thus he avoids what he would consider divisive language that predominantly emphasizes white privilege.

To say, as Wise did, that Obama simply called white resentment of affirmative action "perfectly valid" is a vast oversimplification. Furthermore, Wise's reading of the speech, according to which Obama was "more doting" on the resentments of whites than blacks, does not fit with the evidence. When considering that Obama already had the overwhelming majority of the black vote and was competing for the white vote, the degree to which he did not dote on white fears is what stands out.

When Obama talked about black resentment, he characterized it as unproductive, distracting, and not fully reflecting the progress made, but never questioned the factual legitimacy of the circumstances that generated it. He acknowledged that black politicians may have ginned up black resentment, but they did not make up their own facts, as he strongly suggested did those commentators who fanned white resentment. Obama may have made these distinctions between white and black resentment in more subtle a manner than some critics would have liked, but he believes that his approach is the best way to ultimately bring about greater equality among Americans of all backgrounds.

Even among some of the white people who understand in the abstract that past discrimination against minorities and in particular African Americans truly was awful and did have a devastating impact on members of those groups, there is nevertheless a resistance to sacrificing too much of their own interest in helping those minorities today. Obama expressed an understanding that while such whites might reject receiving favorable treatment for being white, they still may not accept being treated in what seems a less than neutral way compared to, for example, African Americans. They do not want their lives to be less successful than they might otherwise have been in order to make up for the discrimination someone else's ancestors faced in the past—although these whites would likely be more willing to support racial preferences designed to counteract documented, present-day discrimination.

Acknowledging that such feelings among whites are not racist, not immoral, not beyond the pale makes it easier for Obama then to educate those whites to the effects of discrimination, both past and present, so that they can see that strictly neutral treatment may not be enough to give minorities and black Americans in particular a fair shake. Simply telling those whites that their resistance to affirmative action means that they are racist might feel good, but the likely result—Obama's experience has taught him—will be to push those whites into a defensive stance such that they tune out anything else the speaker has to say. He came to believe that emphasizing commonalities among members of different ethnic groups and our unity as Americans will move more people to support measures to combat inequality than the confrontational approach favored by Wise.

The Path to a More Perfect Union

To return to the speech, Obama declared that both blacks and whites must change in order for America "to continue on the path of a more perfect union." For the black community, he urged them to take "full responsibility for their own lives," to do what they are able in order to maximize their chances of success. They should also fight for justice and equality in every arena. Additionally, however, he proposed that African Americans would be most likely to achieve gains if they universalize their plight by "binding our particular grievances . . . to the larger aspirations of all Americans—the white woman struggling to break the glass ceiling, the white man who's been laid off, the immigrant trying to feed his family." Whites, Obama explained, need to recognize that even though America has made progress on race, African Americans continue to face significant obstacles to their success due to racism. These obstacles do "not just exist in the minds of black people. . . . The legacy of discrimination—and current incidents of discrimination, while less overt than in the past—are real and must be addressed."

Here again we see a qualitative difference in the way Obama addresses whites and blacks, this time on what each group needs to do in order to achieve greater equality for Americans. Blacks must do more for themselves and reach out to whites. Whites, on the other hand, have to remove the veil of ignorance that prevents them from seeing the true circumstances that blacks face. This juxtaposition further invalidates Wise's accusation that Obama pandered to the white backlash on racial preferences. Obama told whites, politely but clearly, that they had their facts wrong. By having previously showed understanding for why resentful whites felt the way they did—by validating the emotions behind those feelings rather than condemning them as purely racist—Obama aimed to put himself in a position where he had earned their trust and could then educate them about the reality of racism today.

In order to address the obstacles African Americans face, Obama proposed both changes in attitudes and policy changes along the lines of his prior writings and speeches, namely investment in schools, communities, and institutions that enforce the civil rights laws that ensure equality. Additionally, he called on all Americans to "realize that your dreams do not have to come at the expense of my dreams; that investing in the health, welfare, and education of black and brown and white children will ultimately help all of America prosper." Obama argued that our political system ought to reflect, in the end, the Golden Rule that guides people of all faiths: "Do unto others as we would have them do unto us."

Here we see Obama clearly applying his understanding of American national identity toward the advancement of the progressive socioeconomic policies he supports. Being one people means that we must take collective action, through the institutions of our democratic government, to help ensure that all Americans have an opportunity to succeed and receive equal treatment before the law. This, he believes, is how America can transform our society and create a truly inclusive national unity.

The remainder of the speech focused on unity and on encouraging Americans to resist the divisiveness that had dominated the media's coverage of the election over the previous two weeks. Instead, he wanted Americans to strengthen their sense of being one family and work together to improve "the future of black children and white children and Asian children and Hispanic children and Native American children. . . . The children of America are not those kids, they are our kids."[25]

American unity stood at the center of his political worldview, thus he closed with a story he had already told in the aforementioned January 2008 speech on Reverend King's birthday. Obama spoke about a young white woman, Ashley, who had joined his campaign to help win greater access to health care for those without insurance. She organized a group of volunteers in a largely black area in Florence, South Carolina, and the group had gathered together, each telling why they had joined up. Ashley talked about how when she was nine, her mother got cancer. When she missed work she lost her job and with it her insurance.

Ashley could have become angry and sought a scapegoat. Subtly highlighting again the basic inaccuracies underlying such resentment among whites, Obama speculated that "perhaps somebody told her along the way that the source of her mother's problems were blacks who were on welfare and too lazy to work, or Hispanics who were coming into the country illegally." He presented this information as being little more than vile gossip that Ashley might have heard from someone "along the way." After Ashley told the story of why she had joined, she asked a number of other volunteers to tell their stories. Ashley then asked one older black man why he was there, and he replied, "I'm here because of Ashley."

Obama then concluded, "By itself, that single moment of recognition between that young white girl and that old black man is not enough. It is not enough to give health care to the sick, or jobs to the jobless, or education to our children. But it is where we start." He contended that enhancing fellowship across boundaries does not solve all the problems caused by racism, but it lays a stronger groundwork for doing so. Thus, Obama effectively advanced the American discussion on race by addressing the perspective and concerns of those of all ethnicities and focusing on national unity as well as greater equality and justice. The speech itself stands as one of the core building blocks in his quest to transform our national identity and invigorate our collective feeling that we are one people.

After the Philadelphia speech, Obama hoped to have put the matter of his pastor and his sermons behind him. However, that was not to be. On April 28, Reverend Wright spoke at the National Press Club. He claimed that the U.S. government invented HIV, that Louis Farrakhan was "one of the most important voices in the twentieth and twenty-first centuries," and equated the military efforts of the United States with terrorism.[26]

Obama, who had chastised Wright in Philadelphia but had refused to "disown" him, now found himself forced to do exactly that. The next day, at a press conference, Obama declared that his former pastor's most recent remarks "were not only divisive and destructive, but I believe that they end up giving comfort to those who prey on hate. . . . [What Wright said] contradicts everything that I am about and who I am." The primary mission of his adult life, Obama proclaimed, had been "to insist that we all share common hopes and common dreams as Americans and as human beings." He emphasized the "need to all recognize each other as Americans, regardless of race, religion, or region of the country."

Additionally, in a May 4 appearance on *Meet the Press*, Senator Obama spoke of how, as the child of an interracial couple, it was in his "DNA to believe that we can bring this country together." The fact that Obama had constantly discussed these themes of American unity over fifteen years gave him a well of credibility on which to draw in distancing himself from Wright's comments and, finally, from Wright himself. Ultimately, Obama had to do so because the Reverend's rhetoric stood diametrically opposed to his push to strengthen Americans' sense that we are one family.

Race and the Rest of the Campaign

With some minor exceptions, the question of Obama's views on race became a significantly less prominent issue in the mainstream media from that point forward in the campaign and even for the first couple of months after he took office. It is worth noting that Obama's general election opponent, Senator John McCain (R-AZ), by and large did not make an issue of Reverend Wright or of race in general during the contest for the White House.

In fact, in a Lakeville, Minnesota, rally on October 10, 2008, when a McCain supporter declared that she did not trust Obama because he was "an Arab," McCain reclaimed the microphone and countered, "No, ma'am. He's a decent family man [and] citizen that I just happen to have disagreements with on fundamental issues and that's what this campaign's all about. He's not [an Arab]."[27] McCain clearly had an opening to exploit ethnic-based fear and he chose not to do so. He might have gone further—along the lines of General Colin Powell who was asked about the related question of whether Obama was a Muslim in an October 19, 2008, appearance on *Meet The Press* and pointed out: "The really right answer is: So what if he is?" Nevertheless, Powell was not running for president. McCain certainly deserves real credit for how he handled his supporter's remarks in Minnesota.

After the election, commentators began analyzing Obama's victory and the campaign's approach to discussing race. Journalist Gwen Ifill, in her book, *The Breakthrough*, identified the "Obama effect," a feature of which is that "whites are more comfortable with black candidates who do not seem to carry [racial] anger, while blacks are often more suspicious."[28] She further contended that the campaign had made a conscious decision that "playing up his race" would hurt Obama's chances, and so he would only talk about it "in the context of broader issues."[29] She did not, however, accuse him of not being "black enough." Ifill acknowledged Obama's assertions that it was impossible to transcend race and that ignoring race would not solve America's racial problems.

Appearing in early 2009, at about the same time as Ifill's book, journalist Marc Ambinder claimed that the Obama campaign figured out that, at least after he won Iowa, the candidate could win the votes of African Americans without having to speak the way traditional black candidates had done. The campaign had also strategized that speaking to black voters in that more traditional style would arouse the anxiety of gettable white voters, an anxiety related to the fear that a black candidate would ignore their concerns and look out only for those of African Americans and members of minority groups. According to Ambinder, "polling confirmed that culturally anxious whites were willing to vote for a black candidate so long as they did not meditate on the candidate's blackness."[30] The piece at least implied that Obama's beliefs on race and America were poll-tested and thus insincere, and that he somehow sneaked around racism rather than confronting it directly. However, the consistency of Obama's public rhetoric on race over two decades contradicts these implications.

President Obama on Race

In the White House, Obama has continued to employ targeted universalist rhetoric. For example, when asked at a press conference on April 29, 2009, what he was doing for minority communities hit so hard by the recession, he explained that blacks and Latinos, on average, were more likely to be poor, unemployed, and/or lacking health insurance. Therefore, Obama proclaimed "every step we're taking is designed to help all people, but folks who are most vulnerable are most likely to be helped, because they need the most help."

The first "racial" controversy of the Obama presidency followed his nomination of U.S. Appeals Court Judge Sonia Sotomayor in late May 2009 to be the first Hispanic as well as the first female member of any minority group to the Supreme Court. Shortly after the nomination was announced, President Obama faced questions about Sotomayor's comment that "I would hope that a wise Latina woman with the richness of her experiences would more often than not reach a better conclusion than a white male who hasn't lived that life."[31] On May 29, Obama opined to NBC's Brian Williams that the judge might like the opportunity to restate those thoughts. He went on to dismiss the idea that Sotomayor practiced "identity politics," something he made clear he rejected.[32] Subsequently, Obama largely removed himself from the discussion that continued around that remark, with some on the right making rather incendiary statements (see chapter 8).

That summer Obama directly addressed discrimination in American society once again. In a July 16 speech commemorating the centennial anniversary of the NAACP's founding, he presented a wide-ranging assessment of prejudice, discrimination, and socioeconomic disparities among ethnic groups in America. President Obama spoke both of the great reduction in discrimination faced by members of minority groups in recent decades as well as discrimination's stubborn resistance to eradication. He offered a number of examples ranging from unequal wages earned by black women, to anti-immigrant sentiment against Latinos, to Muslims wrongly targeted based on their religion, to widespread homophobia before declaring that "prejudice has no place in the United States of America." Current prejudice, however, did not even represent the most significant obstacle to equality. Obama went on to emphasize that "the most difficult barriers include structural inequalities that our nation's legacy of discrimination has left behind." He lamented these have been "too often the object of national neglect."

Earlier on that same day, however, another event occurred that led Obama to insert himself into the center of a discussion about discrimination—one that he could have chosen to sidestep—which further elucidates his understanding of racial discrimination and race in America more broadly. These are topics that are central to his effort to transform American national identity.

Henry Louis Gates, a professor of African American studies, was arrested on his own property. Gates, returning from a long trip abroad, had found his front door jammed and, along with the help of his taxi driver, forced his way in. The professor, a fifty-eight-year-old black man of relatively short stature who walks with a cane, verbally sparred with a white police officer, Sergeant James Crowley, who had come to his home to investigate a 911 call reporting two men possibly breaking into that address. Crowley claimed that the professor was causing a public disturbance by screaming at him outside the door of the residence. Gates claimed that the officer refused to show him his police ID, as required by law, and that the arrest was unwarranted. The charges were dropped five days later, on July 21. Further details of this incident and the contradictory responses by the two main participants, Crowley and Gates, are widely available.

At a July 22 press conference devoted to health care, Obama's final questioner asked what the Gates incident meant to him and what it said about race relations in America. The president gave a long and detailed response, but one sentence caused most of the furor: "The Cambridge police acted stupidly in arresting somebody when there was already proof that they [sic] were in their own home." One might wonder whether this statement reflects a divergence from Obama's typically balanced approach toward issues of racial discrimination. Much of the public discussion and media coverage reflected common racial tropes: Has the president, a black man, not simply sided here with the black "suspect" (for lack of a better word) who had been mistreated by the racist white cop? Reading his entire answer to the question, it becomes clear that is not the case.

His answer hewed to the philosophy Obama has expressed for two decades. He did not say or even suggest that Sergeant Crowley had acted in a way that reflects racial prejudice on his part. Obama specifically stated that he did not know what role race had played in this incident. While he did comment that the police had acted "stupidly," he did not attribute their actions to racism. The president acknowledged, as he has on virtually every occasion where he has spoken about race, the "incredible progress" our society has made. Nevertheless, he also noted that statistics show blacks and Latinos are stopped disproportionately as suspects by police, and cited those facts as evidence that "race remains a factor" in America when it comes to criminal justice and law enforcement matters. Obama reminded the audience that these statistics cause some black and Hispanic Americans to harbor suspicion of the police, something that comes into play even in cases of "honest misunderstandings," allowing that this might be one of those cases.

In summary, he condemned the actions of the police in this case as foolish, but described America overall as a place that has both come a long way and still has more to do regarding racial inequality. While this nuance may have gotten lost in the media reaction, in particular on the far right, to his use of the word "stupidly," Obama's answer to the question about the arrest of his friend Professor Gates contained the same balanced approach, tinged with both optimism and realism, that he has always brought to the question of race in America.

Realizing, however, that his remarks had served to increase the tension, Obama responded by making a previously unannounced appearance at a White House press briefing on July 24. Regarding his statements of two days earlier, he acknowledged that he "could have calibrated those words differently." President Obama reiterated that he thought "there was an overreaction" in the arrest of Gates. Obama also did something he did not do in his previous remarks, which was to acknowledge that the professor "probably overreacted as well." He then went on—perhaps in a more even-tempered fashion—to repeat much of the rest of the substance of his initial remarks.

The president urged Americans to remember that "because of our history, because of the difficulties of the past . . . African Americans are sensitive to these issues." He expressed a hope that, ultimately, this event would lead to a "teachable moment" that would bring about more constructive interactions between law enforcement and members of minority communities. Obama concluded: "Instead of flinging accusations we can all be a little more reflective in terms of what we can do to contribute to more unity."

On July 30, the White House hosted a meeting—the "Beer Summit"—of Gates and Crowley, along with the president and vice president, to discuss the events that had transpired. The president issued a statement in which he called on America to learn "a positive lesson from this episode." Whether that happened is open to question, but Obama's handling of the matter demonstrates two things: First, he does not shy away from talking bluntly about matters relating to racial discrimination and how it affects African Americans. Second, when Obama does so, he balances talk of success with a call for more improvement. This approach has brought criticism from the far left that he is too moderate and from the hard right that he is too radical. In any case, this approach reflects his career-long commitments to empathy, justice, and unity.

6

Obama's Vision of National Identity and National Unity

S
ince the founding of the country, Americans have grappled with how much weight to assign, respectively, to unity and diversity in defining our national identity. Focusing solely on unity, as Teddy Roosevelt and Woodrow Wilson did, demands cultural homogenization and rejects people's desire to preserve the cultural heritage and identity of their ancestors. Focusing solely on diversity and one's ethnic identity, as radical multiculturalists advocated, prevents a society from developing a significant degree of national unity, rendering its population unwilling to identify with and sacrifice for the national interest, the common good, or anyone outside their own ethnic community.

President Obama's approach strikes a balance between these two extremes. However, while he values diversity in all its forms, he has prioritized the need to invigorate national unity, with an emphasis on strengthening bonds across group lines. Obama's conception of American national identity makes him what Elizabeth Theiss-Morse called an "inclusive strong identifier."[1] Although he has expressed a deeply felt connection to his blackness and to the black community, he has rejected the more radical elements of multicultural ideology that have garnered support among some black and minority scholars and community leaders, among others.

Obama's America versus Cheney's America

We can gain a better understanding of "Obama's America" by comparing it to the way America is defined by Lynne Cheney, one of the most important figures on the mainstream right during the culture wars of the 1990s. *Of Thee I Sing* is Barack Obama's newest book. Dedicated to his daughters and published in late 2010, it expresses his definition of American national identity, one that is inclusive and unified. Similarly, Cheney published *America: A Patriotic Primer* for her grandchildren in 2002. As children's books, neither was overtly political. Nevertheless, the visions of national identity they presented differ in subtle but profound ways.

But first, the similarities: Both books emphasized pride in America and in being American. Both highlighted the principles of justice, equality, and liberty, as well as the struggles to guarantee them for all Americans. Both were demographically inclusive, although Obama's was a bit more so. Six of his thirteen heroes were non-white and five were women. Obama faced criticism from the right for his inclusion of Sitting Bull, who fought the United States Army to defend his people's land.[2] Of course, so did every Confederate soldier, but that's another story.

The differences in what each author emphasizes are clear. Cheney's American history was more focused on politics and presidents. Five individuals got their own page: Martin Luther King Jr. and four presidents. Obama's thirteen Americans included only two: Lincoln and Washington, along with King, Georgia O'Keeffe, Albert Einstein, Jackie Robinson, Sitting Bull, Billie Holiday, Helen Keller, Maya Lin, Jane Addams, Neil Armstrong, and Cesar Chavez. Obama devoted more space to activists and figures of social and cultural importance. His selections reflect a bottom-up approach to history whereas Cheney's is more traditional. As historian Ed Linenthal put it, Obama's book has "expand[ed] our sense of who counts in our own history."[3]

Cheney moreover defined America specifically as a Judeo-Christian country. One of her pages is "'G' is for God in whom we trust."[4] By declaring that "we" trust in God, she explicitly excluded from that "we" anyone who does not worship God. Obama's book mentioned nothing specifically religious. He did explain that Americans are people of all religions and beliefs.

These two conceptions of America diverge because each author wrote with a fundamentally different purpose, a different understanding of our national identity. Above all, Cheney hoped to inculcate a deep sense of gratitude for what America offers its citizens. Her goal was for us to understand how "blessed we are" because of "the liberty and opportunity" our people enjoy.[5] Her depiction of America was almost wholly celebratory and presented America as a finished product that has already achieved perfection. Obama, on the other hand, when he spoke of "build[ing] upon all that is good in our nation" and "fix[ing] the future" was describing America as a work in progress.[6] He presented those outsiders who sought change as being patriots nonetheless, such as the protestor who held an American flag high while cheering on Cesar Chavez's call for farm workers' rights.[7] In Obama's America, we are still perfecting our union.

The difference between the books on this concerns tone and, yes, empathy, on the part of the respective authors. Cheney, although she mentioned the wrongs done to Americans, did so in a way that seemed perfunctory, as if she considered them to be merely speed bumps on the road to perfection. By presenting a history that more fully reflects the experiences of Americans of every heritage—for example, Obama movingly cited the "broken hearts and broken promises" endured by tribes like the Sioux—he sought to ensure that all of us identify with that history as our own.[8] In order to achieve that goal, his book not only acknowledged but commemorated the pain suffered by those whom this country mistreated and whose descendants— including his own daughters—he nevertheless encouraged to embrace their American identity and their fellow Americans wholeheartedly.

In dealing with diversity, Cheney sometimes simply ticked off groups like she was checking boxes on a list—one page is "'N' is for Native Americans."[9] For Obama, individuals of different ethnicities stood not as representations of their groups, but instead served to illustrate universally American qualities: creativity, intelligence, bravery, strength, respectfulness, kindness, persistence. He described America as "a family" and cited Lincoln, who asked that all Americans "behave as kin."[10] Obama also spoke of how all of us contribute "unique gifts and giv[e] us the courage to lift one another up."[11] Compared to Cheney's book, Obama's vision of America worked harder to cultivate a unity that truly reflects diversity.

Finally, Obama told his daughters that these Americans of every background and region "are all a part of you...you are one of them."[12] This represents a powerful call for us to see ourselves fully and completely as one people, one community. Ultimately, Cheney wanted to strengthen the bond between Americans and their country as an institution. Obama wanted to do this as well, but he also sought to strengthen the ties that bind Americans to one another, to strengthen our sense of being one people. One emphasized national greatness, the other an inclusive national unity. This distinction reflects the essential difference between the mainstream conservative and liberal understanding of our national identity.

Obama: America Is a Gumbo, Not a Melting Pot or Mosaic

In terms of cultural integration, there are many different ways a society can approach balancing unity and diversity. Often, these approaches have been associated with a particular metaphor. The traditional, early to mid-twentieth century assimilationist model described America as a melting pot in which ethnic cultures and identities are broken down, stripped of their distinctive qualities. As a result immigrants are supposed to abandon their previous loyalties as well as their cultures and languages and adopt instead "all-American" (essentially Anglo-WASP) cultural patterns. The immigrants are the ones who do all the adapting in this scenario; the mainstream culture does not change. Many multiculturalists, on the other hand, have utilized the metaphor of the mosaic, wherein each tile within the frame remains distinct and separate from the others but, when viewed together, they make a beautiful picture.

Richard Wolffe related that in a 2008 interview Obama eschewed both the mosaic and the melting pot as metaphors for the form that American unity takes. Instead, he stated: "I think the best analogy I've heard is a sort of a gumbo. . . . It's not a thin soup. It's got these big chunks of stuff in it. But those things are seasoning each other. It's not tomato soup. It's something thick."[13] In *The Audacity of Hope*, Obama remarked that in America today "a constant cross-pollination is occurring, a not entirely orderly but generally peaceful collision among people and cultures. Identities are scrambling, and then cohering in new ways."[14]

By comparison, former presidents Bush or Clinton, for example, would not fundamentally disagree with the way Obama talks about American identity. It is nevertheless clear that Obama has devoted a great deal of energy to thinking about these matters on a theoretical level and has spoken publicly about the need both to strengthen our national identity and to make it more inclusive far more regularly and in greater depth than have previous presidents.

In Obama's American gumbo, the flavors, as he noted, are blending. The elements that make up the national community do not remain separate, unadulterated, and pure, as envisioned by both radical multiculturalism and white separatism/white nationalism. Instead, each element changes as a result of interacting with the others. Obama is thus talking about a comprehensive integration that enhances an all-inclusive and "thick" American national identity.

Unlike in the melting pot scenario, in the gumbo metaphor the mainstream—represented by the thick soup—does in fact change based on the ingredients that are added. However, the newly added ingredients undergo more change than does the soup, with even the most substantial ingredients softening and soaking up the liquid as well as absorbing the flavors of the other ingredients. It's worth noting that the gumbo metaphor stands somewhat closer to the melting pot idea than it does to the mosaic. This accords with the way Obama has focused on strengthening national unity over prioritizing the preservation of each ethnic group's cultural traditions as called for by hard multiculturalism.

Obama's America: Unity, Empathy, Service

The way Obama rhapsodized about American national unity was the most striking feature of the speech that made him a national political figure—the keynote address in Boston at the 2004 Democratic National Convention. Unity stood at the center of his portrayal of the country's history and its values:

> Alongside our famous individualism, there's another ingredient in the American saga, a belief that we're all connected as one people. If there is a child on the South Side of Chicago who can't read, that matters to me even if it's not my child. If there is a senior citizen somewhere who can't pay for their prescription drugs and has to choose between medicine and the rent, that makes my life poorer even if it's not my grandparent. If there is an Arab American family being rounded up without benefit of an attorney or due process, that threatens my civil liberties. It is that fundamental belief—I am my brother's keeper, I am my sister's keeper—that makes this country work. It's what allows us to pursue our individual dreams, and yet still come together as one American family. "E pluribus unum." Out of many, one.

In the section that garnered perhaps the most attention, he declared, "There is not a liberal America and a conservative America. There is the United States of America. There is not a black America and a white America and Latino America and Asian America. There's the United States of America."[15]

This was Obama's first national address, the one that introduced him to the country. Of all the things around which to build this speech, he chose the theme of national unity, of Americans being connected to one another across ethnic lines. That choice demonstrates just how highly Obama prioritizes these issues, issues about which he had already been extensively writing and speaking for over a decade to that point.

Most Americans had never heard this kind of language coming from a progressive politician of color. The speech directly challenged the prevailing notion among many whites that minorities—in particular those who were black and brown—were somehow alienated from an American identity. Obama specifically prioritized unity over a radical multicultural-style identity politics, making clear that bonds of nationhood ultimately trump those of ethnicity, even as he recognized their importance. Unlike the notion of unity pushed by cultural conservatives, however, his construction specifically included not only ethnic minorities but others, such as gay Americans, whom traditionalists were less likely to enthusiastically embrace. (Obama spoke in Boston about how we have "gay friends in the red states.") Like the center-left critics of radical multiculturalism of the mid-1990s, Obama sought a way forward out of the culture wars through the inculcation of a truly inclusive yet unifying definition of American national identity.

Finally, the understanding of national unity Obama put forth in Boston (and elsewhere) centers on empathy, on being one another's keeper, a principle he applied to all Americans. The central tenet of Obama's rhetoric on national unity is the belief that we, as Americans, must serve the common good above solely pursuing our own individual interests. Because we are one people, he has argued, we must be willing to do what is necessary to ensure that all members of the "American family" have the opportunity to achieve success.

Not long after Boston, at the National Press Club on April 26, 2005, Obama endorsed FDR's vision of "the American idea" and further proclaimed, "The freedom to pursue our own individual dreams is made possible by the promise that if fate causes us to stumble or fall, our larger American family will be there to lift us up. That if we're willing to share even a small amount of life's risks and rewards with each other, then we'll all have the chance to make the most of our God-given potential." There are times, he stated, where we simply concern ourselves with our own needs. On other occasions, however, "we are one America, linked by the dignity of each and the destiny of all." This speech, which offered a criticism of George W. Bush's plan to privatize elements of Social Security, demonstrates Obama cultivating support for progressive economic policies based on a particular understanding of American civic nationalism, of what he believes it means to be one America. Similarly, on January 30, 2007, he depicted raising the minimum wage as "a statement of our commitment to each other as Americans."

Serving the common good has been a key theme of Obama's throughout his time on the national stage. In a speech on November 16, 2005, he praised Robert F. Kennedy, who said that national unity meant "we must not limit ourselves to the pursuit of selfish gain, but that which will help all Americans rise together." At the

University of Massachusetts–Boston on June 2, 2006, Obama juxtaposed his conception of an empathy-centered national and broader human unity with another vision, one that tries "to divide us and deny what we have in common." Obama described how this vision relies on the conceit that

> the Americans who sleep in the streets and beg for food got there because they're all lazy or weak of spirit. That the immigrants who risk their lives to cross a desert have nothing to contribute to this country and no desire to embrace our ideals. That the inner-city children who are trapped in the nation's most dilapidated schools can't learn and won't learn and so we should just give up on them entirely. That the innocent people being slaughtered and expelled from their homes half a world away are somebody else's problem to take care of.

In contrast to this kind of cynicism, Obama valorized the Freedom Riders, people of all ethnicities who rode buses from all over the country into the South in the early 1960s to help "their brothers and sisters" and to "change the world." This last phrase represents a transracial reference to the idea of the American family, which bound together Northern whites and Southern blacks in kinship.

In *The Audacity of Hope,* Obama presented detailed reflections on national unity and empathy. He described a long tradition of American politics that centered on unity, one "that stretched from the days of the country's founding to the glory of the civil rights movement . . . based on the simple idea that what binds us together is greater than what drives us apart."[16] Obama criticized the way "our current political discourse unnecessarily divides us" and called for us to "ground our politics in the notion of a common good."[17] Americans are individualistic, he said, but then countered, "Our individualism has always been bound by a set of communal values. . . . We value patriotism and the obligations of citizenship, a sense of duty and sacrifice on behalf of our nation."[18] For Obama, promoting the common good means encouraging empathy, a principle "at the heart of my moral code" that he defined as "a call to stand in somebody else's shoes and see through their eyes."[19]

On the matter of balancing unity and diversity as it applies to religion, Obama here hewed to the same principles he followed regarding ethnicity. He began by noting the incredible religious diversity of this country: "Whatever we once were, we are no longer just a Christian nation; we are also a Jewish nation, a Muslim nation, a Buddhist nation, a Hindu nation, and a nation of nonbelievers."[20] Obama then warned against sectarianism, the attempt to divide Americans along religious lines.

Here, Obama extended his thinking on the test for sound policy, i.e., does it have universal value? And, in this instance: Can it be justified to people outside a particular religious circle? Obama called on those whose politics are motivated by their faith to explain their ideas in universal terms rather than simply cite their own religious texts as evidence. In what Obama called "our deliberative, pluralistic democracy," any position on a given issue must be based on a "principle that is accessible to people of all faiths, including those with no faith at all."[21] His approach on this matter calls on us to put ourselves in the position of an American different from ourselves, a key aspect of his definition of empathy.

It is worth noting that Obama repeatedly included non-religious people and atheists when talking about the diversity of religiosity in the United States, not only in the above-cited passages, but also in his January 20, 2009, inaugural address, where he described the country as "a nation of Christians and Muslims, Jews and Hindus, and non-believers." No previous president had ever acknowledged nonbelievers in his inaugural address.[22] Likewise, in an address that fell during Passover and on the day before Easter, April 3, 2010, Obama noted: "While we worship in different ways, we also remember the shared spirit of humanity that inhabits us all—Jews and Christians, Muslims and Hindus, believers and nonbelievers alike."

On December 1, 2006, Obama addressed the Global Summit on AIDS and the Church sponsored by evangelical pastor Rick Warren on World AIDS Day. Obama drew on ecumenical religious themes to explain his understanding of empathy. He related the story of a South African woman, Leo, who lost a number of siblings to AIDS and was overwhelmed with caring for her nieces and nephews in addition to her own children. And, Obama said: "My faith tells me that Leo's family is my family." He then connected the imperative of helping an AIDS orphan in Africa with helping "the gang member in South Central, or the Katrina victim in New Orleans, or the uninsured mother in North Dakota."

Obama then specifically identified these groups of people as "Americans" ("We can turn away from these Americans"), by which he stressed that members of the first two groups—who are likely black—are just as American as the North Dakotan, whom he is coding by geographic reference as likely being white. All of them—along with the AIDS orphan—deserve our concern and our support. We should not turn away from them, according to Obama, because of an American tradition "that has stretched from the days of our founding to the glory of the civil rights movement, a tradition based on the simple idea that we have a stake in one another—and that what binds us together is greater than what drives us apart." Not only has he equated being American with empathy—specifically empathy across ethnic boundaries—he has defined this empathy as a traditional American value that dates back to 1776.

In numerous speeches he made after announcing his candidacy for president in February 2007, Obama continued to emphasize national unity, empathy, and service. At the March 4, 2007, commemoration of the Selma Voting Rights March, he described the "poverty of ambition involved in simply striving just for money. Materialism alone will not fulfill the possibilities of your existence." Only by serving others as well can one be truly fulfilled.

At Southern New Hampshire University on May 19, 2007, Obama expanded on this theme. He lamented the existence of what he called "our empathy deficit—the ability to put ourselves in someone else's shoes; to see the world through those who are different from us—the child who's hungry, the laid-off steelworker, the immigrant woman cleaning your dorm room [this almost certainly refers to the incident described in *Dreams*, discussed also in chapter 2]." Our society, Obama contended, encourages values that contradict empathy: acquisitiveness, fame-seeking, and other selfish pursuits. He urged the graduates to reject a focus on such values, despite their ubiquity, and instead to "broaden, and not contract, your ambit of concern. . . . Because our individual salvation depends on collective salvation. And because it's only when you hitch your wagon to something larger than yourself that you will realize your true potential."

It is not enough, however, for us as individuals to express and act on our concerns for one another, Obama declared on June 4, 2007. Our obligations to our fellow Americans must also be answered collectively, and not only through voluntary organizations or religious institutions but through our government, the political expression of our nation's values. Additionally, Obama argued on August 9, 2007, that the president must encourage empathy and unity by "talk[ing] about these issues [in this case relating to discrimination against gays] in ways that encourage people to recognize themselves in each other."

Returning to his criticism of divisiveness, in his Ebenezer Baptist Church speech of January 20, 2008, Obama decried the fact that in our society: "We are told that those who differ from us on a few things are different from us on all things; that our problems are the fault of those who don't think like us or look like us or come from where we do. The welfare queen is taking our tax money. The immigrant is taking our jobs. The believer condemns the nonbeliever as immoral, and the nonbeliever chides the believer as intolerant." He demanded that each of us do what we can to counter these messages with a "broadening of our minds, and a broadening of our hearts."

In this condemnation of divisiveness, Obama took aim both at prejudice toward the other in general and at a very specific fallacy, that of the "welfare queen," which conservatives at least since Ronald Reagan's 1976 campaign for the Republican presidential nomination have used to weaken the empathy some Americans might have felt for those in need, thus undercutting support for progressive economic policies designed to alleviate that need.[23] He concluded by warning that this divisiveness distracts us from "the common challenges we face—war and poverty; injustice and inequality."

On October 27, a week before the presidential election, Obama challenged Americans to rise above the attempts by his opponent's campaign to pit them against one another on the basis of who was, in the words of John McCain's running mate Sarah Palin, a part of "real America."[24] Obama called on all of us to "bridge our differences and unite in common effort—black, white, Latino, Asian, Native American; Democrat and Republican, young and old, rich and poor, gay and straight, disabled or not. . . . Because despite what our opponents may claim, there are no real or fake parts of this country. There is no city or town that is more pro-America than anywhere else—we are one nation, all of us proud, all of us patriots."

Unity and Diversity in Obama's America

In his call to "bridge our differences and unite"—a consistent rhetorical theme—Obama prioritizes unity over diversity, and for specific reasons. Supporting diversity does not, on its own, provide an ideological foundation on which to build support for a policy agenda based around promoting the common good and improving economic opportunity for all Americans. One could, for instance, celebrate cultural and ethnic differences and endorse preserving them through strict segregation. Likewise, one could combine support for diversity in a society with a belief that one should only share resources with, and evince concern for, the material welfare of those of one's own ethnic group.

A narrow focus on diversity therefore neither approves of nor rejects a unity centered on empathy of the kind Obama has endorsed; the two concepts are simply not on the same ideological plane. He made this point to the League of United Latin American Citizens on July 8, 2008, noting that his goal is more ambitious than simply having people of different backgrounds represented in government positions, or even showing all American children that people of their group can be leaders, although both of these are important. In order to achieve real national unity, Obama argued, we must "have a government that knows that a problem facing any American is a problem facing all Americans." In his view, a government committed to the common good goes beyond just supporting diversity.

Obama's approach—his emphasis on unity and the need for multiethnic societies to do more than simply celebrate diversity—is echoed in social science literature. The work of Robert Putnam is part of "a growing body of research indicating that more diverse populations seem to extend themselves less on behalf of collective needs and goals."[25] On the other hand, countries that are more ethnically homogeneous and have traditionally had a more cohesive sense of being one people, in particular in Europe, spend more on the socioeconomic needs of their citizens. Economists Alberto Alesina and Edward Glaeser attributed 50 percent of the difference between such spending in Europe and the United States to our greater ethnic "fractionalization."[26]

Another economist, Erzo F.P. Luttmer, found significant ethnic loyalty among Americans on the matter of welfare spending, noting: "Individuals increase their support for welfare spending as the share of local recipients from their own racial group rises."[27] Finally, Alesina, in an article coauthored by Reza Baqir and William Easterly, showed that "the shares of spending on productive public goods—education, roads, sewers, and trash pickups—in U.S. cities are inversely related to the city's ethnic fragmentation, even after controlling for other socioeconomic and demographic factors."[28]

Extrapolating from such data, it is clear that multiethnic societies face particular challenges in convincing citizens to support social spending because many define their community in narrow, ethnic terms. Leaders who hope to strengthen support for the common good among their multiethnic citizenry must, drawing on Putnam's argument, focus on inculcating a sense of national identity that centers on fellowship across ethnic lines. Such a task is not a simple one; it is one that requires a sustained national effort.

Proponents of social spending programs in this country have typically presented them to citizens as a solution to individual economic insecurity, i.e. those who may not need the benefits offered by a given program today should support it anyway because it offers them security against future calamity. In other words, the program is necessary because of what might happen to "you" or perhaps "your family." In countries that see themselves as more homogeneous, supporters justify such programs not only based on what might happen to "you" but also because the programs provide support to a fellow "tribesman." The myth of common descent engenders a strong sense of community that makes people in those countries more willing to share resources.

As Kwame Anthony Appiah noted, identities "create forms of solidarity: if I think of myself as an X, then, sometimes, the mere fact that somebody else is an X, too, may incline me to do something with or for them."[29] Elizabeth Theiss-Morse has added that, typically, those who identify strongly as members of the national community are more likely to define community membership in an exclusionary way, and thus are less likely to support progressive policies that they believe will largely benefit those whom they would exclude. Theiss-Morse's argument therefore suggests that Obama not only must invigorate the national identity of Americans from all backgrounds, but also must transform the way white "strong identifiers" define the nation, so that they truly come to see those of other ethnicities as fellow Americans. His challenge is to help them become inclusive strong identifiers.

It will certainly not be easy to achieve this objective, nor would doing so represent the cure to all of American society's ills. Nevertheless, Obama believes that bolstering American civic nationalism and the notion of the common good will help overcome ethnic and other group prejudices, and will thus bolster support for sharing resources and for broader progressive economic policies that will strengthen the country. His language encourages progressives and, in particular, advocates for immigrants and minorities to promote integration and the unity across ethnic lines that follows from it for exactly this reason.

Obama has pointed us toward a place where Americans, when they interact with or think about someone of a different ethnicity, do not focus primarily on difference but instead see a fellow American first. His intention is not that Americans will be "color-blind," or ignore the history of bigotry and discrimination, but rather that cross-ethnic ties, their sense of being one people, will take precedence.

Speaking of the nation not merely as a mosaic of cultures, or solely as a collection of individuals who adhere to common values, but rather as a family—as Obama has done—proposes a much more intimate relationship binding together its members. The people in such a nation not only participate in the same political system and fight to defend one another's liberty and security when threatened, they also see all of its members as equally deserving of opportunities. This vision therefore provides a civic nationalist justification for progressive economic policies.

People typically don't have their national identity in the front of their minds all day every day; rather national identity is a framework for viewing specific situations. Obama wants people to view social and economic problems through a "national" lens, through the lens of feeling part of a singular, unified American community. The alternative visions encourage either a strict hyperindividualism that justifies laissez-faire conservative policies or a strictly ethnic vision according to which one helps only the members of one's own ethnic group. America may not have ethnic solidarity, but we can have national solidarity. Obama's vision provides a way for people—even those whose ethnic groups have been historically excluded—to feel American and to see all other Americans as part of their family. One hopefully would not deny a family member the resources necessary for survival or the tools needed to have a chance to succeed.

This is exactly the point Obama made in an April 6, 2011, speech to the National Action Network. He spoke of fighting "the problems of joblessness and hopelessness that afflict so many of our cities and rural communities . . . fighting to keep kids off the street, fighting to get them into school, fighting to make sure that they went on to college, fighting to make real the promise of justice in our judicial system." The president then stated that we fight these fights because we are committed to our fellow Americans, because we are one people, declaring: "These causes of justice and equality and opportunity [are] the heart of what makes us Americans." The causes he has fought for in the White House, Obama noted, also reflect these same ideals. Finally, he summarized this vision as follows: "The only way for America to prosper is for all Americans to prosper. . . . In America, we rise and fall together."

On April 14, 2011, Obama further explained that, as Americans, "we're all in this together. . . . We look out for one another . . . not out of charity, but because my life is richer, my life is better when the people around me are happy and the people around me have a shot at the American Dream." Similarly, at Miami Dade College on April 29, 2011, the president stated that one of the defining characteristics of our national identity is "our unshakeable commitment to one another—a recognition that we share a future . . . that we are part of a common enterprise that is greater, somehow, than the sum of its parts." Thus, Obama directly challenges the laissez-faire/Social Darwinist/Ayn Rand conception of America. He once commented, "Reagan offered Americans a sense of common purpose."[30] The forty-fourth president has offered an alternative definition of our national identity built around the idea of empathy, the promotion of the common good, and the march toward greater equality and justice.

Immigration, Integration, and American Unity
Immigration poses perhaps the greatest challenge to strengthening national unity. More than any other individual issue that elected officials have debated in recent years, immigration directly affects the way Americans define ourselves as a people. Are the large numbers of immigrants, in particular from Spanish-speaking countries, fundamentally altering our national identity? If so, what should be done about it? The answers to these questions bear on how we think about immigration. Thus, before examining Obama's rhetoric and positions, a brief discussion of the broader topic of the integration/assimilation/Americanization of immigrants follows.

Sociologists Richard Alba and Victor Nee defined assimilation as "the decline of an ethnic distinction and its corollary cultural and social distinctions. . . . Individuals' ethnic origins become less and less relevant in relation to the members of another ethnic group . . . and individuals on both sides of the boundary see themselves as more and more alike . . . they perceive themselves with less and less frequency in terms of ethnic categories and increasingly only under specific circumstances."[31] They added: "Assimilation . . . does not require the disappearance of ethnicity." This definition fits with the concept of hybridity and the multilayered understanding of identity we see in Obama's rhetoric, according to which members of immigrant groups should become more American over time and adopt an American identity but do not have to dissolve their ethnic ties in order to do so. The same formula applies not only to immigrants but also to those of any heritage.

Alba and Nee compared the path of assimilation into American culture taken by today's immigrants and those from previous periods and, contrary to much recent popular and even scholarly opinion, found strong continuities. They devote an entire chapter (4) to debunking arguments that current immigration is substantively different from the predominantly European immigration of the pre-1924 period, and therefore will not follow similar patterns regarding assimilation. Alba and Nee predicted that today's immigrants, who are predominantly not European in origin, will Americanize successfully to the point that we will see "a break with the conventional equation of the mainstream with white America."[32] The integration of nonwhite immigrants into the American mainstream complements Obama's rhetorical push to help Americanness to transcend whiteness.

Concern that today's immigrants are not assimilating the way the folks who came through Ellis Island did casts a significant shadow over the contemporary debates on integration. For example, political scientist Samuel Huntington controversially asserted that Latino immigrants, and in particular those from Mexico will "divide the United States into two peoples, two cultures, and two languages."[33]

When a group of authors set out to test Huntington's hypothesis, however, their analysis of data from national and Los Angeles–area surveys as well as the U.S. census found that "Hispanics acquire English and lose Spanish rapidly beginning with the second generation. . . . Moreover, a clear majority of Hispanics rejects a purely ethnic identification and patriotism grows from one generation to the next. At present, a traditional pattern of political assimilation appears to prevail."[34] Obama's rhetoric has made clear that he rejects Huntington and shares the optimism of Alba and Nee on this matter.

Muslim Americans as Part of the American Family

Just as on other issues, in his approach to immigration we can see Obama balancing his support for diversity with his desire to enhance national unity. He noted in *The Audacity of Hope* that he had learned that some immigrant groups do have especially urgent and community-specific questions, such as Arab and South Asian immigrants who face added scrutiny and, in some cases, ethnic profiling by law enforcement in our post-9/11 security-minded society. In his 2004 Democratic National Convention speech, Obama reached out to those communities. He made clear that he considers them part of the American family by declaring that the violation of an Arab American's constitutional rights represented a threat to his own civil rights.

In his December 10, 2009, Nobel Peace Prize acceptance speech, Obama reflected back on the eight years since 9/11 and praised "the degree to which America has reaffirmed the extraordinary contributions of the Muslim American community and how they have been woven into the fabric of our nation in a seamless fashion." He also stressed that "the fierce loyalty towards America, the fierce patriotism and integration of Muslim Americans into American life have helped to avoid some of the problems that we've seen in other countries on this issue."

Obama was referring to the relative success the United States has had integrating Muslims in comparison to Western European countries, despite some violent incidents that Muslim Americans have perpetrated or attempted to perpetrate, and despite violent acts committed against them along with some virulent anti-Muslim rhetoric in recent American public discourse. According to a Pew Research Center report released May 22, 2007, "Although many Muslims are relative newcomers to the U.S., they are highly assimilated into American society. On balance, they believe that Muslims coming to the U.S. should try and adopt American customs, rather than trying to remain distinct from the larger society."[35]

Western European countries have until recently largely avoided American-style attempts to encourage Muslims to integrate and adopt the broader national identity.[36] For example, Ed Husain, a former Islamist leader who renounced extremism, described the situation in Britain as follows: "Nobody ever said—you're equal to us, you're one of us, and we'll hold you to the same standards. . . . Nobody had the courage to stand up for liberal democracy without qualms."[37]

According to Obama, an inclusive American national identity that embraces immigrants, members of disadvantaged groups, and everyone else in the population helps improve the country's security. After an aborted attack by a Muslim extremist, albeit in this case by a Nigerian rather than an American, Obama stated on December 28, 2009, "As a nation we will do everything in our power to protect our country, as Americans we will never give in to fear or division, we will be guided by our hopes, our unity, and our deeply held values." From the opposite perspective, according to documents that Navy SEALs discovered in their May 2011 raid on his compound, Osama bin Laden hoped to prey upon racial and religious divisions in order to recruit African American Muslims to commit acts of terrorism inside the United States. He further hoped that such acts would, in addition to any physical damage, further exacerbate those divisions and destroy any attempt to strengthen American unity of the kind described here.

Obama has made a specific effort to reach out to Muslim Americans, having repeatedly emphasized that they are full members of the American community. For example, on September 10, 2010, he spoke of Muslims serving in our military and stated: "They are Americans and we honor their service. And part of honoring their service is making sure that they understand that we don't differentiate between them and us. It's just us. . . . Tomorrow [September 11] is an excellent time for us to reflect on that." Additionally, in his January 25, 2011, State of the Union address, President Obama declared that we will respond to terrorist threats "with respect for the rule of law, and with the conviction that American Muslims are a part of our American family."

The president also sent his deputy national security advisor, Denis McDonough, to deliver a major address at a mosque in Northern Virginia on March 6, 2011. The address was part of the administration's public response to the hearings on radicalization in Muslim American communities then about to start in the Republican-controlled House of Representatives. McDonough made clear he was speaking on behalf of the president, and the speech centered on the importance of strengthening Muslims' feeling that they are embraced by America. The emotional high point of the remarks was the contrast between two ways the United States can approach American Muslims: "We can choose to send a message to certain Americans that they are somehow 'less American' because of their faith or how they look. . . . Or . . . we can send the message that we're all Americans."[38] The Obama administration, he explained, takes the latter approach.

Latino Americans, Illegal Immigration, and American Unity

To return to *The Audacity of Hope*, Obama maintained that members of most immigrant groups—including Muslims, for that matter—have fairly universal concerns relating to bread-and-butter material issues. In terms of their identity, they were simply looking to him, in their meetings, for an "affirmation that they, too, are Americans."[39] The meetings with Latino immigrants in particular provoked Obama "to reflect on the meaning of America, the meaning of citizenship, and my sometimes conflicted feelings about all the changes that are taking place."[40]

In summarizing his views on immigration, Obama endorsed the right of this country to control its borders and set limits on the numbers of those coming across. Additionally, he declared that the privilege of citizenship brings with it obligations on the part of immigrants. They must not only learn English but express loyalty to the United States as well as recognize that they share with their fellow Americans "a common purpose, a common destiny."[41] Immigrants must, in other words, adopt the same general type of American national identity as their fellow countrymen. Obama situated his views within the long tradition of encouraging immigrants to do so, noting that "part of America's genius has always been its ability to absorb newcomers, to forge a national identity out of the disparate lot that arrived on our shores."[42]

On a more tangible level, Obama talked about how the high level of Hispanic immigration has affected both the economy and politics, especially in the cities where these immigrants are achieving political influence in the same way that European immigrants as well as black Americans did in previous decades. Without mentioning

Huntington, Obama also lamented the persistence of a "disturbingly familiar" form of xenophobic nativism built around the fear that Latinos cannot or will not assimilate the way other groups have.[43]

Illegal immigration presents a specific problem within the broader issue of immigration. Obama described how the high numbers of immigrants provoke strong concerns about depressing working-class wages and also dredge up xenophobia that resembles sentiments expressed at the time about some who came through Ellis Island a century earlier. Regarding illegal immigration, Obama contended that for most among native-born Americans, "concerns over illegal immigration go deeper than worries about economic displacement and are more subtle than simple racism. In the past, immigration occurred on America's terms; the welcome mat could be extended selectively, on the basis of the immigrant's skills or color or the needs of the industry."[44] He asserted that part of the discomfort with illegal immigration was related to ethnic prejudice, as America did restrict immigration on the basis of ethnicity and national origin for much of its history up through the mid-1960s.

However, Obama argued that in addition to bigotry, anger about the illegality itself, and fears about being displaced from one's job by an immigrant, immigration has engendered the feeling among the native-born that the country had suffered "a loss of sovereignty . . . that America seems unable to control its own destiny."[45] There exists a sense that the United States had lost control of her own borders, irrespective of any laws we might pass. The country also appeared to some to have lost its ability to assimilate newcomers because of the overwhelming pace and seemingly stronger cultural and linguistic links to their country of origin of recent Latino immigrants—thanks to technology and the proximity of places like Mexico. According to Obama, "Native-born Americans suspect that it is they, and not the immigrant, who are being forced to adapt."[46]

These thoughts have crossed his mind as well, Obama admitted. "When I see Mexican flags waved at proimmigration demonstrations, I sometimes feel a flush of patriotic resentment. When I'm forced to use a translator to communicate with the guy fixing my car, I feel a certain frustration."[47] Here Obama is employing a rhetorical strategy similar to the one he used in his Philadelphia race speech to talk about the anger of some whites over racial preferences, albeit with a slight twist. He acknowledged that those who expressed certain resentments regarding immigrants were not necessarily outright bigots. Obama recognized their feelings and concerns, and did something he could not do when talking about white antipathy toward affirmative action, namely confess that he too had felt the same way at times. On both occasions, he empathized with those in his audience who did feel resentful, perhaps prompting them to let down their guard a bit, to relax from their defensive posture by acknowledging that what they felt was neither completely unreasonable nor motivated simply by prejudice. In this way, Obama gained the credibility to deliver information that contradicted the assumptions that underlay those very resentments.

After his confession, Obama stated that for the most part his interactions with immigrants taught him that "America has nothing to fear from these newcomers, that they have come here for the same reason that families came here 150 years ago. . . . Ultimately the danger to our way of life is not that we will be overrun by those who do not look like us or do not yet speak our language. The danger will come if we fail to recognize [their] humanity . . . if we withhold from them the rights and opportunities that we take for granted."[48] This was the point he was setting up his audience to hear and to accept. He hoped to encourage these culturally anxious native-born Americans to be more welcoming of immigrants, which would then make immigrants more likely to integrate successfully. Each of these developments would then feed on the other, creating a virtuous cycle that would enhance American cohesiveness.

In addition to his comments in *The Audacity of Hope*, Obama spoke about immigration on a number of occasions during the 2008 campaign, although it was not a particularly divisive issue either in the Democratic primaries or in the general election. The major Democratic candidates and Senator McCain all offered generally similar positions in favor of so-called comprehensive immigration reform that included some path to legalization for the over 10 million undocumented immigrants estimated to reside in the United States.

Of interest here is the way Obama talked about aspects of the immigration question that relate to the topic of American unity. In an April 2, 2006, interview he stated that, whatever the outcome of debates on immigration, he wanted to ensure "that we're not using this debate to further divide African American workers who are struggling and Latino or Polish or Ukrainian workers who are struggling. They're all struggling." Similarly, Obama told the audience at a Congressional Hispanic Caucus gala on September 15, 2010, "Some take advantage of the economic anxiety that people are feeling to stoke fear of those who look or think or worship differently—to inflame passions between 'us' and 'them.' I have news for those people: It won't work. There is no 'us' and 'them.' In this country, there is only 'us.'"

It is worth comparing this inclusive, unifying language to the rhetoric on im-migration employed by other political figures. Two Republican candidates for the Senate in 2010, Tea Party favorite Sharron Angle in Nevada (who ultimately lost to Majority Leader Senator Harry Reid) and Senator David Vitter in Louisiana (who won reelection), used the same photo of young, dark-skinned, unsmiling Latino men in ads about illegal immigration designed to evoke fears of criminality by members of that ethnic group.[49] On a related note, Angle also sought to stir up anti-Muslim fears by wrongly claiming that Muslim religious law or Sharia law has already "take[n] hold" in Dearborn, Michigan, and Frankford, Texas (the latter of which hasn't existed since 1975).[50] More broadly, Matthew Yglesias in the *Washington Post* charac-terized the divisive rhetoric coming from conservative politicians on illegal immigra-tion and Islam in the summer of 2010 as an "abrupt slide toward xenophobia" that threatens to "permanently scar our national identity."[51]

In speaking to La Raza on July 22, 2007, Obama spoke in more inspirational tones about America's status as "a nation of immigrants." He went on, however, to document the disparities in many areas, including educational resources and health care for example, that immigrants, members of minority groups, and poor whites face. As he has done elsewhere, Obama went on to assert that the strong sense of community that binds Americans together as a nation requires us to recognize that these disparities represent "not just a Latino problem or an African American prob-lem; [it] is an American problem that we have to solve."

Similarly, in his July 8, 2008, remarks to the League of United Latin American Citizens, Obama described a series of hardships, such as unemployment and sub-standard benefits for those with jobs, that fall disproportionately on Hispanics, both immigrant and native-born. He declared that these are problems that "all of us—black, white, and brown—must solve as one nation. . . . All for one and one for all. . . . It's the idea that's at the heart of America."

Bilingual education is one of the most volatile issues relating to immigration because it directly affects how quickly children of immigrants master English. Many Americans judge a politician's position on bilingual education as a test of how strong-ly he or she prioritizes integration. Bilingual education is a vague term that without a detailed definition provides plenty of room for obfuscation by politicians.

In a debate among the Democratic candidates on February 21, 2008, Obama, as he did in *The Audacity of Hope*, called for everyone who comes to the United States to learn English. Additionally, he underlined how important it was "that we have that process of binding ourselves together as a country." Obama offered his support for bilingual education if the goal was to help Spanish-speaking students catch up in school. On March 28, 2011, he similarly endorsed continued support for both bilingual education and English-language immersion programs. Unsurprisingly, he did not endorse the view expressed by some advocates of bilingual education that government needs to help preserve the language and culture of the country of origin within immigrant communities, a perspective one can characterize as reflecting the more radical multicultural sensibilities Obama has long rejected. On the question of English language acquisition, as well as on immigration as a whole, strengthening national unity has served as a key element of his approach.

Arizona, Immigration Reform, and American National Identity

Immigration emerged as a flashpoint nationally and for President Obama in the spring of 2010, when Arizona passed new state laws relating to illegal immigration. On April 23, Governor Jan Brewer signed SB 1070, and on April 30 signed HB 2162 (which modified the prior law in ways that sought to address concerns about ethnic profiling of suspects). Combined, the laws mandate that all legal immigrants carry their documentation with them or face state penalties (previously only federal law mandated that they do so, and that law was rarely enforced unless a suspect was apprehended relating to another crime). The Arizona laws taken together also require law enforcement officials who are already engaged in a "lawful stop, detention, or arrest" to ask suspects, when feasible, for their immigration-related papers if the officer determines there is a "reasonable suspicion" that they are undocumented immigrants.[52]

In his initial remarks on April 23, Obama condemned SB 1070 as "threaten[ing] to undermine basic notions of fairness that we cherish as Americans, as well as the trust between police and their communities that is so crucial to keeping us safe." After the modifications were passed on April 30, President Obama moderated his criticisms of the law somewhat. Paralleling the occasions when he discussed his own personal reactions to high levels of immigration as well as those of whites who have problems with affirmative action, he explained on May 26 that he understood the frustrations with illegal immigration felt by those who supported the law. On May 19, however, he maintained that this law represented "a misdirected expression of frustration over our broken immigration system."

For the purposes of this book, more relevant than his policy objections are the ways he related his take on the law to his depiction of American identity. On April 27, the president, after criticizing the law as "poorly conceived," reminded his audience that "we are a nation of immigrants. We were founded on immigration. That's what that whole Plymouth Rock thing was about—immigration." Typically, remarks on immigration evoke images of Ellis Island and "foreigners" of various ethnic backgrounds. Obama, however, linked immigration to those who personify traditional, white Anglo-Saxon Protestant Americans, those who sailed across the ocean on the *Mayflower* to Plymouth Rock. He is not the first to note that the Pilgrims were immigrants, but not only did he emphasize that fact, but by doing so in the context of illegal immigration and the controversy surrounding the Arizona laws he connected people who are founding members of the American family to those clandestinely crossing the Mexican-American border today.

Ultimately, Obama spoke against even the modified Arizona law because he believed it would hamper American unity. The law would divide the nation along ethnic boundaries in terms of the way those perceived as being of Mexican or Central American descent would be treated by law enforcement, thus undermining the great achievement of equal rights, the foundation upon which his inclusive vision of America stood. On May 5, 2010, he declared, "We can't start singling out people because of who they look like, or how they talk, or how they dress. We can't turn law-abiding American citizens—and law-abiding immigrants—into subjects of suspicion and abuse. We can't divide the American people that way." On July 1, the president again criticized the Arizona law, calling it "ill-conceived" and "divisive." On July 6, the Department of Justice filed suit to enjoin the enforcement of the Arizona immigration laws, and on July 28 a federal judge issued an order preventing most of the controversial provisions from being enforced.

It is worth noting that Alabama passed an even harsher set of immigration laws on June 9, 2011. Among other provisions that went beyond Arizona's laws, the Alabama law requires public schools to determine whether each newly enrolled student is in the United States legally. The Justice Department sued to block its implementation. On September 28 a federal judge upheld most of it, and Alabama public schools almost immediately experienced what the *Associated Press* called "a sudden exodus of children of Hispanic descent."[53] Additionally, on November 9, Obama criticized the Alabama law in an interview with Spanish-language media.[54]

Public schools can and should play a fundamental role in integrating immigrant children into American society and strengthening their sense of American national identity. Thus, by making immigrant parents afraid to send their children to school—something that has a direct, negative impact on those kids' lives as well as the communities that subsequently have large numbers of uneducated young people—the Alabama law also stands diametrically opposed to Obama's push to invigorate national unity.

Returning to his remarks of July 1, 2010, Obama also reissued his call for comprehensive immigration reform legislation (he had also done so on May 10, 2011, as well as other occasions) and gave a major address on the topic. He argued that we need a system of immigration "that reflects our values as a nation of laws and a nation of immigrants." Most interestingly, Obama reiterated his inclusive civic nationalist definition of the American people and specifically rejected the ethnic definition as being incompatible with our national identity: "Being an American is not a matter of blood or birth. It's a matter of faith. It's a matter of fidelity to the shared values that we all hold so dear. That's what makes us unique. That's what makes us strong. Anybody can help us write the next great chapter in our history." Despite this, neither the U.S. House nor the Senate has, as of early 2012, engaged in serious consideration of such legislation during the Obama presidency.

The House of Representatives, with Obama's support, did pass the DREAM (Development, Relief, and Education for Alien Minors) Act on December 8, 2010, which would grant permanent residency status to those who entered the country illegally as minors, were "of good moral character," and either served two years in the military or completed two years of college. The bill was filibustered by thirty-six Republicans and five Democrats in the Senate, and died on December 18, 2010.

On a number of occasions since then, Obama has reiterated his support for the DREAM Act. On one such occasion, on April 29, 2011, he defined the children of undocumented immigrants who were raised in this country as Americans, stating, "They grew up as Americans. They pledge allegiance to our flag." He went further, declaring: "Whether your ancestors came here on the *Mayflower* or a slave ship; whether they signed in at Ellis Island or they crossed the Rio Grande—we are one people. We need one another. Our patriotism is not rooted in ethnicity, but in a shared belief of the enduring and permanent promise of this country." As discussed earlier, he similarly defined undocumented immigrants as Americans in the epilogue of *Dreams*.

With no legislative solution in sight, Obama announced a new executive branch policy on June 15, 2012. His administration would no longer deport most young undocumented immigrants who had come to the United States as children, and would allow them to work openly, a policy that would temporarily benefit approximately one million people.[55] The president characterized those young people as: "Americans in their heart, in their minds."

In a May 5, 2011, speech, the president referred back to something he saw at the Miami Dade commencement ceremony a week earlier. He described the processional of 181 flags carried by members of the campus ROTC, each representing the country of origin of one or more graduates. The graduates from each country cheered the flag of their birth, but "there was one flag that every single student and spectator cheered loudly and proudly for—and that was when the American flag came through. The American flag. So it was a wonderful reminder—we all come from different backgrounds, we have different beliefs, we have sometimes petty and sometimes not-so-petty political differences. But we all share a set of ideals. We all have a common future."

Additionally, on May 10, 2011, Obama explained: "It doesn't matter where you come from; what matters is that you believe in the ideals on which we were founded; that you believe all of us are equal and deserve the freedom to pursue happiness. In embracing America, you can become American." In the three aforementioned speeches the president defined all of us as members of the American community, whether our ancestors were WASP, Italian, Jewish, Polish, black, or Mexican, or of any other background. He also emphasized that immigrants can simultaneously be proud of their ancestry and proudly embrace their American identity. This is Obama defining and strengthening our national unity.

Although he has not achieved significant legislative successes on immigration, the way Obama speaks about American unity aids the process of integrating those who have felt like outsiders, in particular minorities and immigrants. He has sought to make those Americans traditionally kept outside the circle of the national community to feel truly invited inside by its long-standing members, and, crucially, to give them the resources necessary to fully participate and thrive in the national community. For both immigrants and the native-born of all backgrounds, membership in that community brings the obligation to identify with its interests and those of all its members, not only those who, as Obama said on June 2, 2006, "look like you and act like you and live in your neighborhood." The bond must extend in all directions, and it must extend beyond mere tolerance to empathy and brotherhood.

To return to Arizona, in Tucson, on January 12, 2011, President Obama memorialized the victims shot in the attempted assassination of Arizona Congresswoman Gabrielle Giffords. He described them as "part of our family, an American family 300 million strong." But Obama also talked about how what unites us is stronger than what divides us and described how our national "task, working together, is to constantly widen the circle of our concern so that we bequeath the American Dream to future generations."

One might expect that a president would typically use such language encouraging national unity and empathy for our fellow Americans in a time of tragedy, when the country needed to heal the wounds opened by a hateful, violent act. As this book has demonstrated, however, President Obama has returned to these ideas again and again over almost two decades. They define his conception of American national identity.

7

Obama's Narrative of American History and Our Place in the World

That's how this country was founded, a group of patriots declaring independence against the mighty British empire. . . . That's how slaves and abolitionists resisted that wicked system and how a new president chartered a course to ensure we would not remain half-slave and half-free. That's how the greatest generation . . . overcame Hitler and fascism and also lifted themselves up out of a Great Depression. That's how pioneers went west when people told them it was dangerous. . . . That's how immigrants traveled from distant shores when people said their fates would be uncertain. . . . That's how women won the right to vote, how workers won the right to organize, how young people like you traveled down South to march, and sit in, and go to jail, and some were beaten, and some died for freedom's cause. That's what hope is.[1]

—Barack Obama, February 12, 2008

Obama's depiction of our history as the saga of a people that has fought and—bit by bit—succeeded in enshrining in law equality for those initially denied it stands at the center of his drive to invigorate American national identity. According to Gary Nash, "History . . . is about national identity. . . . It provides so much of the substance for the way a society defines itself and considers what it wants to be."[2] He further explained, "In all modern nations, educators and political leaders have regarded history as a vehicle for promoting amor patriae [love of country], for instilling in young people knowledge and attitudes that promote national cohesion and civic pride."[3]

The battles over radical multiculturalism of the 1980s and 1990s tested the ability of liberal politicians to speak in terms of a coherent, unifying narrative of American history. From the late 1960s, not only radicals but also a significant portion of mainstream liberals had dissociated themselves from patriotism and, to some degree, even from a positive view of America generally, allowing conservatives to connect Americanism to their ideology and their candidates for office over the subsequent generation.[4]

Obama's rhetoric and views therefore represent a profound shift, one that was on display for example, on the night of his victory in Iowa, January 3, 2008, just after he uttered the words, "We're choosing unity over division." The crowd then broke out into an unrehearsed, repetitive patriotic chant: "USA! USA! USA! USA! USA!"[5] One could hear similar chants echoing at Obama rallies during the rest of the campaign.

As the critiques offered over the last two generations have made clear, a wholly positive presentation of American history is inaccurate. So, however, is one that dwells solely or even primarily on oppression. Worse, when liberals present an excessively negative picture that ignores the progress of recent decades, they risk driving moderates and mainstream conservatives in the opposite direction, toward a whitewashed view of our national story. If the only choices are to view America's record as either relatively spotless or intrinsically evil, many people will choose the former. That point of view not only falsely represents the past, it colors one's understanding of the present as well, encouraging a Pollyannaish view of questions relating to discrimination and equality more broadly.

By celebrating America's triumphs and its egalitarian principles while also weaving into the narrative examples of when we have not lived up to them, Obama seeks to ensure that Americans of every heritage remember all of our history and identify with it as their own. We can see this balanced but ultimately optimistic presentation of our history in his discussion of gains won by the civil rights movement at the dedication of the Martin Luther King Jr. Memorial on October 16, 2011:

> We are right to savor that slow but certain progress—progress that's expressed itself in a million ways, large and small, across this nation every single day, as people of all colors and creeds live together, and work together, and fight alongside one another, and learn together, and build together,

and love one another . . . but it is worth remembering that progress did not come from words alone. Progress was hard. Progress was purchased through enduring the smack of billy clubs and the blast of fire hoses. It was bought with days in jail cells and nights of bomb threats. For every victory during the height of the civil rights movement, there were setbacks and there were defeats.

Celebrating publicly the best things America has done gives Obama the credibility to convince people to remember the country's misdeeds as well, in particular those people who might otherwise choose to overlook them. He hopes to get these folks to recognize the effects of such historical misdeeds on Americans today and to increase their support for reforms that can ameliorate those effects. Obama's liberal, civic nationalism thus has two goals: to invigorate national unity and strengthen his political position. Clearly, he thinks that someone who speaks only of the terrible things in our history would not be able to accomplish either task as effectively.

Some on the far left seem to reject out of hand the attempt to characterize America and its history in any sort of positive light. For example, Katha Pollitt, writing in *The Nation* nine days after September 11, said: "The [American] flag stands for jingoism and vengeance and war."[6] Whatever the context, such a statement diverges strongly from Obama's conception of America. Most progressives—people who would be wary of a depiction that downplayed discrimination and its present-day impact—can, however, support his version of the national narrative because they consider it to be multifaceted and balanced. Obama's unambiguous embrace of George Washington and Thomas Jefferson as heroic figures, done in full knowledge that they owned slaves, gives progressives a kind of permission to do so as well. Many liberals feel like they can adopt Obama's brand of patriotism and love of country without feeling like they are betraying those whom the country has wronged in favor of a rose-colored sort of jingoism.

The portrayal of America that Obama has offered is quite different from that of the radical left. His broader testimonial about the country may convince people from all kinds of ethnic backgrounds and political persuasions whom more traditional definitions have alienated to feel differently because it coheres with their commitment to equality and justice. Obama provides a coherent intellectual framework according to which members of these previously alienated groups are able to embrace fully an American national identity as their own.

Obama's Narrative of Our Early History

In *The Audacity of Hope*, Obama laid out two ways of understanding the early history of the American republic. One sees the nation's founders as "hypocrites," condemns the Constitution "as a betrayal of the grand ideals set forth by the Declaration of Independence," and characterizes its compromises over slavery as "a pact with the devil."[7] The other viewpoint accepts those compromises as having been "necessary, if unfortunate" in order to create a structure that the elected representatives from various parts of the country could accept as the basis of a unified system of government. As someone who deeply felt his connection to his blackness as well as his American national identity, Obama stated an unwillingness to accept either interpretation as wholly correct. Instead, he chose both: "I love America too much, am too invested in what this country has become . . . to focus entirely on the circumstances of its birth. But neither can I brush aside the magnitude of the injustice done . . . or ignore the open wound, the aching spirit, that ails this country still." Here we see Obama reconciling the moralistic and the pragmatic view of American history.

Additionally, Obama said that the Constitution, "despite being marred by the original sin of slavery—has at its very core the idea of equal citizenship under the law. . . . Of course racism and nativist sentiments have repeatedly undermined these ideals . . . but in the hands of reformers, from Tubman to Douglass to Chavez to King, these ideals of equality have gradually shaped how we understand ourselves and allowed us to form a multicultural nation the likes of which exists nowhere else on earth."[8] This statement neatly sums up Obama's take on how America dealt with equality over time.

Despite the country's "original sin" on the matter of slavery and the broader sins to which bigotry has given birth, Obama expressed a belief that its founding ideals have provided the opportunity and the means with which the country has been able to go a long way toward redeeming itself. From Obama's 2004 convention speech in Boston, where he characterized this country as "a magical place . . . which stood as a beacon of freedom and opportunity to so many who had come before," to his 2011 State of the Union address, where he spoke of the United States as being "not just a place on a map, but the light to the world," he has consistently spoken of America in these terms.[9]

Here, as on other matters, Obama's view reflects the influence of Martin Luther King Jr. In fact, in President Obama's January 17, 2010, speech commemorating Martin Luther King Jr. Day, he cited the example of civil rights leaders like Reverend

King who fought to make America live up to the ideals it had long betrayed, yet never rejected the country or their identity as Americans: "They didn't give up on this country. . . . Imperfect as it was, they continued to believe in the promise of democracy; in America's constant ability to remake itself, to perfect this union." Obama himself had expressed these ideas as far back as *Dreams*, in which he commented: "We could tell this country where it was wrong . . . without ceasing to believe in its capacity for change."[10]

When focusing on the evolving status of black Americans, Obama spoke much the same way. He detailed the oppression America inflicted on those of African descent and highlighted the eventual achievements—as well as the limitations—of the campaigns to bring about equality, often stressing that both blacks and nonblacks struggled, bled, and died fighting for that cause. Among other examples, Obama did so at an NAACP dinner on May 1, 2005; a June 13, 2005, statement in support of a U.S. Senate resolution apologizing for its role in allowing lynchings to occur; in his Philadelphia race speech of March 18, 2008; at the NAACP Centennial Convention on July 16, 2009; and in a speech to the Congressional Black Caucus on September 27, 2009.

By speaking and writing about the history of racial bigotry in this way, Obama hoped to assuage potential critics from the left who would accuse him of soft-pedaling the degree of oppression black Americans have faced, as well as critics from the right who would charge him with being too pessimistic about the progress that has taken place. As a black politician seeking national office, he could not afford to be seen either as too radical or too Pollyannaish about this history or about racism in America more generally. Nevertheless, the remarks cited in the previous paragraph, all of which Obama made after winning election to the U.S. Senate, are essentially consistent with the sentiments he expressed as far back as 1990.

On a related note, Obama often made sure to remind his audience of the history of bigotry when speaking about topics that ostensibly did not center on that issue. On October 14, 2009, he reflected upon the history of the U.S. Senate and the great personalities who served there, but added, "At its worst, it could be a place where progress was stymied. There was a time, of course, when there were no desks for women, or African Americans, or Latino Americans, or Asian Americans."

When Obama discussed the history of education, he integrated racial discrimination into that narrative. On April 25, 2005, he traced the origins of public schooling, citing the guiding principle laid down by Thomas Jefferson that "talent and virtue, needed in a free society, should be educated regardless of wealth, birth or other accidental condition." Segregation was a violation of that basic Jeffersonian principle. Here he has deftly put Jefferson, a paragon of the traditional chronicle of the United States, on the side of Linda Brown of Topeka, Kansas, and those who fought to desegregate American schools. When presenting virtually any specific topic of American history, Obama included how prejudice affected the path of its development.

We can contrast the way Obama has done so to the way other contemporary politicians have integrated (or not) the history of racism when discussing the story of America in their public remarks and actions. We can laugh (perhaps) at off-the-cuff mistakes, such as that made by then presidential candidate Representative Michele Bachmann (R-MN) in Iowa on January 21, 2011, where she claimed that the Founders, the men who wrote documents like the Declaration of Independence, "worked tirelessly until slavery was no more in the United States," when of course most of the Founders did no such thing, and many of them owned slaves their entire lives.[11]

But we have to take it more seriously when such whitewashing is clearly pre-planned. On April 2, 2010, Virginia governor Bob McDonnell issued a proclamation declaring April "Confederate History Month." The proclamation asserted that the Confederates "fought for their homes and communities and Commonwealth in a time very different than ours today."[12] He also called on "all Virginians to reflect upon our Commonwealth's shared history, to understand the sacrifices of the Confederate leaders, soldiers, and citizens." Nowhere in the proclamation, however, did the governor mention slavery and its relationship to secession, the Civil War, or the Confederacy. When asked about this omission, McDonnell replied on April 6, "There were any number of aspects to that conflict between the states. Obviously, it involved slavery. It involved other issues. But I focused on the ones I thought were most significant for Virginia."[13]

The notion that slavery was not one of the more significant issues for Virginia during the Civil War era is not only inaccurate but also reflects a particular ideological approach to that history, as James M. McPherson, the preeminent historian of the conflict, explained in his reaction to McDonnell's proclamation: "The people that emphasize Confederate heritage and the legacy, and the importance of understanding Confederate history, want to deny that Confederate history was ultimately bound up with slavery. But that was the principal reason for secession—that an antislavery party was elected to the White House."[14] A day later, the governor backtracked, issuing an apology and a rewritten proclamation that referred to slavery as "an evil and inhumane practice" upon which all Virginians should reflect and from which they should learn.[15] However, he issued the apology and change of language only after facing significant criticism.[16]

Irrespective of historical accuracy, the original proclamation and the justifications McDonnell offered for omitting slavery clearly diminished the importance of racism in our history. His initial narrative spoke specifically to and about white Virginians—certainly not all of whom accept his historical interpretation—under the guise of speaking to and about "all Virginians." Such a narrative works against the strengthening of an inclusive national identity, as Obama himself pointed out in an April 9 interview on *Good Morning America*. He called on all of us to remember that when we speak about our history we need to recognize that the national story we present can affect Americans' "sense of whether they're part of a commonwealth or part of . . . our broader society." Obama is saying here that public figures can use history to invigorate or to weaken the degree to which members of various groups identify themselves as Americans.

Obama on America's Role in the World

Another aspect of Obama's portrayal of this country and its history is the way he described its role in the world, both regarding its cultural and ideological values and its relations with other countries. In *The Audacity of Hope*, Obama traced back to the early Republic the national desire both to remain isolated from European affairs and to expand and dominate the North American continent, a drive motivated by belief in manifest destiny. He cited the violence done to American Indians as well as to Mexico, both of whom lost territory to the expansion of the United States. On Native Americans, he further lamented on December 16, 2010, the fact that, "by virtue of the longstanding failure to tackle wrenching problems in Indian Country, it seemed as though you had to either abandon your heritage or accept a lesser lot in life; that there was no way to be a successful part of America and a proud Native American." Obama rejected this as a "false choice," one that is inconsistent with "our basic values . . . that [have] always defined who we are as Americans. E pluribus unum. Out of many, one." Here we see the president referring back to the broader definition of our national identity that is central to his entire political worldview.

To return to *The Audacity of Hope*, the taking of lands from Mexico and from American Indians was like slavery in that all of these "contradicted America's founding principles and tended to be justified in explicitly racist terms, a conquest that American mythology has always had difficulty fully absorbing but that other countries recognized for what it was—an exercise in raw power."[17] Expansion continued after the Civil War, as America in the 1890s and early 1900s projected its power beyond its own continent, from the South Pacific to the Caribbean, based on motives that were "barely distinguishable from those of the other great powers, driven by realpolitik and commercial interests."[18]

At the end of World War I, Obama continued, Wilson's ambitious plans for the League of Nations failed, as the country turned inward. At the end of World War II, the country embraced a multilateral approach to international relations, in particular because the Cold War created a need for allies all over the world as well as international institutions to increase global stability and reduce conflict. Although Cold War containment policy achieved its main goals over the course of fifty years, and Obama found much to praise in America's role in ultimately defeating Soviet communism, he did not shy away from pointing out instances where he believed the country had made mistakes. We backed anticommunist regimes even when they were themselves authoritarian, and helped overthrow democratically elected regimes that were too close to the Soviet Union. The former policy led directly to the Vietnam War, which Obama described as having divided us in ways we had not been before, with sharply negative consequences for American society. On Ronald Reagan's foreign policy, Obama struck a middle course, praising his approach to the Soviet Union and the Cold War while bemoaning his lack of focus on oppression by noncommunists in other parts of the world.[19]

In his October 2, 2002, speech announcing his opposition to the Iraq war, then state senator Obama also offered remarks on other conflicts in which the United States has fought as part of his argument that he did not oppose all wars, only ones he considered foolish ventures. He characterized World War II, for example, as an unalloyed good in which our country "triumphed over evil."

As Obama has taken a nuanced approach when discussing our history in front of a domestic audience, he has done the same when speaking in front of a foreign audience. For instance, in Strasbourg, France, on April 4, 2009, he was asked whether he subscribed "to the school of American exceptionalism that sees America as uniquely qualified to lead the world." President Obama answered, "I believe in American exceptionalism, just as I suspect that the Brits believe in British exceptionalism and the Greeks believe in Greek exceptionalism." Speaking more broadly, he recognized that although America had erred from time to time, in terms of its overall record he was "enormously proud of my country and its role and history in the world."

Here we see Obama embracing American exceptionalism while also recognizing that people of every nation may well feel similarly when assessing their own group's achievements. We don't see this kind of balance from those conservatives who each try to outdo the other in proclaiming just how exceptional America is.[20] These conservatives condemned what they called Obama's "apology tour" simply because he gave a speech abroad that acknowledged that America had, on occasion, made a mistake, that it was and is in fact human.[21]

Those who adhere to the conservative conception of American exceptionalism seem to believe that America is literally flawless, infallible, and incapable of ever doing anything that it might have to reconsider later on, let alone apologize for. Frankly, they sound like five-year-olds. Mitt Romney even titled his most recent book *No Apology: The Case for American Greatness.* He also closed a presidential campaign ad in late 2011 with a line he had used repeatedly on other occasions to contrast himself to Obama: "I will never apologize for the United States of America."[22] Similarly, Newt Gingrich's 2011 book is called *A Nation Like No Other: Why American Exceptionalism Matters.* This has already become a campaign issue in the 2012 presidential election, another version of the game played in 2008 when his opponents questioned Obama's patriotism by complaining that he didn't always wear a flag pin.

Even more incredibly, Sarah Palin's 2010 book *America by Heart* clearly mischaracterized Obama's remarks cited in the paragraph above. Palin wrote: "President Obama even said that he believes in American exceptionalism *in the same way* 'the Brits believe in British exceptionalism and the Greeks believe in Greek exceptionalism.' Which is to say, he doesn't believe in American exceptionalism at all (emphasis mine)."[23] She could have presented the full sentence from Obama's speech, which makes his meaning clear. Her use of the words "in the same way" represents a subtle but fundamental twisting of what Obama said. He simply stated that he believes in American exceptionalism and acknowledged that members of other nations think they are exceptional as well. Rather than be as boorish as Palin would have liked and finish the comment by baldly stating, "But I'm right and they're wrong," Obama simply stated these things as facts and left it at that. It's called diplomacy.

To push that last point a bit further, President Obama's understanding of American exceptionalism—because it lauds our achievements while simultaneously showing humility—is far more likely to actually enhance America's ability to lead than the arrogant jingoism of the likes of Palin, Romney, and Gingrich. Obama's modest yet proud way of talking about America is one that can strengthen alliances, while the conservatives' boastful chest-thumping will only alienate our friends and potential allies while doing nothing to materially weaken our enemies.

In accepting the Nobel Peace Prize on December 10, 2009, Obama reflected in more detail on America's role in global affairs since the 1940s, starting with World War II. Once again, he acknowledged that this country had made its share of mistakes. Nevertheless, he proclaimed, "The plain fact is this: The United States of America has helped underwrite global security for more than six decades with the blood of our citizens and the strength of our arms. The service and sacrifice of our men and women in uniform has promoted peace and prosperity from Germany to Korea, and enabled democracy to take hold in places like the Balkans." By first acknowledging America's imperfections, Obama hoped to demonstrate that he was not simply another jingoistic booster who refused to see any imperfections in the record of his country. Therefore, when he delivered an ultimately positive assessment of its role on the world stage, it would carry more weight with his international audience.

In terms of its role in spreading the values of democracy and human rights, Obama talked about the importance of America staunchly defending those values. In his Nobel Prize speech, he accompanied his balanced portrayal of his country's actions over time and his pledge to respect the "unique culture and traditions of different countries" with a rejection of the idea that "the failure to uphold human rights is excused by the false suggestion that these are somehow Western principles, foreign to local cultures or stages of a nation's development."

In a December 10, 2010, statement issued upon the awarding of the 2010 Nobel Peace Prize to imprisoned Chinese democracy advocate Liu Xiaobo, Obama remarked similarly, "The rights of human beings are universal—they do not belong to one nation, region, or faith." This rhetoric coheres with his approach to diversity and unity within American society as well. The values of democracy are universal and those values ultimately trump his otherwise strong respect for cultural diversity in the rare instances when the two clash.

In his June 4, 2009, speech at Cairo University in which he reached out to the Arab and Muslim world, Obama similarly cited the country's founding ideal of equality and underscored the fact that Americans have "shed blood and struggled for centuries to give meaning to those words—within our borders, and around the world." He went on to explain that America is an egalitarian society that is pluralistic—

"shaped by every culture, drawn from every end of the Earth"—but unified. Finally, the president described the United States as centered on the principle that our "common aspirations" transcend ethnicity, religion, class, and other forms of identity. These common aspirations are, in fact, "the hope of all humanity."[24]

These themes came together in remarks Obama made to American troops at Bagram Airfield in Afghanistan on March 28, 2010. The president made explicit the contrast between the model represented by the United States and a fundamentalist model that relies on a clash of civilizations and cultures, one that sees pluralism as an abomination thwarting the purity its adherents seek. He extolled the troops for demonstrating "what's possible when people come together, not based on color or creed, not based on faith or station, but based on a commitment to serve together, to bleed together, and to succeed together as one people, as Americans."

Obama then juxtaposed our core principles and those of its enemies, whom he defined in terms of their fundamentalism: "But all of you want to build—and that is something essential about America. They've got no respect for human life. You see dignity in every human being. That's part of what we value as Americans. They want to drive races and regions and religions apart. You want to bring people together and see the world move forward together. They offer fear, in other words, and you offer hope."

In the late spring and summer of 2010, a controversy broke out that provided an opportune moment for Obama to highlight this contrast once again. The country found itself divided over the proposal to build Cordoba House (also known as "Park 51"), a Muslim community and cultural center that was to include a Muslim prayer space along with an auditorium for performance arts events, basketball court, gym, lecture hall, restaurant, culinary school, and swimming pool.[25] The site for the center, which would require the tearing down of the existing Burlington Coat Factory building (in which weekly Muslim prayer services had been held starting in September 2009), is two blocks from Ground Zero in Lower Manhattan.[26]

President Obama spoke about the matter at a White House iftar dinner on August 13, 2010. He began by noting that commemorating the events of Christians, Muslim, Jews, and Hindus, for example, at the White House is "an affirmation of who we are as Americans." Obama here asserted that pluralism is central to how we ought to understand what it means to be American. Then, echoing his Bagram speech, he defined America as "a nation where the ability of peoples of different faiths to coexist peacefully and with mutual respect for one another stands in contrast to the religious conflict that persists around the globe."

Going further on that theme, Obama contrasted America's core principles with those expressed by al Qaeda and other violent extremists who practice, in his words, "not Islam [but instead] a gross distortion of Islam."[27] He spoke in similar terms on May 2, 2011, when—in remarks announcing the death of Osama bin Laden at the hands of U.S. forces—the president noted, "Our war is not against Islam. Bin Laden was not a Muslim leader; he was a mass murderer of Muslims."

To return to the August 13, 2010, iftar speech, Obama highlighted America's democracy, guarantees of freedom, "the laws that we apply without regard to race or religion; wealth or status. Our capacity to show not merely tolerance, but respect to those who are different from us—a way of life that stands in stark contrast to the nihilism of those who attacked us on [September 11, 2001], and who continue to plot against us today." As for the controversy over the building in Lower Manhattan, Obama then expressed his support for the right of Muslims to build Cordoba House/ Park 51, grounding that support in the traditions of religious freedom and equality that are core aspects of our national identity: "Muslims have the same right to practice their religion as anyone else. . . . That includes the right to build a place of worship and a community center on private property in Lower Manhattan. . . . This is America, and our commitment to religious freedom must be unshakeable. The principle that people of all faiths are welcome in this country, and will not be treated differently by their government, is essential to who we are." He concluded by noting the long history and contributions of Muslim Americans, describing them as "part of an unbroken line of Americans that stretches back to our founding; Americans of all faiths who have served and sacrificed to extend the promise of America to new generations."

A Florida pastor's call to make September 11, 2010, "International Burn a Quran Day" prompted Obama to use that day to reiterate some of the above themes, and to contrast further the fundamental ideals espoused by al Qaeda and by the United States. In remarks delivered at the Pentagon, he declared that on 9/11 nine years earlier al Qaeda had "attacked the very idea of America itself. . . . They may wish to drive us apart, but we will not give in to their hatred and prejudice. . . . Those who attacked us sought to demoralize us, divide us, to deprive us of the very unity, the very ideals, that make America America—those qualities that have made us a beacon of freedom and hope to billions around the world." Likewise, in Indonesia on November 10, 2010, President Obama stated, "Our national motto is E pluribus unum," and then explained that our country demonstrates "that hundreds of millions who hold different beliefs can be united in freedom under one flag."

Presidents have long spoken in such terms. Just as Obama characterized this country as a beacon of freedom, Ronald Reagan in his January 11, 1989, farewell address called America "a beacon . . . for all who must have freedom."[28] Obama, however, is subtly but unmistakably redefining that notion. Traditionally, people around the world have admired what they see as the freedoms Americans enjoy and the democratic principles on which our political system rests. In the above speeches, especially those at the Pentagon and in Indonesia, Obama added another element, emphasizing that America's democratic values allow us to generate unity while showing respect for diversity. These values mandate that we recognize Americans from every background as full members of the national community. He is defining a twenty-first-century American mission according to which this country provides a model not only of democracy as opposed to tyranny, but of a pluralistic democracy as opposed to fundamentalist tyranny. This mission is central to Obama's conception of American exceptionalism.

With the Oslo and Cairo speeches and the remarks at Bagram, at the White House iftar dinner, at the Pentagon, and in Indonesia, Obama essentially assigned America the dual role of promoting our common humanity and modeling its formula of democratic pluralism for the rest of the world. His hope is that this formula can help all societies—including his own—ease the dislocation and insecurity people feel regarding their ability to preserve their traditional identities in a rapidly globalizing world. Obama's vision of America stands as an alternative to both a rootless cosmopolitanism that ignores the need for belonging and a fundamentalist-type retrenchment that rejects difference completely and typically seeks to impose conformity through violent means.

Obama's Broad Narrative of American History

On many other occasions, Obama went beyond discussing a specific topic or a single aspect of the country's history or its values. His speeches often chronicled in long brushstrokes a sweep of events that define America's common story. On June 4, 2005, he gave a commencement address at Knox College, founded in 1837 by abolitionists and activists in the Underground Railroad and which was among the first U.S. colleges to admit women and nonwhites. Obama began by comparing the lack of rights and freedoms of a servant in Imperial Rome, a peasant in eleventh-century China, or even a British subject in one of the thirteen colonies before 1776, to the ideals upon which the newly created American republic rested. He lauded the

American Dream that drew people from all over the world, but also noted that that dream "was scarred by our treatment of native peoples, betrayed by slavery, clouded by the subjugation of women, shaken by war and depression." Even though he was not yet president, Obama here referred to "our" treatment of native peoples, rather than attempt to separate himself rhetorically from America's crimes by defining that treatment as something that whites did.

Other than war and economic depression, America had inflicted each of these scars on itself; they resulted from Americans' own bigotry. Obama placed them front and center in our national history. Nevertheless, he explained, America has worked to overcome these betrayals of our core values and move towards perfection, even if that is not something we can ever achieve: "The test is not perfection. . . . The true test of the American ideal is whether we are able to recognize our failings and then rise together to meet the challenges of our time."

This depiction of America, as well as the previously discussed commentary on America's role in the world, reflects the influence of Reinhold Niebuhr, whom Obama claimed as "one of my favorite philosophers."[29] Niebuhr, an American theologian who became a leading liberal thinker in the mid-twentieth century, argued that no human being and, by extension, no society is purely good or evil. Obama's reading of Niebuhr helped convince him that a society, even one that commits serious transgressions against its own citizens or other countries, is not necessarily unworthy of admiration and respect. Just as all human beings have good and evil within them, so do societies and countries, which are nothing more than collections of individual human beings. Obama was thus able to acknowledge the wrongs American society has done and yet consider our overall impact to be strongly positive. This further separates his view of America from that of radical multiculturalists, who rely on a Manichean worldview that considers this country and the Western world more broadly as unredeemable due to their racism.

We can also see evidence of the influence of Niebuhr on Obama in the way the latter spoke about Abraham Lincoln just six weeks earlier, on April 20, 2005. In his speech at the Lincoln Presidential Library and Museum, Obama praised his fellow Illinoisan for his will, self-discipline, commitment to his moral beliefs, and ability to constantly improve himself in order to overcome new challenges. Yet Obama did not shrink from describing Lincoln's flaws, both personal and ideological, noting that "Lincoln was not a perfect man, nor a perfect president. By modern standards, his condemnation of slavery might be considered tentative; his Emancipation

Proclamation more a military document than a clarion call for justice. He wasn't immune to political considerations."

Even in this speech, most of which was devoted to praising Lincoln, Obama did not whitewash the sixteenth president's views on race. However, even though those views do not comport with contemporary standards, Obama did not use this to discredit Lincoln, or to depict him as something other than a towering figure in the fight for racial equality, as some purists might have. He judged Lincoln on the whole body of his work, and further proclaimed, "And yet despite these imperfections, despite his fallibility . . . indeed, perhaps because . . . of this essential humanity of his, when it came time to confront the greatest moral challenge this nation has ever faced, Lincoln did not flinch." Here Obama framed his take on Lincoln through the prism of the Niebuhrian principle that having flaws does not make great men less great, it is what makes them human.

To return to the Knox College address, Obama noted that America has faced a series of challenges in different eras. During the Gilded Age, the greed of robber barons and their exploitation of the working class provoked a pushback from laborers seeking to improve their working conditions by organizing into unions as well as from progressive forces in government looking to maintain competition by breaking up monopolies. In the depths of the Great Depression, the New Deal furthered the tempering of hypercapitalism through regulation and the implementation of measures to create a safety net for those who fell on hard times. Obama expanded on these details in a July 25, 2005, speech at the AFL-CIO national convention where he traced the broad history of the labor movement and the push for economic security for Americans.

Later in the Knox College speech Obama returned to slavery, which he called a "moral cancer [that] ate away at the American ideals of liberty and equality." He then noted that growing numbers of Americans came to believe that slavery was incompatible with the country's ideals. Obama spoke of the risks faced by abolitionists and, in particular, those who aided escaped slaves. As to why they took such risks, he offered, "Perhaps it is because they knew that they were all Americans; that they were all brothers and sisters; and in the end, their own salvation would be forever linked to the salvation of this land they called home." He attributed similar motivations to those of all ethnicities and regions who fought for civil rights a century later.

Obama returned to this theme on March 4, 2007, in Selma, when he explained that civil rights leaders "battled not just on behalf of African Americans but on behalf of all of America. . . . [They] battled for America's soul." These remarks reveal a connection that is fundamental to his understanding of America; he has expressed a belief that a strong sense of American national identity and unity motivates us to sacrifice for one another and enables this country to achieve things that are both great and just.

In a speech at the EMILY's List annual luncheon on May 11, 2006, Obama talked about meeting Marguerite Lewis, a black woman born in 1899, and about all that has changed since then. There were few cars and no airplanes in 1899, nor could most African Americans exercise the right to vote due to Jim Crow laws. She saw millions of immigrants arrive and unions emerge to protect workers' interests. In between two world wars, she saw American women win the right to vote and the country get through the Depression. Finally, the initial successes of the civil rights movement told her, in Obama's words, that "maybe it's my turn." The victories of 1964 and 1965 meant that she could vote, which she had done in every election since, she told Obama. He spoke in very similar terms, tracing the country's progress through the life of a single American, on election night in 2008, and in speeches of January 6, 2005, and June 14, 2006.

On June 2, 2006, at the University of Massachusetts Boston, Obama conflated the granting of equal rights and suffrage to women and black Americans with the entry of millions of immigrants into our society, characterizing all these steps as part of the process of "broaden[ing] the American family." Rather than simply note that rights were won, Obama emphasized that these victories fundamentally altered the boundaries of who could claim full membership in the national community. Later, Obama localized the legacy of exclusion by linking events in Boston's history: the prejudice faced by its Irish immigrants, the rocks hurled at black students being bused into South Boston, and the decision of the owners of the city's beloved Red Sox not to sign Jackie Robinson.

On a related note, on April 29, 2011, he similarly linked together the challenges faced by Americans of different ethnic backgrounds, some white and some nonwhite, stating: "When waves of Irish and Italian immigrants were derided as criminals and outcasts; when Catholics were discriminated against, or Jews had to succumb to quotas, or Muslims were blamed for society's ills; when blacks were treated as second-class citizens and marriages like my own parents' were illegal in much of the country—we didn't stop. We didn't accept inequality. We fought. We overcame. We carried the dream forward."

Obama's message at UMass Boston was clear: the city and all its people have been harmed by prejudice (think what the Red Sox could have won with Jackie Robinson in the lineup). Therefore, Bostonians, and by extension every American should reject prejudice and come together as one people if we want to reach our full potential. Toward that end, he detailed a number of "amazing and unlikely things" that have occurred throughout the country's history, including the great heights Abraham Lincoln and Martin Luther King Jr. reached and the fact that, on that day, so many students would be the first in their family to earn a college degree. Certainly, placing the accomplishments of the students alongside two such luminaries aimed not only to inspire them but also to enhance their identification with the American story, within which he placed their own lives as personified by these two accomplished figures, one black and one white.

Presidential Candidate Obama's American History

The speech announcing Obama's candidacy for the presidency on February 10, 2007, in Springfield, Illinois, contained an early version of the historical narrative he repeated, with minor variations, over and over during the campaign. He highlighted America's capacity for change as represented by a series of events: "In the face of tyranny, a band of patriots brought an empire to its knees. In the face of secession, we unified a nation and set the captives free. In the face of Depression, we put people back to work and lifted millions out of poverty. We welcomed immigrants to our shores, we opened railroads to the West, we landed a man on the moon, and we heard a King's call to let justice roll down like water, and righteousness like a mighty stream."

Obama then pivoted to the theme of unity, noting that these changes, in particular those that won equality and freedom for those previously denied it, ensured that we now face the future as "one people—as Americans." He further concluded, "Beneath all the differences of race and region, faith and station, we are one people." By presenting American history as building toward this kind of explicitly cross-ethnic national unity, Obama's rhetoric encouraged his audience to embrace that national unity as well. During the subsequent months of the campaign, He offered similar narratives built around the theme of expanding freedom and/or equality. Obama chronicled struggles led by activists as well as wars fought at home and abroad. He did so on May 7, 2007; on June 23, 2007; on August 1; on August 21; on January 3, 2008, in Iowa; and five days later in New Hampshire.

On December 5, 2007, Obama underscored service to one's fellow Americans as the unifying thread running through the nation's storyline. Along these lines, Obama praised those who serve the nation by teaching or caring for the sick, who worked to build railroads and enforce the law in the West, men who worked in the Civilian Conservation Corps during the Depression, women who joined the assembly lines during World War II, and those who volunteered for the Peace Corps. In the speech, Obama criticized President George W. Bush for not asking more of Americans as a whole after September 11. Obama then called on his audience to show their love of country by taking action to make it a better place, equating patriotism with empathy toward and service on behalf of one's fellow Americans.

In Madison, Wisconsin, on February 12, 2008, Obama catalogued a particularly extensive series of significant signposts in our national history (see the quotation that opens this chapter), starting with the Revolutionary War, and including the antislavery movement, the settlement of lands west of the Mississippi, immigrants coming to our shores, the women's suffrage movement, the union-organizing campaigns, the challenge of surviving the Great Depression, the victory over Nazism, and the civil rights movement—each serving as an example of "what hope is."[30]

In a return to Iowa on May 20, 2008, Obama's chronicle of America this time included the 1848 Seneca Falls convention, which was arguably the beginning of the women's rights movement in the United States, as well as specific mentions of other locations where important events took place: Lexington and Concord, Normandy, Selma, and Montgomery. The inclusion of Seneca Falls, Selma, and Montgomery alongside major battle sites represents a significant refashioning of the traditional roster of the great place-names in our national history that many Americans had heard, particularly those educated before the 1970s. Such a list effectively elevated the campaigns for equal rights to a place of primacy equal to that of military campaigns for freedom, offering the audience a broadly inclusive understanding of the plotline of American history.

On the night of the last primaries in the 2008 race for the Democratic nomination, June 3, Obama selected for inclusion in his narrative another aspect of the fights for equality, as he praised "the women who shattered glass ceilings." This specific language certainly owed something to his desire to reach out to Hillary Clinton and her supporters. Nevertheless, going back to the Knox College commencement speech in 2005, Obama had talked about the struggle for gender equality on a regular basis; moreover, in virtually every one of the speeches in which he discussed American history he mentioned some historical aspect thereof.[31]

The content of Obama's own American identity derives directly from his understanding of the country's history. He explored this connection in his "The America We Love" speech of June 30, 2008. Obama noted that some of his opponents had questioned his patriotism, and he certainly wanted to push back. He began by pointing out that questioning an opponent's patriotism—as well as the enactment of policies that have punished Americans because of a supposed lack of patriotism—are themselves traditions that date back to the country's founding.

The speech then became more personal, as Obama talked about how and why he came to love America and linked the wider narrative of America to his own life story. He drew on memories of his grandparents talking about their service during World War II, his grandfather having fought with George Patton's army in Europe and his grandmother having worked in a factory that assembled bombers. During Obama's years in Indonesia he had learned about the principle of equality enshrined in the Declaration of Independence, a principle his mother told him applied to Americans of every color, and how the rights guaranteed in the Constitution protected the liberties of Americans. Even after Obama got older and he learned of what he called the country's "imperfections" on matters of racism, poverty, and the abuse of power by government officials, this knowledge did not weaken his identification with America. He explained that when he was "a young man of mixed race, without firm anchor in any particular community . . . it is this essential American idea—that we are not constrained by the accident of birth but can make of our lives what we will—that has defined my life."

This kind of identification with America cannot be mandated, Obama continued. It must be "cultivated in the heart of our culture, and nurtured in the hearts of our children." He called on our schools to teach the history of America so that students develop this connection with the nation. Obama sought to ensure that all Americans "see ourselves as part of a larger story, our own fates wrapped up in the fates of those who share allegiance to America's happy and singular creed." That sense of American community was "what we strive to build."

Two speeches in which Obama laid out his vision of American unity by talking about the events and movements that have defined our common history bookended the general election campaign. He did so in front of millions of television viewers both in his acceptance speech at the 2008 Democratic National Convention in Denver on August 28 and in his victory speech in Chicago's Grant Park on election night, November 4, 2008.

In an event titled "We Are One," which took place on January 18, 2009, and celebrated the coming presidential inauguration (the title itself served as a sign of the importance Obama placed on enhancing national cohesion), he stood in front of the Lincoln Memorial and, in one of his most poetic formulations, placed Martin Luther King Jr. in the pantheon of heroes whom we have honored with monuments on the National Mall. This pantheon included Washington and Lincoln as well as the "Greatest Generation" that won World War II:

> Rising before us stands a memorial to a man who led a small band of farmers and shopkeepers in revolution against the army of an empire, all for the sake of an idea. On the ground below is a tribute to a generation that withstood war and depression, men and women like my grandparents who toiled on bomber assembly lines and marched across Europe to free the world from tyranny's grasp. Directly in front of us is a pool that still reflects the dream of a King, and the glory of a people who marched and bled so that their children might be judged by their character's content. And behind me, watching over the union he saved, sits the man who in so many ways made this day possible.

President Obama's American History Narrative

In his inaugural address, Obama placed slaves within a broader list of ancestors who sacrificed to make our lives better today, one that included immigrants, sweatshop laborers, those who settled the West, and soldiers who died fighting for freedom. He did something similar in his speech at the bicentennial celebration of Lincoln's birth on February 12, 2009, noting that slaves as well as immigrants built the Capitol, a key piece of history that reminds us of the contributions of African Americans to our nation—in particular during the time of their enslavement—that older histories have typically overlooked. By giving a place to those who have often been invisible in the standard narrative of American history, Obama encouraged Americans of all backgrounds to reclassify as a central element of our national saga something that they might have associated only with a particular ethnic group.

On a related note, when his remarks detailed the contributions of individual African Americans or historical matters of great importance to the black community, Obama often pointed out that these were not simply part of African American history, but events that we must integrate into our national narrative.[32] In a statement issued on March 25, 2009, honoring the passing of John Hope Franklin, the preeminent historian of the African American community, Obama did not use the words "black" or "African American." Instead Obama proclaimed that, thanks to Franklin, "we all have a richer understanding of who we are as Americans and our journey as a people."

Similarly, on July 16, 2009, Obama prefaced his review of the changes wrought by the civil rights movement over the past century by characterizing it as "the journey we, as Americans, have traveled." Addressing the attendees at Hampton University's commencement ceremony on May 9, 2010, the president incorporated the founding of historically black colleges into the tale he wove of America's past and future. At the West Point commencement on May 22, 2010, he spoke of the country's great military accomplishments at home and abroad over more than two centuries, the ultimate results of which—in the case of the Civil War—included freeing the slaves and eventually ensuring that equal rights and opportunities were available to Americans of all backgrounds.

On June 19, 2010, the forty-fourth president issued a proclamation marking Juneteenth (i.e. June Nineteenth), the day 145 years earlier when a community of still-enslaved African Americans in Texas finally learned that they were free, over two months after the end of the Civil War, and some two-and-a-half years after Lincoln issued the Emancipation Proclamation. Many African Americans have celebrated the day ever since. In his proclamation, Obama noted that Juneteenth offered "a time to reflect on the common values and ideals that we share as Americans." He continued: "This is why Juneteenth, while rooted in the history of a people, can be celebrated by all Americans." Rather than mark these things as exclusively black in nature, Obama invited all of us to see them as part of the national patrimony. Ultimately, he explained in an interview, "we as African Americans are American. . . . Our story is America's story . . . by perfecting our rights we perfect the Union—which is a very optimistic story, in the end."[33]

Throughout his tenure as president thus far, Obama has returned on many occasions to this familiar role as history teacher. On Independence Day, 2009, and on Martin Luther King Jr. Day, 2010, he outlined our national chronicle in some detail, although he did not break new ground in terms of the historical events or themes he discussed. At Arizona State University on May 13, 2009, however, his list of those who embodied the American spirit grew to include Cesar Chavez, the entrepreneurs Hewlett and Packard, as well as the first responders who rushed into the World

Trade Center towers on 9/11, and the volunteers who went to New Orleans to help the survivors of Katrina. Obama included these last two groups again on October 16, 2009, when he cited various examples throughout our history of service to one's fellow Americans.

By linking those who helped the largely black population of the city devastated by Hurricane Katrina to those who acted so selflessly on September 11, Obama connected a tragedy that disproportionately affected African Americans to an event that other Americans perhaps considered more patently national in scope, namely an attack on American soil. Making this connection integrates more fully the experiences of black Americans into the broader narrative.

In his State of the Union address on January 27, 2010, Obama began by recounting "moments of great strife and great struggle" over the 220 years since the Constitution went into effect. Obama listed four key crisis points: the Civil War, the Great Depression, World War II, and the civil rights movement. The ultimate success of the nation depended on achieving success in each of these moments. Ultimately, Obama declared "America prevailed because we chose to move forward as one nation, and one people."

Here we see President Obama crafting an inclusive, unifying historical narrative and accentuating the importance of national unity in another speech that millions of Americans heard. Speaking more broadly, such a narrative strengthens two kinds of connections: it reminds black Americans and members of other minority groups that events like the Revolution are not simply white or white male American history, but are part of their national history because they too are part of the American family; it also reminds whites that abolition and the civil rights movement and all the struggles for equality are part of that family history as well.

Additionally, without comment other than to say that it is "going to be on loan to us," on Martin Luther King Jr. Day 2010 the president oversaw the installation in the Oval Office of one of forty-eight authorized copies, signed by Lincoln, of the Emancipation Proclamation.[34] The White House invited African Americans over the age of eighty along with their grandchildren to witness the event. Obama also called for all of us to honor the holiday by performing acts of service in our communities, and participated in such an activity himself on that day.

Other actions Obama has taken have made similar statements about inclusion. On May 25, 2009, he became the first president to send a wreath to the African

American Civil War Memorial on Memorial Day.[35] There were also two meaningful redecorations within the White House. The first was President Obama's placing of a bust of Martin Luther King Jr. in the Oval Office in the first month after the inauguration.[36] The second was Obama's selection in the summer of 2011 of Norman Rockwell's *The Problem We All Live With* to hang on a wall near the Oval Office. In a call to Tom Joyner's radio show on August 30, the president described how seeing the painting—as well as a framed program from the 1963 March on Washington that resides in his office—serve as "reminders . . . that we stand on the shoulders of a lot of people who made a lot of sacrifices."[37] Rockwell bluntly depicted white resistance to racially integrated schools in the South, showing six-year-old Ruby Bridges— escorted by U.S. marshals—entering a New Orleans elementary school. In the painting, the girl is walking past a wall with "NIGGER" and "KKK" scrawled across it. A tomato that someone had clearly just thrown at her lay on the ground, having made a stain on the wall just at the height of her head.[38] Just as Obama can advance his understanding of America and the narrative of its history through spoken rhetoric, such actions can do so as well.

Obama's Vision of American Society and Governing Philosophy

In a number of speeches as president, Obama has linked together the nation's historical narrative with his governing philosophy and vision of American society in a comprehensive fashion. We can see this, for example, in a commencement speech at the University of Michigan on May 1, 2010. The president chronicled high points along the path our country has followed, hewing to the familiar inclusive narrative described earlier. Obama then integrated a different storyline into the discussion, tracing two "strands" in the country's political "DNA." One, going back to the Revolution, represents a tradition of Americans being "understandably skeptical of government." The other strand, however, recognizes that "there are some things we can only do together, as one nation—and that our government must keep pace with the times." Obama quoted Jefferson in support of the latter part of that statement, then detailed how the idea of national greatness and the need to work together has motivated America—through its government—to assemble railroads across the continent, to build a strong system of public secondary schools, to create financial safeguards in the wake of the market crash of 1929 and the Great Depression, to plan and construct the Interstate Highway System, and to strengthen the social safety net and form a Great Society.

Just over a month later, in a speech at Carnegie Mellon University on June 2, 2010, President Obama similarly offered that government has to do the things that "individuals couldn't do and corporations wouldn't do," such as, among other things, pass laws that require oil companies to reimburse those damaged by spills for which the company is at fault. Here he was referring to the BP oil spill, which resulted in the death of eleven platform workers and the release of approximately five million barrels of crude oil into the Gulf of Mexico.

On a related note, in a speech to the U.S. Chamber of Commerce on February 7, 2011, the president spoke about the relationship between American businesses and the United States as a society. He acknowledged that corporations are responsible to their shareholders, but also reminded them of their responsibilities toward their fellow Americans and to the national interest. Obama noted that government had a responsibility to make America "the best place on earth to do business," but then called on businesses to think about "what you can do for America. Ask yourselves what you can do to hire more American workers, what you can do to support the American economy and invest in this nation." He referred to a "spirit of patriotism, and that sense of mutual regard and common obligation, that has carried us through far harder times than the ones we've just been through." Obama urged his audience of business leaders to heed the spirit embodied in a simple remark made by the former head of General Motors, who—when FDR asked him to put GM's industrial capacity toward the effort to prepare for our entry into World War II— offered in response: "This country has been good to me, and I want to pay it back."

At Kalamazoo (Michigan) Central High School's commencement ceremony on June 7, 2010, Obama contrasted service to one's community and, more broadly, one's country to a more selfish attitude that maintained, "other people's problems aren't really your responsibility." He traced examples throughout our history where Americans had served their country, citing the Founding Fathers, those who took part in the abolitionist and civil rights movements, and those who served in the armed forces, some of whom never returned from that service.

Here again we see Obama integrating those who participated in the campaigns for inclusion and equality into the national narrative alongside those who served their country in more traditional arenas such as politics and the military. He next called on all of us to continue that tradition of service, mentioning a series of challenges the country faces, including areas of priority for his administration like developing clean energy. The president then remarked, "Service binds us to each other—and to our communities and our country—in a way that nothing else can. It's how we become more fully American." He directly connected his more inclusive notion of service to the strengthening of our sense of community as Americans.

President Obama brought these themes together and tied them to specific budgetary and policy recommendations in two major speeches in 2011. In the first, delivered on April 13, 2011, he laid out a fiscal plan for the coming dozen years. He began by revisiting some of the ideas from the University of Michigan speech regarding the two contradictory strands of thought running through our history on the appropriate role and size of government. Obama then got more specific and directly connected his progressive economic vision to the idea that we are connected as one people:

> Part of this American belief that we are all connected also expresses itself in a conviction that each one of us deserves some basic measure of security. We recognize that no matter how responsibly we live our lives, hard times or bad luck, a crippling illness or a layoff, may strike any one of us. "There but for the grace of God go I," we say to ourselves, and so we contribute to programs like Medicare and Social Security, which guarantee us health care and a measure of basic income after a lifetime of hard work; unemployment insurance, which protects us against unexpected job loss; and Medicaid, which provides care for millions of seniors in nursing homes, poor children, and those with disabilities. We are a better country because of these commitments. I'll go further—we would not be a great country without those commitments.

After giving the specifics of his budget proposal, Obama returned to his broader discussion of how the policies we pursue through government reflect what it means to be a member of the American community: "In order to preserve our own freedoms and pursue our own happiness, we can't just think about ourselves. We have to think about the country that made those liberties possible . . . about our fellow citizens with whom we share a community . . . about what's required to preserve the American Dream for future generations. This sense of responsibility—to each other and to our country—this isn't a partisan feeling. . . . It's patriotism." Here Obama equated patriotism with a strong sense of national unity built around progressive policies. He is also, at least indirectly, characterizing the Ayn Rand/Social Darwinist/

laissez faire approach to social policy as being not patriotic and fundamentally not American.

The president again married this historical narrative and governing philosophy to a set of concrete legislative proposals, the American Jobs Act, in his September 8, 2011, address to a joint session of Congress. At the time of this crucial speech, his approval ratings had reached a new low in most polls, and the country's economic situation, in terms of both growth and employment, had gotten worse after showing signs of recovering earlier in 2011. The proposal—totaling $447 billion—amounted to a second stimulus that on an annual basis would pump about as much money into the economy as the 2009 stimulus package. After echoing many of the aforementioned themes and detailing his plan, Obama declared: "No single individual built America on their own. We built it together. We have been, and always will be, one nation, under God, indivisible, with liberty and justice for all; a nation with responsibilities to ourselves and with responsibilities to one another."

On September 27, 2011, the president characterized this idea as "quintessentially American." He continued: "Those of us who've done well should pay our fair share to contribute to the upkeep of the nation that made our success possible because nobody . . . did well on their own. A teacher somewhere helped give you the skills to succeed. Firefighters and police officers are protecting your property. You're moving your goods and products and services on roads that somebody built. That's how we all do well together. We got here because somebody else invested in us."[39] Obama toured the country throughout September and October drumming up support for the American Jobs Act, and his language made clear that this premise would stand at the center of his reelection rhetoric.

In Osawatomie, Kansas, on December 6, 2011, the president presented his philosophical approach on these matters as an updated version of Teddy Roosevelt's "New Nationalism," which Roosevelt had laid out on August 31, 1910, in the same Kansas town. Obama, in this speech, thus explicitly characterized his philosophy of governance as a form of nationalism. More strongly even than in the speeches described earlier, the "New Nationalism" speech saw Obama rail against the extreme degree of economic inequality in our society, something he characterized as incongruous with our definition of American national identity. He spoke in the language of the Occupy Wall Street movement that spread across the country in the fall of 2011, calling attention to the tremendous wealth disparity that exists between the top 1 percent and the remaining 99 percent of Americans. Obama declared "this kind of gaping inequality gives lie to the promise that's at the very heart of America: that this is a place where you can make it if you try."

The 2012 State of the Union address, delivered on January 24, stands as the capstone of this series of speeches. Obama centered his remarks around the themes of economic fairness, shared responsibility, and national unity, building upon the populist chord he had been striking in the preceding weeks. He contrasted two visions of the economy, explaining: "We can either settle for a country where a shrinking number of people do really well while a growing number of Americans barely get by, or we can restore an economy where everyone gets a fair shot, and everyone does their fair share, and everyone plays by the same set of rules. What's at stake aren't Democratic values or Republican values, but American values." On February 13, when the president released his proposed budget for fiscal year 2013, he repeated this quotation almost verbatim in his remarks, and members of his administration characterized the budget as reflecting the principles laid out in Osawatomie and in the State of the Union address.[40]

In these nine speeches we see Obama embedding in the country's historic traditions his vision of national unity as well as his understanding of the active role government must play in supporting the common good, exemplified by the specific policies he was proposing (or defending) in the moment. In these speeches, he described his approach as sidestepping an anachronistic debate between those who want a smaller or a larger government. Obama described the dangers he saw in taking either of those approaches to an extreme. Ultimately, his legislative agenda flows directly from his understanding of our national identity and our history.

Another section of the University of Michigan speech focused on a call for civility as a necessary component of a healthy democracy. Obama urged us all to expose ourselves to ideas that differ from our own. He then transitioned to a more expansive appeal, challenging Americans to broaden our horizons in a more personal way by engaging "in different experiences with different kinds of people. If you grew up in a big city, spend some time with some who grew up in a rural town. If you find yourself only hanging around with people of your race or your ethnicity or your religion, broaden your circle to include people who've had different backgrounds and life experiences. You'll learn what it's like to walk in someone else's shoes, and in the process, you'll help make this democracy work." Here Obama was underlining the societal benefits of empathy, one of his core values. He defined empathy as having the ability to understand, intellectually and even emotionally, the ideas and perspectives of others. Obama was suggesting that practicing empathy would help temper some of the more corrosive and divisive language that permeates our political discourse.

The president was also calling here for a more thorough integration of American society, the creation of bonds across all kinds of lines, not just those of ethnicity but also geography/region and even broad life experiences. Integration is another of his core values. He described integration and empathy as working symbiotically with one another. The more integrated American society becomes, the more we are able to empathize with others among us who come from different backgrounds. Furthermore, that empathy encourages cooperation and compromise, both of which are central to his common good-centered approach to governance. Finally, empathy and integration foster national unity, thus enhancing the ability of Americans to work together to build, in one of Obama's favorite historical phrases, a more perfect union.

In sum, Obama's narrative of our history balances between highlighting America's glorious achievements and acknowledging the failures that have stained its history and even recent past. A people needs a history and a definition of national identity that all its members can adopt as their own. Such things encourage Americans to recognize that we all benefit when those denied freedom and equality obtain it. Obama hopes that his version of American history can help us to see that we share a past, and that we must work together to shape our future.

President Obama has crafted a history of our country and a vision of our national identity that includes the perspectives of Americans from all backgrounds yet unifies us by drawing together those perspectives into a single narrative. According to that national story, America proclaimed its universalistic ideals at its founding, and gradually, painfully, made tremendous strides toward living up to those ideals over time, while also spreading its sovereignty over a continent and emerging as a world power. He has told our history as the story of people acting—struggling, fighting, arguing, dying, and living with each other—to create the country we are and the country we will become.

8

Rejecting Obama's America

Right-Wing Exclusionists and Left-Wing Race Critics

Many voices have expressed opposition to President Obama's inclusive and strongly unified definition of American national identity and his balanced yet hopeful narrative of our history. On the far left, critics have accused him of glossing over the oppression that America and its white majority have inflicted on its ethnic minorities over time. A different kind of antagonism has arisen from a certain segment of the right wing, especially from those who see Obama's vision of America as a threat to their more exclusionary understanding of what American national identity means. Figures on the far right have played on cultural, religious, and ethnic grievances to divide Americans from one another as part of their criticisms of the forty-fourth president.

Political players on all sides criticize their opponents' policies and proposals. However, many right-wing personalities have gone much further, employing rhetoric that appears specifically designed to bind together white, straight Christians who subscribe to traditional gender roles, and to drive a wedge between them and the rest of America. This wedge is based not only on opposing views on policy or philosophical issues such as capital gains taxes, abortion, or the proper role of government, but specifically on ethnicity, religion, culture, and/or sexual orientation.

Some of these extremists have defined our national identity in such a way that only members of certain groups and/or those who hold certain religious beliefs are truly considered part of the American family. Such a definition is the exact opposite of Obama's push for unity—which centers on the cultivation of an inclusive American national identity. The sweeping conservative victories in the 2010 midterms—and in particular the exclusionism expressed by some on the right—have set up the 2012 elections as a potentially decisive clash over whether Obama's America will become the blueprint of our future or remain a far-off dream.

Obama's Impact on Race Relations

Measuring the influence Obama ultimately has on redefining and strengthening America's national identity is beyond the scope of this book and something that may not be done fruitfully for a generation. That is why I have talked about Obama's potential impact on transforming that identity. Determining the long-term impact of any person's ideas on the collective mentality of a society—or even assessing the content of that collective mentality—are challenging tasks for social scientists. Having said that, numerous surveys done (*New York Times*/CBS, Pew, ABC/*Washington Post*, CNN/Opinion Research) in the years since the 2008 election indicated that Americans of all ethnicities and African Americans in particular believed that race relations had already improved, and the one that asked (Gallup) also found strong optimism about the long-term impact of an Obama presidency on race relations.[1]

There is preliminary evidence that after Obama's election Americans began to feel more comfortable talking about racial issues with those of different backgrounds; this applied in particular to whites talking to blacks. Psychologist E. Ashby Plant conducted a study that found Obama had positively affected whites' general impressions of black Americans. Between Obama's nomination and election day, Plant interviewed nearly four hundred white college students in Florida and Wisconsin and found "little evidence of antiblack bias."[2] This result strongly differs from that of a previous study by Plant as well as studies conducted by other scholars, which found that roughly 80 percent of whites displayed at least some bias toward blacks.

Another study found that in tests administered immediately after two of Obama's high visibility successes—his acceptance of the Democratic nomination and his election as president—the achievement gap between whites and blacks virtually disappeared. The study is described in "The Obama Effect," an article published in the 2009 edition of the peer-reviewed *Journal of Experimental Social Psychology*.[3] This is of course only one study and does not by any means suggest that America has permanently overcome all ethnic disparities in education. Still, it is something.

In *The End of Anger*, Ellis Cose offered a thorough analysis of race relations in America during the Obama presidency that tracks with the aforementioned surveys and studies. Cose's 1994 book, *The Rage of a Privileged Class*, had documented widespread, seething anger over the racism that continued to hold back even relatively successful African Americans. His most recent book is based on in-depth, qualitative surveys of and interviews with a cohort of economically and professionaly successful blacks—people thus similar to those he interviewed in the early 1990s—as well as discussions with African Americans from lower socioeconomic strata. Cose found that, even if America is not yet fully free of bigotry, there has been a decisive, fundamental shift from what he found two decades earlier among upper-middle-class blacks and among blacks more broadly: "Black hopes, once held in check by the weight of prejudice and discrimination, have begun to soar free and . . . black rage—corrosive, hidden, yet omnipresent—is ebbing."[4] He added, "There is a growing sense that things may be turning around," and attributed at least some of this shift to the election of Obama.[5]

The Postinaugural Honeymoon: We Focus on Obama's Ability, Not Color

Since his election to the presidency, Obama's language on American national identity and related topics such as ethnicity and prejudice/discrimination has hewed to the same basic principles he has followed throughout his public career. One comment stands out as representative of his broad approach. When asked on March 24, 2009, about the role race had played in the first two months of his presidency, Obama offered that his election had evoked "justifiable pride on the part of the country that we had taken a step to move us beyond some of the searing legacies of racial discrimination in this country." Then he noted, "But that lasted about a day."

The president added that he focused mostly on repairing the economy, something that "affects black, brown, and white." Furthermore, he noted that the American people would judge him on how successfully he accomplished that task. Obama recognized the tremendous milestone he and the country achieved by his election as the first black president, as well as the limitations of that achievement. He then pivoted to his need to—in simple terms—get to work, because voters as well as history would assess how his administration affected the lives of the whole of the American people.

In this comment, we see Obama acknowledging the importance of discrimination, of the hatreds that have divided the American community far too long and deeply, as well as how important it is for us as a society to defeat that hatred and undo the material harm it continues to inflict on members of minority groups. Ultimately, he explained, most of our collective energy—as expressed through government—

ought to be focused on improving the lives of all Americans through universal rather than race-specific measures. On other occasions the president has also reminded those who find universal measures lacking because they ignore the specific concerns of minority groups that universal measures will disproportionately aid the members of those groups because of their generally lower socioeconomic status. They can only do so, however, if there is political support to enact them, and Obama has typically utilized universal rather than race-specific rhetoric because he believes that doing so is more likely to garner such support.

Eugene Robinson, writing in the *Washington Post* fewer than ten days after the press conference described above, was pleased to agree with Obama's assessment of the role race was playing in his presidency. The columnist pointed out that "already it tends to slip the nation's collective mind that the first black president of the United States is, in fact, black. There may be hope for us after all."[6] Robinson stated that criticism as well as praise of Obama had largely avoided mentions of race, and added: "That's only natural, since race could hardly be more irrelevant to the multitude of urgent problems Obama wrestles with every day. Watching him in action . . . we witness a daily demonstration of the irrelevance of race. And that, potentially, is nothing short of transformative." He concluded, "We focus on Obama's ability, not his color. In doing so, we are a better nation."

That all-too-brief moment began to dissipate almost as soon as Robinson noticed it. Perhaps the moment was itself an illusion, or at least represented our collective desire to believe we actually had made race irrelevant. Clearly, much of the country did feel euphoric over electing a black president, especially on Inauguration Day as we witnessed an event that suggested we were getting close to achieving Martin Luther King Jr.'s vision. But the celebration of that moment gave way to a return to reality, in the form of a deepening economic crisis and the realization that, as Obama himself repeatedly noted after assuming office, ethnic discrimination and prejudice remain powerful forces in our society.

The Honeymoon's Over: The Right Wing Accuses Obama of Racism

The issue of ethnicity began to seep back into public discourse with Sonia Sotomayor's nomination to the Supreme Court, and the aforementioned controversy surrounding her "wise Latina" remarks. On his show Rush Limbaugh opined on May 29 that Judge Sotomayor, whom he compared to former KKK leader David Duke, would "bring a form of bigotry or racism to the court." Limbaugh also asserted that her nomination indicated that the way to "get promoted in the Barack Obama administration" is to "hat[e] white people."[7] Limbaugh's use of such ethnically divisive language in fact predated this particular affair. Speaking more broadly, the affair itself offered a harbinger of things to come later that summer.

Ethnic matters returned, front and center, to the Obama administration with the Henry Louis Gates affair. President Obama made his initial remarks concerning Gates's arrest on July 22, 2009, and the following day on his self-titled Fox News show Glenn Beck asserted: "[Obama's] goal is creating a new America, a new model, a model that will settle old racial scores through new social justice." Four days later Beck told his Fox viewers: "We have demonstrated President Obama's desire for racial justice. But how is he setting out to achieve it? Exactly the way a community organizer would: through intimidation, vilification, bullying, a system, an underground shell game." Finally, during an appearance on the *Fox & Friends* morning program on July 29, Beck capped off the week by calling Obama a "racist" who has "a deep-seated hatred for white people or the white culture." Beck stood by those remarks the following day, repeating the sentiments on his radio show.

Limbaugh weighed in similarly on July 24, 2009: "Here you have a black president trying to destroy a white policeman." On July 27 Limbaugh offered, "I do believe [Obama is] an angry black guy!" Thus, Limbaugh and Beck, by openly exploiting the still significant bigotry and resentment among some whites toward black and other minority Americans and, specifically, about the fact that an African American is their president, threw down a direct challenge to Obama's quest to invigorate national unity and strengthen bonds across ethnic lines.

In the weeks after Gates's arrest, the health care debate became the major political story in the media. At town hall–style gatherings in congressional districts across the country, screaming matches broke out in which opponents of reform shouted down their own representatives. Sarah Palin, on August 7, accused the president of proposing the creation of "death panels" in which "bureaucrats can decide, based on a subjective judgment of their 'level of productivity in society,' whether [a person is] . . . worthy of health care. Such a system is downright evil."[8] Obama, of course, had proposed nothing that comes even close to resembling this system. After weeks of heated and at times over-the-top language, President Obama addressed both houses of Congress in a rare joint session on September 9. After he explained, "The reforms I am proposing would not apply to those who are here illegally," South Carolina Congressman Addison Graves ("Joe") Wilson shouted out, "You lie!"[9]

Thus, less than half a year after Eugene Robinson issued his hopeful analysis that race played little role in the way Americans were judging the forty-fourth president, that analysis now seemed hopelessly naïve. *New York Times* columnist Maureen Dowd wrote on September 12 what many Obama supporters and media observers had been thinking, namely that antiblack bigotry motivated at least some of the most virulent opposition to the administration's policies. Dowd noted that when she heard Wilson's outburst—a unique breach of protocol up to that point (perhaps since surpassed when Jan Brewer stuck her index finger in President Obama's face on the tarmac in Phoenix, Arizona, on January 25, 2012, an image captured by a photographer and seen by millions)—she heard more than just the two words Wilson actually uttered: "Fair or not, what I heard was an unspoken word in the air: You lie, boy!"[10] The columnist traced the evolution in her own thinking over the course of the previous weeks: "I've been loath to admit that the shrieking lunacy of the summer—the frantic efforts to paint our first black president as the Other, a foreigner, socialist, fascist, Marxist, racist, Commie, Nazi; a cad who would snuff old people; a snake who would indoctrinate kids—had much to do with race. . . . But Wilson's shocking disrespect for the office of the president . . . convinced me: some people just can't believe a black man is president and will never accept it."

On September 15, former president Jimmy Carter followed up in a similar vein, stating unequivocally in a speech in Atlanta that the "You lie!" eruption was "based on racism."[11] He further proclaimed, "There is an inherent feeling among many in this country that an African American should not be president." That night on *NBC Nightly News*, Carter added, "An overwhelming portion of the intentionally demonstrated animosity toward President Barack Obama is based on the fact that he is a black man." By mid-September 2009 the question of how much of the criticism of Obama from the right was racially motivated began to dominate the media.

Some conservatives responded with outrage that anyone would accuse a federal elected official such as Representative Joe Wilson of racism without providing proper evidence, notwithstanding the fact that many of those same people had done exactly the same to President Obama. Glenn Beck, for example, fits into both categories. Having previously called Obama a "racist" who has "a deep-seated hatred for white people," he complained on his September 16 radio broadcast about the "false cries of racism on Joe Wilson when there's absolutely nothing to back it."

After more rhetorical crossfire, with tensions rising on all sides, Obama sought in a September 20 appearance on ABC's *This Week* to lower the temperature of the public debate. He acknowledged that while some Americans oppose him because of his race, others support him for that reason. That same day on *Meet the Press*, Obama commented that, in general, the discussion around health care and other issues "is not about race, it's about people being worried about how our government should operate."

The president succeeded in his short-term goal, and the question of his opponents' racism faded—at least for a while—from the mainstream media. His comment did not deny that racism motivates some who disagree with him; however, he sought to frame the situation in as positive a light as possible. As was the case with the Beer Summit that helped end the controversy over Henry Louis Gates's arrest, Obama sought to defuse tension when tempers flared on an issue relating to racism. Both of these instances reflect his belief that divisive disputes over racism are counterproductive. Obama believes that the most effective strategy for combating the effects of racism has two elements: pointing out discrepancies and injustices that need rectifying, and transforming the way Americans view their fellow citizens of other races by unifying them around the notion of the common good. In his view, achieving the latter buttresses support for doing the former.

In February 2010, *Washington Post* columnist E. J. Dionne offered a nuanced look back at the question that Obama, Dowd, and Carter had addressed the previous September. Dionne noted the belief on the left that opposition to Obama's proposals reflects, "a reaction among some whites against the multiracial, multicultural political coalition he has brought together."[12] Dionne went on, however, to note that while such feelings were a factor for some, "it would be a mistake to see the hostility toward Obama only in terms of race." The other primary aspect of the opposition derived from anti-statism, a deep antipathy toward federal authority. Essentially, Dionne's balanced comments parallel the comments the president himself made on the previous September 20. Both rejected racism as the sole cause of white opposition, but both acknowledged that it is a cause for some of it.

Right-Wing Exclusionism
In his study of the rhetoric of the far right, journalist David Neiwert explained that such extremists simply define anyone who opposes their radical vision of America as being not American. He further noted that those on the radical right "hate the very idea of an inclusive America."[13] They believe that only they represent "the 'true' national identity."[14] They exclude from the national community large swathes of

American society; including a majority if not all Obama supporters. According to Neiwert, the far right has targeted the following groups for exclusion: "liberals, gays and lesbians, Latinos, blacks, Jews, feminists" among others.[15] He summarized this viewpoint as follows: "The kind of unity [the far right wing] promotes is one in which Americans can come together only under the banner of their ideology; otherwise they will face exclusion."[16] While certainly not all conservatives fit this description, it does accurately depict what I would call the "exclusionist" view of American national identity.

To be clear, opposition to President Obama's policies does not necessarily make one an exclusionist, as many conservatives have called for a more limited role for government without objecting to the inclusive, cross-ethnic American unity Obama has sought to enhance. Moreover, this exclusionist challenge from the right is not monolithic. Those on the moderate end of the exclusionist spectrum encourage ethnic divisiveness indirectly, while that divisive rhetoric grows more direct and extreme the further one moves along that spectrum.

On the less extreme end—by comparison—of the exclusionist spectrum stands Sarah Palin. In chapter 7, I briefly mentioned her "real America" remarks and focused on Obama's juxtaposing them to his own call for us to come together as Americans. Let's explore those remarks in more detail. On October 17, 2008, the Republican vice presidential nominee offered the following thoughts: "We believe that the best of America is in these small towns that we get to visit, and in these wonderful little pockets of what I call the real America, being here with all of you hard working very patriotic, um, very, um, pro-America areas of this great nation. . . . This is where we find the kindness and the goodness and the courage of everyday Americans."[17] Comparing these remarks to the way Obama spoke about rural America, for example, on April 27, 2010, reveals how one can praise its virtues without being divisive. There, the president commented, "These visits are reminders that when you get out into the heartland and you talk to folks, there's a lot to learn from rural America— because it's towns like this that give America its heartbeat."

Dividing the nation into "real" or "everyday Americans" and, presumably, "not real" Americans exemplifies an exclusionary definition of our national identity. Palin made that division based on where people live, but their status as small-town residents served as a stand-in for their culture, values, and, more ominously if indirectly, their religion and their ethnicity. Her equating rural/small-town folk with real

America evokes an image of white, straight, Christian people and separates them from those who do not fit into those categories. Such an equation stands in direct contrast to Obama's inclusive definition of American national identity. The differences between these two definitions track the difference described in the academic literature between a civic and an ethnic form of nationalism. Ultimately, Obama's America is open to whomever wishes to join and accept the responsibilities that go along with it, while Palin's America is one in which certain people decide who is worthy of admission into the American family and who is not.

The language George W. Bush and his surrogates used to define patriotism through his presidential campaigns and his time as president was politically divisive, but differed qualitatively from that of Palin and from exclusionists in general. The rhetoric of Bush, Dick Cheney, and Karl Rove insinuated that those who, for example, opposed the war in Iraq were unpatriotic. The Bush team's rhetoric did not, however, define such people as outside the circle of the American national community because of who they are. That is exactly what Palin did.

The difference between Palin's exclusionary definition of the American people and Bush's language of patriotism is that whereas Bush's was merely ideologically divisive, Palin's language carried a whiff of *völkisch* (i.e., ethnically divisive) nationalism. Her reference to "real America" evokes the Klan's Anglo-Protestant definition of the American people, an ideology that, like her remarks, draws on the traditional small-town antagonism toward the city and toward cultural change more broadly. Palin's America harkened back to a simpler time when Americans were—or at least seemed—more like one another in terms of culture, religion, and outlook, a time when those who were different knew their place. Palin's rhetoric offered the promise of a return to such a mythic time and, playing on fear of and resentment toward those defined as the other, suggested that her political opponents would take the country on a path that rejected everything good and right about that mythic America.

Chuck Norris, the actor turned right-wing activist, issued a call on September 22, 2009, that, like Palin's, was indirectly but unmistakably divisive in terms of ethnicity. Norris urged those who preferred his vision of the country to President Obama's to eschew flying the contemporary American flag in favor of a "revolutionary" flag (i.e. the Betsy Ross flag or the "Don't Tread on Me" flag) that "makes a stand for our Founders' vision of America."[18] As an alternative, he suggested flying a modern flag that was "tea-stained," as that would also "show your solidarity with our Founders."

This originalist approach maintains that the "true" America existed at the time of the American Revolution and that we have since lost our way. Interestingly, Obama has argued so as well, albeit differently, in his suggestion that bigotry long prevented the United States from fully realizing the egalitarian values expressed in the Declaration of Independence. In Obama's view, America most resembles its true self now as opposed to then because of our gradual progress toward achieving equality over the past two hundred-plus years and especially since the 1960s. In this view, the future offers the promise of continued movement toward perfection.

We see an even more direct rejection of contemporary America in the growing calls for various states to secede from the Union. Although these calls predate January 2009, they have grown louder since the inauguration of President Obama. At a Tea Party rally of April 15, 2009, Texas governor and 2012 presidential candidate Rick Perry toyed with the possibility of his state seceding, musing: "We've got a great union. There's absolutely no reason to dissolve it. But if Washington continues to thumb their nose at the American people, you know, who knows what might come out of that?"[19] Not coincidentally, Chuck Norris declared that someday he might himself run for president of an independent Texas.[20] Can there be a more direct rejection of American unity than calling for the country's dissolution?

On July 23, 2010, Congressman Zach Wamp, a Republican candidate for governor of Tennessee, praised Perry as a "patriot" and echoed his flirtations with the idea of secession, commenting: "I hope that the American people will go to the ballot box in 2010 and 2012 so that states are not forced to consider separation from this government."[21] The following day, Wamp felt it necessary to declare that if he were elected, "of course we will not secede from the union. But we will also not have a governor who will cave in to Barack Obama."[22]

Even during the time when Alabama governor George Wallace was declaring "Segregation now, segregation tomorrow, segregation forever!" in 1963, Southern conservative political leaders did not speak openly of secession. Yet Wamp and Perry, two prominent conservatives, have done so during the presidency of Barack Obama. Such talk of secession makes clear that there are some who would rather tear this country apart than accept the idea of a black president.

This kind of secession talk represents an ironic turn in the long-running debate over American national unity. On the one hand, we have those who agree with Samuel Huntington's fear that America will be hopelessly divided because those of

Mexican descent—whom the Huntingtonians believe are unassimilable—will eventually want to break off territories where they are a majority and rejoin those lands to Mexico. This fear remains so strong that in May 2010 Arizona passed a law banning classes from public high schools if they "advocate ethnic solidarity instead of the treatment of pupils as individuals."[23] The law's champion, Arizona Superintendent for Public Instruction Tom Horne, apparently designed the bill to force Tucson to abandon its program in Mexican American studies.[24] The Tucson Unified School did exactly that in January 2012, shortly after a judge had ruled that the program did in fact violate the law Horne had championed. Had they not ended the program, Tucson would have lost $15 million annually in state aid.[25]

On the other hand, we see (almost exclusively) white conservatives in such states as Texas and Tennessee—many of whose ideology would suggest an affinity for Huntington and support for efforts such as those of Horne—who want their state to secede from the United States of America. Many of them support secession because they oppose liberal policies, but also—underneath that political opposition—they do so because they are motivated by a white, Christian identity politics (which I will discuss later in this chapter) that parallels the radical multiculturalism they so strongly reject when it comes from those of Mexican descent or other nonwhites. Essentially, it appears that some of the same conservative whites who were most concerned about separatism and about America's territorial integrity being threatened by nonwhite immigration and, in particular, Mexican "ethnic solidarity" are the same people who demanded secession after a liberal—not to mention black—American won the presidency and his party won a majority in Congress. Nevertheless, even Perry and Wamp, like Norris and Palin, shied away from utilizing rhetoric that one could characterize as openly or directly bigoted in ethnic terms.

Religious-Based Exclusionism

In addition to his remarks about secession, Perry also put forth an explicitly exclusionary definition of American national identity. On September 14, 2011, not long after becoming a candidate for president, he stated: "America is going to be guided by some set of values. The question is going go to be: Whose values?"[26] The governor then declared that it should be "those Christian values that this country was based upon." Here Perry directly equated his version of Christianity with America. Thus, people who either belong to other religious faiths or none at all are—in Perry's America—are simply less American.

Another prominent candidate for the Republican nomination, former Godfather's Pizza CEO Herman Cain, spoke on more than one occasion about Muslim Americans in a clearly exclusionary way. On March 21, 2011, Cain told the magazine *Christianity Today*: "Based upon the little knowledge that I have of the Muslim religion, you know, they have an objective to convert all infidels or kill them."[27] Five days later, a reporter asked him, "Would you be comfortable appointing a Muslim either in your cabinet or as a federal judge?"[28] Cain answered that he would not, and continued: "And here's why. There is this creeping attempt, there's this attempt to gradually ease Sharia law and the Muslim faith into our government. It does not belong in our government." In a March 28 appearance on Fox News's *Your World with Neil Cavuto*, Cain further explained: "A reporter asked me would I appoint a Muslim to my administration? I did say no. And here's why . . . I would have to have people totally committed to the Declaration of Independence and the Constitution of the United States. And many of the Muslims, they're not totally dedicated to this country."

During much of the early fall of 2011, Cain placed at or near the top in most national and state polls asking Republican voters whom they wanted to nominate for president. At the very least, these widely discussed and rebroadcast remarks did not prevent him from winning a significant degree of support from Republican primary voters for a time, at least until revelations regarding his interactions with a number of women ended his campaign in early December. We can compare what Perry and Cain have said to Obama's fundamentally inclusive statement (see chapter 6) about religious diversity ("we are no longer just a Christian nation; we are also a Jewish nation, a Muslim nation . . . "). The difference between Obama's America and the vision of America put forth by Perry and in particular by Cain could not be clearer.

Beck and Limbaugh: Openly Divisive Race-Based Exclusionism

Going beyond Palin and more "moderate" (in relative terms) exclusionists into direct divisiveness and race-based fear mongering, we have media figures like Beck and Limbaugh, among others. Although as of this writing Beck no longer has a daily television platform—his run on Fox lasted from January 19, 2009 to June 30, 2011—I offer a discussion of his rhetoric here alongside that of Limbaugh because of the amount of media attention it drew at the time.

Beyond their remarks on the Sotomayor and Gates incidents, Limbaugh and Beck have taken aim at Obama's entire agenda. They have done so not merely from an ideological perspective that criticized what they see as an over-expansive role for government in society. The two hosts have gone much further: they have accused the president of seeking to undo the effects of racial discrimination by literally taking from whites and giving to blacks purely on the basis of race. They have claimed that this goal underlies Obama's domestic policy agenda.

Limbaugh summarized this perspective on June 4, 2009, in one of the most pernicious formulations heard from a major media voice since Obama became a national figure—one that could have no purpose but to sow the toxic combination of hatred and fear among white members of his audience and pit Americans against one another along ethnic lines: "The days of them not having any power are over, and they are angry. And they want to use their power as a means of retribution. That's what Obama's about, gang. He's angry, he's gonna cut this country down to size, he's gonna make it pay for all the multicultural mistakes that it has made, its mistreatment of minorities."

In this brief, vitriol-laden rant, Limbaugh defined Obama and his nonwhite supporters ("they") as anti-American and angry, and set their interests in opposition to those of whites, whose interests he defined as in line with those of America. It's Obama and his people vs. America. Moreover, Limbaugh insinuated or perhaps tried to subconsciously evoke the idea that this was a street fight by using the term "gang." In his view, the battle between Obama's and Limbaugh's gangs would determine whether whites or nonwhites will ultimately wield "power."

Limbaugh did not choose these words lightly. His statement resembles rhetoric that goes back to the eighteenth century, according to which poor whites should rally together with slave owners around their shared whiteness, because if black slaves ever got free they would enact vengeance on all whites. It draws on the image of blacks as bloodthirsty savages bent on destroying the white civilization that has oppressed them for so long, without of course mentioning what that oppression says about how "civilized" are those who have carried it out. The greatest fear of the slave-owning elite was always an alliance of the common folk of all races. Limbaugh's use of the trope of white racial unity as the only defense against retribution for past mistreatments is not original, but that makes it no less disgraceful.

The general theme of ethnic-based retribution and redistribution appears repeatedly in Limbaugh's and Beck's broadcasts in reference to specific legislative proposals, including the economic stimulus package passed in early 2009 and, in particular, health care reform. Limbaugh told his audience on May 11, 2009, that the goal behind the president's entire domestic agenda was "forced reparations." Reparations refers to the idea of reparations for slavery, that is, a payment to the descendants of slaves either made by the government or, according to the believers in even more outlandish conspiracy theories, taken from white Americans exclusively through a special tax. The question of paying reparations to freed slaves goes back to the Civil War and remains a highly contentious issue for many Americans of all ethnic backgrounds. Earlier, on February 22, 2009, Limbaugh had characterized the health care reform effort similarly, asserting, "This is a civil rights bill. This is reparations." It is worth noting he equated civil rights legislation broadly with the specific claim for reparations, support for which lacks consensus even among civil rights activists. Four months to the day later, Limbaugh further asserted, "Obama's entire economic program is reparations."

Not to be outdone, on Fox on July 23, 2009, Beck summarized the president's legislative agenda as follows: "Everything that is getting pushed through Congress, including this health care bill, are transforming America. And they are all driven by President Obama's thinking on one idea: reparations." There can be little doubt about the intention behind such rhetoric. It is worth noting that Obama specifically rejected the implementation of a race-based reparations program both during his run for the U.S. Senate in 2004 and during the 2008 campaign.[29]

On July 13, 2010, Beck went far beyond anything he said in the remarks above. On Fox he showed a video of two white members of the Weather Underground espousing what he called black liberation theology: "White youths must choose sides now. We must either fight on the side of the oppressed or be on the side of the oppressor. If you sit in your house and live your white life and go to your white job and allow the country that you live in to murder people and to commit genocide, and you sit there and you don't do anything about it, that's violence."

Then Beck went further, telling his audience: "This is how they and the Black Panthers and others who follow this line of thinking can eventually find themselves rationalizing the killing of babies, because they've convinced themselves that you are either a victim or you are the oppressor." He next introduced another video, this one of Dr. Khallid Abdul Muhammad, whom he identified as the former chairman of the New Black Panther Party, by stating that black liberation theology is "exactly how you get crazies like this one." Here Beck is conflating black nationalism and black liberation theology, essentially characterizing them as identical. The video showed Muhammad talking about what black people should do to white people, "We kill the men, we kill the women, we kill the children, we kill the babies, we kill the blind, we kill the cripple, we kill the crazy, we kill the (expletive), we kill the lesbians, I say, damn it, we kill them all! . . . [Because] they're going to grow up one day to rule your babies."

After briefly commenting further on the video, Beck then brought up Jeremiah Wright, characterizing him as "a liberation theology creature." After more commentary and an interview with a "black liberation theology expert," Beck showed a clip of Obama stating that he came to Christianity through Reverend Wright. Beck then made the connection directly for his audience, the connection he had been building toward with his commentary, his interview with an expert, and his videos talking about black people rising up in murderous vengeance against white people all over America. He told the audience, "Barack Obama's spirituality comes from the prism of liberation theology." Beck then returned to the issue of reparations and stated that black liberation theology is the reason "why Obama said he doesn't support reparations because, quote, 'They don't go far enough.' Why don't they go far enough? Because to blot out *the* collective sin, the white man has to give everything up" (emphasis in original).

In this segment, Beck accused President Obama of literally wanting to take every material possession from every white American and redistribute them to African Americans, as well as believing in an ideology whose practitioners countenance the murder of all white men, women, and children. This is the kind of thing that millions of Americans have been hearing on a daily basis about Barack Obama from conservative media figures like Glenn Beck in recent years.

Fox News and Racially Divisive Media Coverage

More broadly, Fox News—by which I am referring to the daytime programming and the news stories posted on the Fox News website, not the evening opinion hosts like Beck, Sean Hannity, Bill O'Reilly, et al.—has played a decisive role in spreading a number of racially divisive stories since Obama took office, including those of Van Jones, ACORN (Association of Community Organizations for Reform Now), the New Black Panther Party, and Shirley Sherrod, the details of which are widely available.

Sherrod garnered the most media attention. On July 19, 2010, she was forced to resign as Georgia State Director of Rural Development for the U.S. Department of Agriculture after a video of a speech she made at an NAACP event surfaced. The video seemed to indicate that she, an African American, had discriminated against a white farmer who had sought her help while she was in her current position at the USDA, i.e., under President Obama. In fact, the truth was essentially the opposite: Sherrod, after initially feeling hesitant, put aside her own ambivalent feelings about helping a white person and realized her job was to fight for any wronged person, whatever their ethnicity. Moreover, she was speaking about an incident that was more than two decades old, one that occurred when she did not work for the USDA.

The video was deceptively edited and presented falsely on BigGovernment.com, a conservative website run by Andrew Breitbart, under the headline "Video Proof: The NAACP Awards Racism–2010."[30] The story quickly spread from Fox News—which posted it on its website even before Sherrod was fired—into the mainstream media.[31] The USDA—and many others, including the NAACP and other media outlets—jumped to the wrong conclusion without seeing the full video and condemned Ms. Sherrod.

This was one instance where the Obama administration clearly failed to get it right on a matter pertaining to racism. Secretary of Agriculture Tom Vilsack took responsibility for Sherrod's firing and denied that the White House had anything to do with the decision.[32] Irrespective of the specific role the president or members of the White House staff played in the decision to force Sherrod out, the whole affair was ultimately an embarrassment for a president who had spoken as Obama has about racism.

After the full video came out and vindicated Ms. Sherrod, Obama on July 29, 2010, decried the "bogus controversy" around her remarks and acknowledged that his administration is one of the "many" who share "blame" for her dismissal from the USDA, adding that she "deserve[d] better." Obama also noted that her "story about overcoming our own biases and recognizing ourselves in folks who, on the surface, seem different is exactly the kind of story we need to hear in America." After initially turning down a return to the USDA, in May 2011 Sherrod took a new position focusing on improving the agency's performance in the area of civil rights.[33]

Elements of each of the four aforementioned stories were either presented on Fox News in a misleading fashion or were blatant falsehoods. They share a common theme: under President Obama, black people are using their newfound positions of power to discriminate against white people. Journalist Joan Walsh offered a detailed synthesis of Fox News's treatment of these four stories and asserted that "the network hypes one 'scary black people' and 'Obama's a racist' story after another." She continued, "Fox News has, sadly, become the purveyor of a fifty-state 'Southern strategy,' the plan perfected by Richard Nixon to use race to scare Southern Democrats into becoming Republicans by insisting the other party wasn't merely trying to fight racism, but give blacks advantages over whites."[34] Like Limbaugh and Beck, Fox News is playing on the age-old white fears of racial revenge.

Speaking more broadly, this is the core of political strategy on the right: convincing whites that those of darker complexion are going to change America—or perhaps already have—in a way that disadvantages them. In good times and bad, the right wing realizes that when the white middle and working classes are focused on their economic anxieties and interests, the right will lose. Therefore, they have to distract those whites with dog whistles aimed at raising their cultural anxieties. White cultural anxiety is the wet blanket that right-wing conservatives are desperate to throw on the flames of cross-ethnic unity.

Right-wing demagogues play on white fears about the growing diversity in America in order to prevent what they really fear—a cross-ethnic "American" coalition of middle- and working-class people who recognize that the real problem in this country is the concentration of wealth and political power in the hands of the economic elites. The Occupy Wall Street movement represents exactly this kind of coalition. There's a reason why their most effective slogan is "We are the 99 percent!"

Likewise, Obama seeks to invigorate strong bonds uniting Americans across ethnic lines, to strengthen their sense of being one people so that whites will see nonwhites as full members of the American national community, and vice versa. Regarding white cultural anxiety specifically, he wants to inoculate the potentially anxious whites so that the ethnically divisive, exclusionist rhetoric of the right fails to influence their political outlook.

Presenting Obama as "Not American"

Although Limbaugh and Beck are the most well-known and influential of those employing such directly antagonistic language, other reasonably widely heard figures on the right have gone even farther in rejecting Obama's America. They seriously question or even reject Obama's status as an American. Wesley Pruden is the former editor in chief of the stridently conservative *Washington Times*, which the respected antiracist watchdog Southern Poverty Law Center characterized as being, under Pruden's leadership, "a reliable source for extremist views on race, religion, [and] immigration."[35] In a November 17, 2009, *Washington Times* piece, Pruden juxtaposed

Obama and an America defined by whiteness: "It's no fault of the president that he has no natural instinct or blood impulse for what the America of 'the fifty-seven states' is about. He was sired by a Kenyan father, born to a mother attracted to men of the third world, and reared by grandparents in Hawaii, a paradise far from the American mainstream."[36]

Pruden here clearly defined Obama as outside the circle of America because of his "blood" and "natural instincts," and painted him as foreign and exotic, "outside the mainstream." The use of "sire," a term typically used to describe the breeding of horses or, in popular culture, the process by which vampires reproduce, suggests something unnatural or even nonhuman about Obama. Pruden's highlighting of Ann Dunham's two "third-world" husbands plays on old racial tropes, whereby women in interracial sexual relationships must be somehow morally suspect. In sum, the statement is a bald attempt to other Obama.

The cryptic-seeming mention of "the fifty-seven states" alludes to a verbal slip Obama made on May 9, 2008: "It is wonderful to be back in Oregon. Over the last fifteen months, we've traveled to every corner of the United States. I've now been in fifty-seven states? I think one left to go. Alaska and Hawaii, I was not allowed to go."[37] The context of the remark makes clear that Obama meant to say forty-seven states (fifty minus three: one other unnamed continental state plus Alaska and Hawaii). Pruden's mention of the remark is almost certainly a dog-whistle reference to a rumor, spread via email during the campaign, that Obama's "fifty-seven states" comment unwittingly revealed that he is, in fact, a "secret" Muslim because there are fifty-seven member states of the Organization of the Islamic Conference.[38]

Employing such an absurdly spurious claim, yet one that has credence among the extreme far-right, further indicates that Pruden sought to other Obama and to paint him negatively both as a Muslim—something that would in itself disqualify him from the Oval Office for some—and as a sort of Manchurian Candidate, a traitor being planted into a position of power from which he would work to destroy the country.[39] Pruden's article clearly places him farther along the extreme end of the exclusionist spectrum even than Limbaugh and Beck.

On a similar note, Michael Savage, host of *The Savage Nation*, asserted on his radio show on February 24, 2010, that President Obama's mother "had contempt for America" and cited as evidence the fact that she married two "third-world men" who were both Muslim. To Savage and his followers, the combination of their religion (in reality Barack Obama Sr., whose father was indeed Muslim, declared himself an atheist early in life) and non-Western origin indicates that any American woman attracted to them must be anti-American. This despite the fact that both Obama's father and stepfather chose to study at American universities where each met and fell in love with his mother.

This kind of language may well have had the desired effect. A Pew research poll conducted from July 21 to August 5, 2010, found the percentage of respondents who believe Obama is a Muslim went up significantly, as did the percentage who said they didn't know what his religion is, while the percentage of those who believe he is a Christian dropped sharply compared to Pew polls taken in 2008 and 2009.[40] Similarly, a *Newsweek* poll administered August 25 to 26, 2010, found that the percentage of respondents who believed Obama is Muslim was almost double what *Newsweek* had found in two polls they conducted in mid-2008.[41]

In addition to media commentators, politicians have also sought to other Obama, to discredit his status as an American. Rick Santorum commented on June 28, 2010: "Obama is detached from the American experience." Santorum continued, "He just doesn't identify with the average American because of his own background—Indonesia and Hawaii."[42] *New York Times* writer Matt Bai offered, "It was a dubious remark, heavy with racial implications."[43] Additionally, on December 31, 2011, just four days before narrowly winning the Iowa caucuses, Santorum stated that Obama has engaged in "absolutely un-American activities."[44]

At a Santorum town hall gathering in Florida on January 23, 2012, an audience member declared: "I never refer to Obama as President Obama because legally he is not. . . . He is an avowed Muslim and my question is, why isn't something being done to get him out of government?"[45] Rather than correct the questioner on the matter of Obama's religion, not to mention the legality of his presidency, as John McCain had done in a similar situation in 2008 (see chapter 5), Santorum ignored those aspects of the question and replied that he intended to win the election and thus "get him out of the government right now." He later told CNN's John King, "I don't think the president's a Muslim, but I don't think it's my obligation to go out and repeat that every time someone who feels that way says something." As of this writing, Santorum went on to win caucuses in Minnesota and Colorado, as well as a non-binding primary in Missouri, and in mid-February briefly led most national polls for the Republican nomination. He won seven more contests before withdrawing on April 10.

On September 11, 2010, Newt Gingrich asked, "What if [Obama] is so outside our comprehension, that only if you understand Kenyan, anticolonial behavior, can you begin to piece together [his actions]?"[46] He added, of Obama, "That is the most accurate, predictive model for his behavior." In late November and throughout much of December 2011, Gingrich held the lead in most national polls for the Republican presidential nomination, and did so again for a few days in late January 2012 after winning the South Carolina primary. The remark clearly did not hurt Gingrich with Republican primary voters any more than Santorum's aforementioned comments hurt him. In fact, some voters appear to have been drawn to Gingrich at least in part because of such rhetoric. For example, when he criticized Obama at a rally in Sarasota, Florida, on January 24, 2012, a number of those in the crowd began chanting, "Kenya, Kenya."[47] Similarly, on December 7, 2011, Mitt Romney, the putative front-runner throughout much of the primary season, said of Obama: "I don't think he understands America." A *New York Times* editorial commented: "It's not quite Newt Gingrich's saying Mr. Obama has a 'Kenyan' worldview, but it's close."[48]

On March 2, 2011, former Arkansas governor Mike Huckabee, then near the top of polls for the Republican presidential nomination (he ultimately did not run), stated on the American Family Association radio show *Focal Point* that Obama "has a different worldview and I think it is, in part, molded out of a very different experience. Most of us grew up going to Boy Scout meetings and, you know, our communities were filled with Rotary Clubs, not madrassas." Furthermore, when the interviewer asked whether there "may be some fundamental anti-Americanism in this president," Huckabee replied that "that's exactly the point I make in [my] book."

Journalism professor Susan Moeller has explained that—due to the way the term "madrassa" has been discussed in the media—Americans have been "led to infer that that all [madrassas] are anti-American, anti-Western, proterrorist centers having less to do with teaching basic literacy and more to do with political indoctrination."[49] It is important to note that Obama did not attend a madrassa—i.e., a religious Muslim school—in Indonesia, although in *Dreams* he did write of being a member of the Boy Scouts while living there. Nevertheless, Huckabee's intent could not be clearer.

It is worth noting that John McCain, as he had during the 2008 presidential campaign (see chapter 5), continued to speak out against attempts to paint Obama as somehow not American and/or working against America's interests. In a January 16, 2011, piece in the *Washington Post*, McCain praised the remarks Obama made after the shootings in Tucson, Arizona, and added, "I disagree with many of the president's policies, but I believe he is a patriot sincerely intent on using his time in office to advance our country's cause. I reject accusations that his policies and beliefs make him unworthy to lead America or opposed to its founding ideals."[50] One can contrast McCain's remarks to those of Mitt Romney who, in a December 15, 2011, post-debate interview on Fox News with Sean Hannity, characterized Obama as, "Someone who is now so desperate to get reelection that he's doing things that are very much counter to the interest of the country and he knows it."

Like McCain, former Utah governor Jon Huntsman refused to question the forty-fourth president's status as an American. In a June 21, 2011, speech that kicked off his presidential campaign, Huntsman declared that he and Obama "have a difference of opinion on how to help a country we both love. But the question each of us wants the voters to answer is who will be the better president; not who's the better American."[51] McCain and Huntsman deserve credit for rejecting the exclusionism too many on the right have embraced when it comes to talking about Obama.

Speaking more broadly, anxiety and anger about the fluidity of a country's national identity is not merely an academic or even a political question. It is a question of life and death, as seen in the mass killings in Norway on July 22, 2011, by a right-wing nationalist fired with hatred against multiculturalism and Muslims.[52] When conservative politicians like McCain and Huntsman speak out the way they have, it might ease at least some of the anxiety on the far right. One hopes.

The desire to define Obama as un-American/foreign/other also motivates the so-called birther movement, which maintains that the president was born on foreign soil (Kenya) and is thus not constitutionally eligible to hold office, despite conclusive and widely available evidence to the contrary. The birthers reject the very idea of his presidency. According to J. Richard Cohen, the president of the Southern Poverty Law Center, "This particular conspiracy theory was first developed by an open anti-Semite and circulated by right-wing extremists who cannot accept the fact that a black man has been elected president of the United States."[53]

Support for birtherism by an individual or within a movement or organization stands as a measure of political extremism and of exclusionism, i.e., not only opposition to Obama's policies but to the kind of inclusive national identity he has expounded. It is worth noting that in a Public Policy Polling survey of four hundred Republican primary voters administered between February 11 and 13, 2011, a majority said that the president was not born in the United States. Barely one-quarter of those polled affirmatively stated that he was, whereas the rest were unsure.[54] Further demonstrating the links between birtherism and exclusionism, among those Republicans who erroneously claimed Obama was not born here, a seven-to-one majority viewed Sarah Palin favorably, but among those who definitively knew Obama was born here, a slim but clear majority viewed Palin unfavorably.

The noise surrounding the birther movement reached a fever pitch in the spring of 2011 after Donald Trump adopted it as the main focus of his flirtation with running for president. Finally, at that point President Obama petitioned the state of Hawaii to release his "long-form" birth certificate, something that it does normally not do for anyone born in the state. Obama had previously released copies of the document he did possess, known as a "certificate of live birth," and had shown the original of that document to members of the media. Additionally, officials in the state of Hawaii from the governor on down had officially verified the legitimacy of the original long-form birth certificate residing in the state's archives. The release of the long-form birth certificate significantly reduced the media coverage of birther claims, at least to this point. Additionally, a few weeks after the president had the long-form certificate issued, Trump announced that in fact he would not be seeking the presidency.

The Tea Party and Exclusionism

The Tea Party ideology is certainly built around small government conservatism, i.e., an opposition to a robust role for government in society and the economy. However, the Tea Party movement has also contained—from some important quarters—clear denunciations of the inclusive and unified vision of America that Obama has put forth. For example, Dale Robertson, the founder of the Houston-based TeaParty. org, was photographed in early January 2009 outside a Tea Party event in Houston, Texas, holding a sign that read: "Congress = Slaveowner, Taxpayer = Niggar."[55] *The Washington Times* identified Robertson as a "founder of the 'tea party' movement."[56] Later that month Robertson sent an email asking for donations to his organization with the title "Obama Pimping Obama-Care, One Last Time!" that included a photograph of the president doctored to make him look like a pimp out of a 1970s blaxploitation movie, i.e., with "a pencil-thin mustache and a zebra-striped, fur-brimmed fedora, complete with a feather."[57]

Many Tea Party members reject such sentiments to be sure. Additionally, the Houston Tea Party Society, the group that hosted the February 27, 2009, event, stated after the photo surfaced in the *Washington Independent* in January 2010 that they "do not choose to associate with people that use his type of disgusting language."[58] Nevertheless, racially divisive and/or nakedly racist signs have appeared at Tea Party rallies since they began. In a Madison, Wisconsin, rally on April 15 (tax day), 2009, one sign read: "Obama's Plan: White Slavery."[59] Additionally, by September 2009 signs with a digitally altered photograph depicting Obama as a tribal African witch doctor had become popular at Tea Party rallies across the country.[60]

Former congressman Tom Tancredo (R-CO), a long-time exponent of divisive anti-immigrant rhetoric, spoke at a February 4, 2010, Tea Party convention. He asserted that Obama was elected because "we do not have a civics literacy test before people can vote in this country. People who could not even spell the word 'vote,' or say it in English, put a committed socialist ideologue in the White House, name is Barack Hussein Obama."[61] The Tea Party crowd cheered.

Tancredo has here defined Obama's supporters as foreigners who do not even speak proper English and as people unfamiliar with our country's civic values. He has clearly sought to divide the American community. E.J. Dionne called the speech "astonishingly offensive" and added: "Tancredo harkened back to the Jim Crow South that denied the right to vote to African Americans on the basis of 'literacy tests' that called for potential black registrants to answer questions that would have stumped PhDs in political science."[62] In a press conference the following day, Tea Party convention organizer and Tea Party Nation founder Judson Phillips made clear that he endorsed the sentiments Tancredo expressed regarding a connection between a lack of knowledge of American politics and Obama voters.[63]

Finally, on March 20, 2010, the day before the final vote in the House of Representatives on health care reform, a crowd of a couple of hundred Tea Party protesters just outside the Capitol building showed their bigotry when pro-reform congressmen walked toward the building to cast their votes. The Tea Partiers taunted Representative Barney Frank (D-MA), calling him a "faggot" and a "homo." They also chanted "Kill the bill, nigger!" over and over at Representative John Lewis (D–GA) and Representative Emanuel Cleaver (D–MO).[64] One protestor spat on Representative Cleaver and was arrested by Capitol police. Additionally, health care reform opponents called Representative Ciro Rodriguez (D–TX) a "wetback" at a gathering in his district, while another called Representative Rodriguez's home and said, "Go back to Mexico."[65]

Again, to be clear, these incidents do not mean that the Tea Party is a racist or exclusionist movement from top to bottom. In fact, Joe Wierzbicki, a coordinator of the Tea Party Express, one of the most important elements of the movement, said: "That [witch doctor] image is not representative at all of what this movement is about."[66] As for the health care reform–related bigotry of March 2010, Tea Party

Express coordinator Amy Kremer declared, "It's disgraceful and the people in this movement won't tolerate it because that's not what we're about."[67]

However, racist statements made by some of its leaders have tainted even the Tea Party Express itself. Mark Williams, then chair of the Tea Party Express, appeared on CNN's *Anderson Cooper 360°* on September 14, 2009. He denounced the racist signs appearing at Tea Party Express rallies that month. However, Cooper then confronted Williams with having called Obama "an Indonesian Muslim turned welfare thug and a racist in chief."[68] Williams responded, "Yes. That's the way he's behaving." When Cooper asked Williams again, directly, if he believed that those words still accurately describe Obama, Williams replied, "He's certainly acting like it." Williams, however, was able to remain as chairman of the Tea Party Express even after this CNN appearance, despite having made these and other ethnically charged comments about Obama.[69] On June 18, 2010, Williams stepped aside as chair in favor of Amy Kremer, but remained as the spokesman of the organization for another month.[70]

The issue of racism within the Tea Party reemerged when, on July 13, 2010, the NAACP formally condemned racist elements within the Tea Party and called on the movement's leaders to "condemn extremist elements within the Tea Party [and]…to repudiate those in their ranks who use racist language in their signs and speeches."[71] The next day, the aforementioned Mark Williams responded by posting on his blog a satirical, fictional letter from NAACP president and CEO Benjamin Jealous to Abraham Lincoln that further confirmed Williams's racial bigotry. For example, Williams had the pretend Jealous criticize the Tea Party demand for lower taxes and then ask, "How will we coloreds ever get a widescreen TV in every room if noncoloreds get to keep what they earn?"

The National Tea Party Federation subsequently expelled Williams and, shortly thereafter, the Tea Party Express as a whole when it refused the federation's request to eject Williams from their organization.[72] In a July 18 appearance on *Face the Nation*, the federation's spokesman David Webb also referred to Williams as "an embarrassment to the Tea Party movement" and characterized the expulsions as "an act of self-policing within the federation." Tea Party Express chair Amy Kremer stated that, although she personally disagreed with Williams's post, she would not "throw a fellow conservative under the bus."[73] Nevertheless, Williams resigned his position as Tea Party Express spokesman and ended his association with the organization on July 23, 2010.[74] The above-outlined incidents indicate that exclusionist and baldly racist sentiments clearly exist among significant elements within the movement and its leadership, despite the fact that others within that leadership have publicly denounced such sentiments and sought to distance the movement from them.

Another indication of exclusionist sentiment among Tea Party members is what appears to be an extensive inclusion of birthers in its ranks. Tea Party Nation founder Judson Phillips stated directly that he "does not believe Barack Obama" on the matter of his birthplace.[75] Phillips added that there are "a lot of really sane Americans . . . like us," who question whether Obama was born in this country. Additionally, at the Tea Party rally held in Washington, D.C., on September 12, 2009, there were quite a number of birther-type signs charging that President Obama had been born in Kenya.[76] A California Field Poll taken January 5 through 17, 2010, produced more empirical evidence of disproportionate support for the birther conspiracy among Tea Party members, greater support even than exists among Republicans more broadly.[77]

Similar results appeared in a national poll conducted by CBS and the *New York Times* between April 5 and April 12, 2010. Once again, the attitudes of white Tea Party supporters were more extreme than those of white Republicans in general (there was significant overlap between the two groups) on the question of whether Obama was foreign born, on race-related questions such as whether the Obama administration "favors blacks over whites," and whether "too much has been made of the problems facing black people."[78] To further connect the dots along the exclusionist spectrum, a strong majority of Tea Party supporters in this poll expressed a favorable opinion of Glenn Beck, whereas he received far less support among respondents as a whole. On a related note, another poll conducted for a University of Washington survey done February 8 through March 15, 2010, found that even after "account[ing] for conservatism *and* partisanship, support for the Tea Party remains a valid predictor of racial resentment (emphasis in original)."[79]

It is worth noting that prominent conservative politicians have spoken in ways that can only serve to feed that white racial resentment, telling white Americans that they cannot hope to receive fair treatment from the Obama administration. For example, on June 13, 2010, Representative Steve King (R-Iowa) offered the following during an appearance on G. Gordon Liddy's nationally syndicated radio show: "The president has demonstrated that he has a default mechanism in him that breaks down the side of race—on the side that favors the black person."[80]

In summary, professor of political science and law Nathaniel Persily characterized the Tea Party movement as "a combination of localism, nativism, and populism."[81] E. J. Dionne similarly noted that "yes, parts of this movement do seem to be motivated by a new nativism and by racism."[82] William Jelani Cobb, a historian of race in America, offered: "I suspect the Tea Party crowd believes that the currency of whiteness has been devalued."[83] Mark Potok, director of the Intelligence Project of the Southern Poverty Law Center, stated: "Anyone who's looked at some of the signs at the various 'tea parties' knows perfectly well that race is a significant part of this backlash."[84]

In October 2010 the NAACP supported the publication of a detailed report on racism in the Tea Party movement that followed up on their statement of that July.[85] NAACP leader Benjamin Jealous noted that nakedly racist groups, including the Council of Concerned Citizens and Stormfront, had publicly allied themselves with the Tea Party movement. Jealous also cited David Duke's support for the Tea Party as evidence of the racist nature of its appeal.[86] In 2010 Duke posted a YouTube video titled "David Duke Speaks to the Tea Party Movement" in which he praised its members as "American people who have watched in silent anger while the nation of our forefathers has been destroyed." According to Duke, the Tea Party "is about preserving our heritage and our freedom." The video makes clear that "our" refers to white Christians. Additionally, a recent academic study based on in depth interviews and interactions with Massachusetts Tea Party members found a clear element of racial prejudice motivating support for the Tea Party.[87]

Exclusionism, White Nationalism, and White Anxieties

The nexus that links these figures along the exclusionist spectrum, from Palin on the (relatively) more moderate end, to Limbaugh and Beck, to Tancredo and other nativists, and to Pruden, Savage, and the birthers and other open racists like David Duke on the far end is the fear that America will continue along the path toward transcending its whiteness as nonwhites fully integrate into our society and culture. According to the aforementioned Massachusetts study, this fear also drives the members of the Tea Party movement.[88]

Figures like Palin cloak that fear when they talk of traditional, small-town values representing the real America, while blatant bigots like Pruden and Savage stoke that fear more openly, but there is little doubt the underlying theme remains consistent. Having a black president is the most potent evidence that the change they fear has arrived.[89] Pat Buchanan, a long-time exclusionist, argued however that the roots run much deeper:

The alienation and radicalization of white America began long before Obama arrived. . . . In their lifetimes, they have seen their Christian faith purged from schools their taxes paid for and mocked in movies and on TV. They have seen their factories shuttered in the thousands and their jobs outsourced in the millions to Mexico and China. They have seen trillions of tax dollars go for Great Society programs, but have seen no Great Society, only rising crime, illegitimacy, drug use and dropout rates. They watch on cable TV as illegal aliens walk into their country, are rewarded with free educations and health care and take jobs at lower pay than American families can live on—then carry Mexican flags in American cities and demand U.S. citizenship. They see Wall Street banks bailed out as they sweat their next paycheck, then read that bank profits are soaring, and the big bonuses for the brilliant bankers are back. Neither they nor their kids ever benefited from affirmative action, unlike Barack and Michelle Obama.[90]

White, straight, Christian Americans are, in Buchanan's mind, the primary victims of the past fifty years' worth of changes in American society. It is worth emphasizing that he identified "white America" by "their Christian faith," leaving no room for non-Christians in his definition of the white community or, presumably, in the American community either. Although there are differences on some economic issues between Buchanan and other exclusionists like Beck, Limbaugh, and Palin, what unites these figures—their common embrace of an exclusionary definition of our national identity—more than outweighs the differences. Ultimately, exclusionists would rather destroy the more inclusive definition of America put forth by Obama—one that invigorates the bonds between whites and nonwhites and strengthens our sense of national community—than see their power diminish.

Buchanan also serves as a link between less explicit exclusionists who have a larger media platform and the even more extreme voices of white nationalism. White nationalism rejects the idea that membership in the American nation is based solely on citizenship and is neutral regarding ethnicity. According to antiracist activist Leonard Zeskind, "By contrast, white nationalists turn their skin color into a badge of a distinct national identity. . . . They are dedicated to the proposition that those they deem to be 'white' own special rights: the right to dominate political institutions, the economy, and culture. They believe that a 'whites-only' nation exists in fact, if not in name. And they swear to a duty to create a whites-only nation-state on soil that was once the United States of America."[91] Louis Beam, a high-ranking official in the neo-Nazi paramilitary organization Aryan Nations and a major figure in the violent white nationalist movement, commented in 1991: "People occupying the North American continent today now define themselves more by race than by any other criterion. . . . There are in fact no more 'Americans,' only competing racial groups."[92]

Whereas Palin implicitly identified America with only certain types of people—equating white, rural Christians with being authentically American—white nationalists and extreme racists identify with being white even above being American, or, as Beam's comment makes clear, not at all with being American. The bridge between Palin's moderately exclusionist rhetoric and Beam's unadulterated white racial nationalism is Pat Buchanan–style explicitly white Americanism, which openly declares what Palin implied, that America is and indeed should be a white, Christian country, culture, and people. In the 1992 and 1996 Republican primary campaigns for president and his far less successful 2000 run for president as the nominee of the Reform party, Buchanan attracted a following that included (among others) many of the same kind of racially conscious white voters who had previously helped give David Duke a majority of the white vote in Louisiana in two separate statewide campaigns in the early 1990s. Zeskind noted that "Buchanan was a white Christian nationalist first and foremost, and his voters understood that."[93]

A fear exists among white racists that America has become a place hostile to them as whites, Zeskind explained. They fear what will ensue if and when they become a racial minority in America, which will occur sometime around 2050 if present trends continue. "In the white nationalist mind, becoming a racial minority is only one step away from racial extinction."[94] Obama's election stoked that fear among those who already held such an extreme position.[95]

In April 2009, the Department of Homeland Security issued a report on right-wing domestic terror threats that found "right-wing extremists have capitalized on the election of the first African American president."[96] The report also mentioned anger about immigration as motivating white supremacists and right-wing extremists in general. In July 2011 the report's primary author, Daryl Johnson, reiterated that one factor driving the increase in right-wing extremism is the fact that there is "a changing demographic in America shifting away from a predominantly Caucasian nation."[97]

Hua Hsu, writing in the *Atlantic* in early 2009, addressed a broader "white identity" movement among white Americans that mirrors, in terms of its ideological foundations, the ethnic identity–based movements of minority groups that grew out of multiculturalism.[98] He characterized it as "a racial pride that dares not speak its name, and that defines itself through cultural cues instead—a suspicion of intellectual elites and city dwellers, a preference for folksiness and plainness of speech (whether real or feigned), and the association of a working-class white minority with 'the real America.'"[99]

Hsu did acknowledge the possibility that a politics fueled by the white identity movement could grow more powerful if whites grow more fearful along the lines of the extreme white nationalists Zeskind detailed. Hsu predicted, however, that another outcome was more likely to occur as result of the coming demographic transformations in the United States: these changes "are likely to reduce the power of racial hierarchies over everyone's lives, producing a culture that's more likely than any before to treat its inhabitants as individuals, rather than members of a caste or identity group . . . a social structure that treats race as just one of a seemingly infinite number of possible self-identifications."[100] Such a future is in line with the conception of America Obama has depicted.

By strengthening the identification of nonwhites with America, Obama would be strengthening the multiethnic character of our national identity and thus preventing white racists from claiming America as exclusively theirs. Furthermore, Obama's definition of America directly opposes bigotry by emphasizing fellowship and amity among Americans and—by extension—human beings of all ethnicities.

The fears held by some whites represent a fundamental threat to American unity and our country's ability to be a successful multiethnic democracy. These whites fear that as nonwhites become a majority in the United States one or both of the following will occur: America will become a place that they, as whites, feel alienated from culturally and whose values they cannot abide; or, even worse, that nonwhites will use their majority status to do to whites what the white power structure did to them for centuries, i.e. oppress them on the basis of race/ethnicity.

This is exactly the fear Beck and Limbaugh have sought to exacerbate. It is exactly the fear on display at a panel discussion titled "Will Immigration Kill the GOP?" held at the 2011 Conservative Political Action Conference (CPAC)—the premier political gathering of conservatives in the United States. Both the panelists (who included the aforementioned Tom Tancredo, former representative Virgil Goode (R-

VA), current representative Lou Barletta (R-PA), and Pat Buchanan's sister Bay) and audience members framed their general opposition to immigration around their fear that the country is becoming less white. One audience member actually asked the panel how to convince more "Caucasian communities" to oppose immigration reform.[101] The audience included a number of recognizable white nationalists.[102] One of them was William Johnson, chair of the white nationalist political party American Third Position, who once called for an amendment to the Constitution that would read, "No person shall be a citizen of the United States unless he is a non-Hispanic white of the European race."[103]

In 2012, CPAC included a panel whose premise directly opposes the very foundation of Obama's understanding of American identity, namely his belief that a society such as ours can be both diverse and strongly unified. This panel, "The Failure of Multiculturalism: How the Pursuit of Diversity is Weakening the American Identity," included as a panelist Peter Brimelow, the founder of VDARE.com, a website named for the first white English child born in North America.[104] The Southern Poverty Law Center lists VDARE.com as a white nationalist extremist group.[105] On April 2, 2009, Brimelow proclaimed that "an explicitly white nationalist party it seems to me . . . would be a perfectly legitimate response to the immigration-driven ethnic shift and the rise of ethno-centric politics on the part of the minorities."[106]

Newt Gingrich, Mitt Romney, and Rick Santorum all held events at the 2012 CPAC and said nothing about Brimelow, his rhetoric, or his panel. However, the aforementioned Rep. Steve King not only attended the panel but personally gushed to Brimelow about having read his books and praised the white nationalist for having written "eloquently . . . about the balkanization of America."[107]

Obama understands the fear some whites have of an America with a nonwhite majority, and the danger posed by demagogues willing to stoke it, and so he has taken special care to counteract it. These anxious whites are, in fact, one of the prime target audiences for Obama's push for American unity. In the 1990s, as the debates over radical multiculturalism and ethnic separatism raged, one primary concern among whites was that nonwhites were rejecting America, identifying far more with their ethnic group than the broader national community, if they identified with it at all.

While the anti-American rhetoric among radicals on the left was loud and received a disproportionate amount of attention in the media, there was never any significant mass political movement among nonwhites in the United States that expressed truly anti-American sentiments. Many in white America, however, had heard and still remembered that extreme rhetoric, in particular after the videotaped snippets of Reverend Jeremiah Wright's sermons brought it back to them. Some among the more anxious whites believed that many or even most nonwhites—particularly black and Hispanic Americans—really did reject America and thus reject whites. Obama's rhetoric, long before the 2008 Philadelphia speech, has reflected his understanding of this misperception and its potential danger.

As long as whites were 80 percent or more of the population, the belief that black and Hispanic Americans were rejecting America may have made anxious whites disappointed or even angry, but not especially afraid, at least not in terms of the large-scale impact of black and brown alienation. The coming demographic changes do add a powerful element of fear to this anger. This kind of fear, I would argue, has little basis in reality, but that does not matter to those afraid and to those willing to exploit that fear. The actual, tangible effect of Obama's policies—whose lack of ethnic vengefulness will be confirmed over time—should help to assuage those fears as the Chicken Little–like ravings of Limbaugh, Beck, et al. are proven false, when the sky does not fall on white America. At least one hopes so.

Furthermore, Obama's message of national unity aims at cementing the already-existing bond between America and the members of minority groups whom anxious whites feared had rejected her. His hope appears to be that as middle of the road or even right-of-center whites—who were themselves worried two decades ago about ethnic separatism in America—now see nonwhites ever more enthusiastically embracing an American national identity, these whites will feel a stronger connection to their nonwhite fellow citizens as a result. This connection would be based on shared membership in the American family and does not require agreement on ideological issues. As President Obama said on October 16, 2011: "To say that we are bound together as one people, and must constantly strive to see ourselves in one another, is not to argue for a false unity that papers over our differences and ratifies an unjust status quo."

Conservatives, moderates, and liberals can certainly recognize one another as fellow Americans despite their political differences. Whites and nonwhites, or at least many of them, have wanted to deepen ties with one another but have too often felt that the other group needed to make the first step toward reconciliation. To be clear, it is not the responsibility of either group alone to take that first step. The point is that reducing the fear and anxiety that impedes the strengthening of national unity is all of our responsibility.

Obama's rhetoric, which extends the hand of America as personified by its president, encourages blacks in particular but nonwhites in general to take that hand more unambiguously than before, or perhaps simply in a way that the media makes more visible to their white fellow Americans. Many whites of good faith, seeing that happen, will feel more motivated to then extend their hand to nonwhites as well. Obama's goal is to ensure that this virtuous cycle feeds on itself.

From the Other Direction: The Far Left Accuses Obama of Ignoring Racism

While they received far less media attention than their counterparts on the far right, some commentators and political figures opposed Obama's conception of America from his left. They urged him to take a more directly confrontational approach to issues relating to racism and other forms of bigotry. Likewise, these critics from the left also argued that Obama's depiction of racism in contemporary America and in its history presents a rose-colored, Pollyannaish story that significantly underplays the depths of oppression blacks and members of other nonwhite groups have faced.

The aforementioned Tim Wise offers an instructive example of the critique coming from Obama's left. Wise denigrated the account of American history Obama offered in his Philadelphia race speech as "sunny and warm" but "not an accurate one" because it ignores the depth of racism.[108] Wise contended that Obama has "embrace[d] the dominant national narrative generally accepted by the white majority."[109] Obama, however, has done so such thing. His chronicle of our history has, in fact, placed the crimes America has committed in the name of bigotry front and center, not only those it committed against enslaved Africans but also those against American Indians and women among other misdeeds and mistakes. The president has refused, however, to allow those crimes to be the whole story, as Wise seems to demand, and to ignore the advances—even if they remain incomplete—the country has made toward full equality and inclusion.[110]

Wise further criticized Obama for supposedly not speaking the truth about the economic conditions and severe discrimination faced by black Americans today. He accused the president of having done "everything he could to be nonthreatening" by avoiding discussing racism during the campaign, thus "distanc[ing] himself from the larger black community."[111] This book—in particular chapters 4 and 5—provides clear evidence to the contrary.

Additionally, Obama has helped further transform the perception that acting and speaking the way he does equates to being white, although he is far from the first African American to do so. He has thus broadened white people's idea of what it means to be black and has challenged white stereotypes of black people, according to which whites see African Americans as—in Wise's words—"uneducated, dysfunctional, and lower class."[112] Most importantly, Obama's election and the truly inclusive narrative of American history he has presented signify we are moving in the direction of redefining our national identity in a way that fully includes both whites and nonwhites.

In addition to Wise, others have also taken aim at Obama from the left since Inauguration Day. In late 2009, echoing the criticisms made early in the presidential campaign, a number of African American politicians and commentators began talking about how Obama did not sound "black enough" when talking about race. In an interview with American Urban Radio Networks on December 22, 2009, a questioner asked the president what he thought about "the fact that black leadership is grumbling. . . . They thought that there would be a little bit more compassion for black issues."[113] After listing an array of initiatives from his administration that he contended will "make a huge difference" for African Americans, Obama continued: "The only thing I cannot do is . . . pass laws that say I'm just helping black folks. I'm the president of the entire United States." He was focused on "passing laws that help all people, particularly those who are most vulnerable and most in need. That in turn is going to help lift up the African American community." This is exactly the argument Obama has been making for fifteen years.

In early January 2010, a book about the 2008 presidential campaign was published that contained off-putting comments made by Harry Reid. Reid, speaking in support of Obama running for the presidency, noted that it would benefit Obama that he was "light-skinned" and that he could speak without a "Negro dialect."[114] Reid apologized for the comments and President Obama accepted the apology. As far as he was concerned, "the book is closed" on the matter.[115]

Sociologist Michael Eric Dyson, however, condemned Obama's reaction as weak and accused the president of avoiding racial issues, contending, "This president runs from race like a black man runs from a cop."[116] Dyson continued: "[Obama] is loath to speak about race. . . . You ain't talking about civil rights, you ain't talking about affirmative action, you're not pressing the issue. . . . If Barack Obama was standing forth in America to speak brilliantly and courageously about the issues of race, he'd sound a lot more black too."

Whether Obama has spoken brilliantly, courageously, both, or neither about racism in America is open to interpretation, as is the question of whether he has "sound[ed] black." However, this study has demonstrated that he is anything but loath to talk about racism. Obama has spoken about it over and over again, has spoken about civil rights, and has spoken about discrimination. He has pressed the issue. As the Henry Louis Gates affair demonstrated, Obama has even chosen to inject himself into an already brewing race-related media storm that did not directly involve him. In that case, the president could quite easily have responded to the question about the arrest, which was asked at the end of a press conference specifically devoted to health care, by saying that he was there to talk about health care and would comment at a later time. Dyson, Wise, and others who have criticized Obama for not speaking about race in the way they would like are choosing to ignore the record.

Just after Obama delivered the State of the Union address on January 27, 2010, the Kirwan Institute criticized the speech because "race was altogether absent from his remarks."[117] The Kirwan editorial condemned Obama for not mentioning the "racially disparate impact of our economic crisis" or the "underlying dynamic." The fact that Obama has done so on dozens of occasions before and after becoming president may not be relevant to a criticism of this one speech, but it is worth noting. Additionally, it is simply incorrect to assert that Obama did not discuss race in that speech. I have argued that he did so, but in a different way, by emphasizing, at the outset, the racially inclusive American narrative that he believes is an important and effective way to build support for solving problems of racial inequality.

About one month after the Reid story broke in the media, a *New York Times* article reported rising disenchantment among Obama's black critics. The article cited criticisms from members of the Congressional Black Caucus, from black journalists and political analysts, from the Kirwan Institute, as well as other scholars including Dyson, who quipped, "All these teachable moments, but the professor refuses to come to the class."[118] The article also cited praise for the way Obama has discussed racism from other African American scholars and political figures, including law professor Charles Ogletree and Dorothy Height, the chairwoman of the National Council of Negro Women, who was a matriarch of the civil rights activist community.

Like Tim Wise, many of these critics from Obama's left argue that the story of America told by Reverend Wright is more accurate than the one the president has offered. For example, in an open letter to Obama written on March 26, 2008, just eight days after the Philadelphia speech on race, a collection of almost four dozen social science scholars said that they appreciated Obama's "willingness to be a risk-taker" in even broaching the subject of racism, but added, "we are concerned that your remarks incorrectly reduce racism to mere racial prejudice. You remarked that Reverend Jeremiah Wright 'expressed a profoundly distorted view of this country— a view that sees white racism as endemic.' We believe that Wright is exactly right, that racism is not only endemic but is at the core of American society as reflected in a large and well established body of social scientific research."[119]

Fundamentally, his left-wing critics want Obama to talk about racism and America the way Wright did because they believe that doing so is the only way to undo the destruction that racism continues to wreak, as indicated by Wise's admission that, on this topic, "I am being, of course, deliberately provocative. . . . Provocation is often what is needed in order to shake the complacency from the minds of the masses."[120] Obama, in contrast, has for more than fifteen years consistently expressed a more balanced but ultimately hopeful depiction of America, one that he believes will prove far more effective in undoing racism's continuing effects than the one put forth by Reverend Wright, Tim Wise, Michael Eric Dyson, and his other critics on the left.

It is arguably to Obama's benefit that these critics from the left condemn him, particularly regarding the way he talks about racism in America, because these condemnations allow him to position himself as being more firmly within the bounds of the mainstream. As those on the far left criticize him for not being radical enough, while those on the far right simultaneously attack him as too radical, Obama's views appear all the more reasonable. He can thus argue that he stands in the center of the broader debate on racism and what to do about it. Thus, Obama may well appreciate these critics on his left for giving him more room, in political terms, to propose policies and employ rhetoric that might otherwise seem more radical were it not for the existence of these figures repeatedly denouncing him for being too soft or too moderate on racial issues.

Although the opposition from the left to the way Obama depicts America is important, it is neither as politically powerful nor as potentially destructive as that coming from the extreme right. Fundamentally, Obama's left-wing critics do not seek to increase tensions among Americans of different ethnicities, whereas those on the far right simultaneously draw on and feed the anxiety some white Americans feel as their percentage of the population drops ever closer to 50 percent.

The message of national unity and amity across ethnic boundaries Barack Obama has expounded can potentially assuage that white anxiety by strengthening the feeling that all Americans—white and nonwhite—are one family. The alternative, exclusionist vision of America is one in which the political parties become even more divided along ethnic and cultural lines. The Republican party would come to represent primarily white, culturally conservative Christians, and the Democratic party would be the party of most gays, non-Orthodox Jews, and nonwhites, as well as those dwindling number of Christian white liberals who clung to a nonracial way of approaching politics. My work on multiethnic societies throughout history tells me that this is a recipe for disaster. When political parties break down along ethnic and/or cultural borders, the possibility for a vibrant sense of national unity that includes members of all groups disappears. Now is the time to invigorate the sense of connectedness among whites and nonwhites, to break down the fear of the other on both sides. I argue here that Obama's rhetoric offers the possibility of achieving significant success in unifying Americans. The 2012 elections will be the decisive moment in determining whether and how soon that possibility becomes a reality.

Conclusion

My Country 'Tis of Thee. Think of the words and the meaning of this song. Marian Anderson sang it in 1939 on the steps of the Lincoln Memorial after, ironically, the Daughters of the American Revolution had vetoed her proposed concert in front of a racially integrated crowd in Constitution Hall. The lyrics surely evoked different feelings on the part of minority and especially black Americans compared to, for example, those felt by the members of the Daughters of the American Revolution.

In 1963, on those very same steps, Martin Luther King Jr. drew inspiration from the lyrics of that song again in his "I Have a Dream" speech. He said:

> And this will be the day—this will be the day when all of God's children will be able to sing with new meaning:
>> My country 'tis of thee, sweet land of liberty, of thee I sing.
>> Land where my fathers died, land of the Pilgrim's pride,
>>> From every mountainside, let freedom ring!

In this speech, King explicitly noted how the song meant something different to those who had not yet won the full measure of equality promised by America's ideals. That day had not yet come.

At the presidential inauguration on January 20, 2009, Aretha Franklin chose to sing that particular song. While listening, I couldn't help but think about the fact that now, maybe for the first time in our history, all Americans of every background could fully and without reservation believe that the lyrics applied to them just as much as to any descendant of those who sailed across the ocean on the *Mayflower*. All of us can now unequivocally sing, "*My* country . . . of *thee* I sing . . ."[1] (emphasis mine). It has been more than three years since that day, and the feeling of profound satisfaction over history being made has become a distant memory. Nevertheless, it remains a feeling worth remembering.

For centuries, a gap—or in many cases a chasm—existed between what America has promised to all and what it has delivered to some. Starting with those promises made by Thomas Jefferson in the summer of 1776, many of our greatest American leaders have inspired us with words that exalted our most sacred principles, liberty and equality, yet our country did not apply them universally. The remarks Abraham Lincoln delivered at Gettysburg, along with the actions he took to end slavery, significantly shrunk the gap between those grand principles and the reality of inequality and oppression in the United States, but the gap remained stubbornly wide. The soaring language of Martin Luther King Jr. helped cajole a generation of leaders finally to bring the laws of the land mostly in line with those Jeffersonian promises.

The election of Barack Obama as president demonstrates continued progress toward fulfilling those promises. Even more so, his rhetoric has declared that America will stand for all its citizens; it will indeed fully include nonwhites as well as whites in the American family. Without question, the more people Obama can convince to accept his vision of America, the more support he will likely garner for the progressive economic and social policies he advocates. Additionally, he has acknowledged that he believes that the way he talks about America and race specifically will prove more successful in political terms than speaking in a more confrontational way about racism in America's past and present.

The practicality of and the politics behind Obama's rhetorical strategy are clear and important. Those realities do not change the fact that his depiction of America has inspired people. He has inspired them not only to vote for him but also to strengthen their relationship with America and with other Americans, particularly those of a different ethnicity. Strengthening these relationships can spark the virtuous cycle of reconciliation and integration I have spoken of throughout this book, one that can significantly invigorate American unity across ethnic boundaries.

By embracing America and its saga in full, all its truths both sweet and bitter, Obama has offered a narrative through which members of ethnic minority groups can identify with American history as their own, and even be proud of that history without denying the struggles of their ancestors because those struggles—along with those of women, workers, gays, and all those of every background and creed who have fought hardship and prejudice—are placed at the center of America's common story. Furthermore, Obama's embrace of America reinforces the fact that members of those minority groups do want to belong to the American family; they do want to be one people united with whites in a single national community that shares a multifaceted but ultimately unifying history.

That history is one of national redemption. It includes America having sinned by ignoring its founding principles of freedom and equality, and having overcome that sin through struggle, both violent and nonviolent. That history also includes the indispensable role the United States has played in the fights to defeat those who have sought and those who still seek to create a world that denies those democratic principles, and who reject the very idea that a diverse society can have real unity. That is Obama's America.

The implications of America's success or failure in the endeavor of invigorating its national unity are profound, not only for our country but for the world as well. People all over the planet instinctively understand this, which helps explain the high expectations for the Obama presidency voiced by so many non-Americans. Beyond that, the clash between two diametrically opposed philosophies—fundamentalism and pluralism—arguably defines our world today. The fundamentalist worldview, which some in virtually every region of the globe espouse, seeks to create a society in which every person adopts identical beliefs and practices; such a worldview tolerates neither dissent nor diversity. Fundamentalism can impose a religion or a nonreligious ideology. A world that embraces pluralism holds out the potential for peace and prosperity for people of all backgrounds, whereas a world where fundamentalism reigns supreme condemns humanity to constant war and/or harsh oppression as well as the forced abandonment of all cultural and religious traditions those in the minority in any society hold dear.

America, because of its diversity as well as its vibrant democracy and its position as the world's primary military and economic power, can lead humanity toward democratic pluralism and can defeat fundamentalism. We have the chance to demonstrate to the world that a society of many races and cultures can truly become one people. Such an achievement would enhance America's ability to influence global affairs by improving its moral standing in the eyes of the populations of other countries. Furthermore, doing so would provide a powerful rebuke to the fundamentalists around the planet who want to create societies—in some cases a world—where only one way of life is permitted.

Despite the serious flaws in its past and even its present-day shortcomings, this country has for more than two centuries offered an inspiring example of constitutional democracy to many around the world. In a new century where we face terrorism and other threats to our security, Obama's response centers on a powerful and inspiring choice to offer a new and truly inclusive American narrative. By redefining America this way, he aims to give opponents of violent extremists something positive with which they can identify. Obama wants America to seize the opportunity to continue serving as a model, this time as an alternative not simply to undemocratic governments, but also to the kind of fundamentalist worldview that threatens to destroy the hope for a peaceful future. Our country's ability to carry out this mission is at the core of his understanding of American exceptionalism. Whether President Obama succeeds in strengthening American unity will help determine whether we live in world defined by pluralism or one dominated by fundamentalism. The stakes could not be any higher.

Notes

Introduction

1. Elizabeth Theiss-Morse, *Who Counts as an American? The Boundaries of National Identity* (Cambridge: Cambridge University Press, 2009), 30.
2. David Miller, *On Nationality* (Oxford: Oxford University Press, 2005), 25–26.
3. Juliet Hooker, *Race and the Politics of Solidarity* (Oxford: Oxford University Press, 2009), 24.
4. To save space I will not provide citations with links to Obama's speeches (other than where the remarks delivered differ substantially from the prepared text), broadcast interviews, or debate remarks. These are all available at Project Vote Smart: http://votesmart.org/candidate/public-statements/9490/barack-obama-ii, which has an easily searchable database. I will provide a citation and a link when the source is not available at that site.
5. Remarks by Barbara Jordan, Keynote Address, Democratic National Convention, July 12, 1976, http://www.americanrhetoric.com/speeches/barbarajordan 1976dnc.html. Jordan was the first African American woman to deliver the keynote address at a major party's national convention. She represented Texas in the House of Representatives from 1973 to 1979.
6. There are important distinctions among these various types of groups, in particular the different nature of discrimination faced by members of groups defined by physical characteristics like skin color. Nevertheless, having to say "ethnic, cultural, religious, racial, etc. groups" every page or so would make the book unreadable. For the purposes of discussing identity, I have grouped them together because these "ethnic" groups are the kinds of groups around which a nationalist-type movement that seeks political autonomy in or sovereignty over a given territory can feasibly be organized. Therefore, these "ethnic" identities have a po-

tentially conflictual relationship with the national (i.e. country-based) identity in a society where, as virtually all do, there is more than one "ethnic" group.

7. The Diversity within Unity Platform, http://communitariannetwork.org/diversity -within-unity/. See also Amitai Etzioni, "Minorities and the National Ethos," *Politics* 29, no. 2 (June 2009): 100–110, accessed February 20, 2012.

8. Much has been written on the question of Obama and race, to say the least. Two strong academic article collections are: *Du Bois Review: Social Science Research on Race, Special Issue: Obama's Path* 6, no. 1 (Spring 2009), in which I would recommend in particular Rogers M. Smith and Desmond S. King, "Barack Obama and the Future of American Racial Politics," 25–35; and *Journal of Black Studies: Barack Obama's Improbable Election and the Question of Race and Racism in Contemporary America* 40, no. 3 (January 2010).

9. Barack Obama, *The Audacity of Hope: Thoughts on Reclaiming the American Dream* (New York: Vintage, 2006), 275.

10. Barack Obama, interview with Richard Wolffe, in Wolffe, *Renegade: The Making of a President* (New York: Crown Publishers, 2009), 324.

11. The quotation is from Tim Wise, *Between Barack and a Hard Place: Racism and White Denial in the Age of Obama* (San Francisco: City Lights, 2009), 87.

12. The fact that Lincoln and King did so is well known. Douglass exemplified this kind of thinking when he broke with the radical abolitionist William Lloyd Garrison over the sustainability of the U.S. Constitution. Garrison had publicly burned a copy of the document, terming it irredeemably pro-slavery.

13. Remarks as delivered by Barack Obama, Madison, WI, February 12, 2008, http://www.washingtonpost.com/wp-dyn/content/article/2008/02/12 /AR2008021203144_pf.html. The speech differs from the prepared text, which appears at http://votesmart.org/public-statement/318670/remarks-of-senator -barack-obama-potomac-primary-night/?search=wisconsin.

14. Gary B. Nash, Charlotte Crabtree, and Ross E. Dunn, *History on Trial: Culture Wars and the Teaching of the Past* (New York: Vintage Books, 2000), 101.

15. Theiss-Morse, *Who Counts as an American?*, 129.

16. Mary E. Stuckey, *Defining Americans: The Presidency and National Identity* (Lawrence: University Press of Kansas, 2004), 3.

Chapter 1. American National Identity: From the Revolution through the 1960s

1. For a singularly harsh yet lively criticism of those particular liberals written by a close friend of Rushdie, see Christopher Hitchens, *Hitch-22: A Memoir* (New York: Twelve, 2010).

2. Eugene Robinson, "The Moment for This Messenger?," *Washington Post*, March 13, 2007.

3. Michael Lind, *The Next American Nation: The New Nationalism and the Fourth American Revolution* (New York: Free Press, 1995), 380.

4. David Walker, *Walker's Appeal to the Coloured Citizens of the World* (Boston: David Walker, 1829), 85.

5. Frederick Douglass, "The Meaning of July Fourth for the Negro," in *Frederick Douglass: Selected Speeches and Writings*, ed. Philip S. Foner (Chicago: Lawrence Hill Books, 1999), 196–97.

6. Mia Bay, "See Your Declaration Americans! Abolitionism, Americanism, and the Revolutionary Tradition in Free Black Politics," in *Americanism: New Perspectives on the History of an Ideal*, eds. Michael Kazin and Joseph A. McCartin (Chapel Hill: University of North Carolina Press, 2006), 42–43. For more on Americanism in black thought, see pp. 40–45.

7. W. E. B. Du Bois, "Of Our Spiritual Strivings," in *The Souls of Black Folk* (New York: Dover, 1994), 2–3.

8. Colbert I. King, "Two Speeches, Two Truths about America," *Washington Post*, July 5, 2008. In addition to the surface parallels regarding both men's biracial ancestry, Obama himself expressed admiration for what he described as Douglass's ability to speak to all Americans across ethnic boundaries. See Jodi Kantor, "Teaching Law, Testing Ideas, Obama Stood Slightly Apart," *New York Times*, July 30, 2008.

9. Scott L. Malcomson, "The Nation; An Appeal Beyond Race," *New York Times*, August 1, 2004.

10. Robinson, "The Moment for This Messenger?"

11. See Rogers Brubaker, "The Manichean Myth: Rethinking the Distinction Between 'Civic' and 'Ethnic' Nationalism," in *Nation and National Identity: The European Experience in Perspective*, ed. Hanspeter Kriesi et al. (Zurich: Ruegger, 1999), 59–67.

12. Oliver Zimmer, "Boundary Mechanisms and Symbolic Resources: Towards a Process-Oriented Approach to National Identity," in *Nations and Nationalism* 9, no. 2 (2003): 178–79. See also Louise Bergström, "Rethinking the Boundaries between Civic and Ethnic Forms of Nationalism—Twentieth-Century European Nation Formation," unpublished paper presented at the Association for the Study of Nationalities Conference, April 24, 2009.

13. On the identity-related difficulties faced, for example, by ethnic Koreans in Japan, please see Sonia Ryang, ed. *Koreans in Japan: Critical Voices from the Margin* (London: Routledge, 2000).

14. See, for example, Imogen Foulkes, "Long Road to Swiss Citizenship," *BBC News*, September 20, 2004, http://news.bbc.co.uk/2/hi/europe/3673736.stm.

15. Robert Putnam, "E Pluribus Unum: Diversity and Community in the Twenty-first Century," *Scandinavian Political Studies* 30, no. 2 (2007): 137.

16. See David Remnick, *The Bridge: The Life and Rise of Barack Obama* (New York: Alfred A. Knopf, 2010), 305–6.

17. Maureen Healy, *Vienna and the Fall of the Habsburg Empire: Total War and Everyday Life in World War I* (Cambridge: Cambridge University Press, 2004), 311. The reference is to Benedict Anderson's concept laid out in his book, *Imagined Communities: Reflections on the Origin and Spread of Nationalism* (London: Verso, 1983). See also Ian Reifowitz, *Imagining an Austrian Nation: Joseph Samuel Bloch and the Search for a Multiethnic Austrian Identity, 1846–1919* (Boulder, CO: East European Monographs, distributed by Columbia University Press, 2003).

18. Steven Erlanger, "France Debates Its Identity, But Some Question Why," *New York Times*, November 29, 2009.

19. Hector St. John Crèvecoeur, *Letters from an American Farmer and Sketches of Eighteenth-Century America* (Harmondsworth, UK: Penguin Classics, 1986), 68.

20. For a synthetic discussion of the understanding(s) of American national identity that existed in the early Republic, i.e. from the 1780s into the 1820s, see Stuckey, *Defining Americans*, 23–32.

21. Crèvecoeur, *Letters from an American Farmer*, 68. Well into the twentieth century, the term "race" was used much more loosely than today.

22. See also Lind, *The Next American Nation*, 30, and Desmond King, *Making Americans: Immigration, Race, and the Origins of the Diverse Democracy* (Cambridge, MA: Harvard University Press, 2000), 294.

23. For more, see Aristide Zolberg, *A Nation by Design: Immigration Policy in the Fashioning of America* (Cambridge, MA: Russell Sage Foundation Books at Harvard University Press, 2006), and Noah Pickus, *True Faith and Allegiance: Immigration and American Civic Nationalism* (Princeton, NJ: Princeton University Press, 2005).

24. For more on nativist anti-Catholicism, see Philip Gleason, "American Identity and Americanization," in *Harvard Encyclopedia of American Ethnic Groups*, ed. Stephan Thernstrom (Cambridge, MA: The Belknap Press of Harvard University Press, 1980), 34–38. Although thirty years old, this article offers an excellent discussion of the broad changes to American identity, and the forces behind those changes, that occurred from the American Revolution through the 1970s.

25. Herbert Baxter Adams, "The Germanic Origin of New England Towns," *Johns Hopkins University Studies in History and Political Science* 1, no. 2 (1883). See also Thomas Bender, "Introduction: Historians, the Nation, and the Plenitude of Narratives," in *Rethinking American History in a Global Age*, ed. Thomas Bender (Berkeley: University of California Press, 2002), 3. For a more detailed discussion of the then widely held ethnogenetic view of Americans as Anglo-Saxons in the late colonial period and the early Republic, see Lind, *The Next American Nation*, 17–30, and, on Jefferson specifically, see 353–54. A more recent scholarly analysis can also be found in Eric P. Kaufmann, *The Rise and Fall of Anglo-*

America (Cambridge, MA: Harvard University Press, 2004), 16-19. Kaufmann analyzes more broadly the persistence of the Anglo-Protestant ethnic element at the core of the dominant American nationality from colonial times into the twentieth century. See pp. 11–36.

26. Gleason, "American Identity and Americanization," 38.
27. Ralph Waldo Emerson, *Journals of Ralph Waldo Emerson* (Boston: Houghton Mifflin, 1910–14), 115–16.
28. Herman Melville, *Redburn, His First Voyage: Being the Reminiscences and Confessions of the Son-of-a-Gentleman in the Merchant Service*, ed. Harold Beaver (Harmondsworth, UK: Penguin, 1976), 239.
29. Wendell Phillips, "The United States of the United Races," *National Era* 7 (September 1853). See also Martha Elizabeth Hodes, *Sex, Love, Race: Crossing Boundaries in North American History* (New York: NYU Press, 1999), and Gilbert Osofsky, "Wendell Phillips and the Quest for a New American National Identity," *Canadian Review of Studies in Nationalism* 1 (1973): 14–46.
30. Garry Wills, *Lincoln at Gettysburg: The Words That Remade America* (New York: Simon & Schuster, 1992).
31. King, *Making Americans*, 294.
32. Among others, Israel Zangwill is most responsible for popularizing the term "melting pot." It is worth noting that Zangwill himself included not only whites but people of all races in the American nation, listing "Celt and Latin, Slav and Teuton, Greek and Syrian—black and yellow—Jew and Gentile." See Zangwill, *The Melting Pot* (New York: MacMillan, 1909), 199. In the years around 1900, most of those who discussed the coming together of various ethnicities to form the American people did not include nonwhites. See David Hollinger, "Amalgamation and Hypodescent: The Question of Ethnoracial Mixture in the History of the United States," *American Historical Review* 108, no. 5 (December 2003): 1366–67.
33. For example, see Karen Brodkin, *How Jews Became White Folks: And What That Says about Race in America* (New Brunswick, NJ: Rutgers University Press, 1998).
34. Woodrow Wilson, "Americanism: Address to Convention Hall," Philadelphia, May 10, 1915, in *Immigration and Americanization: Selected Readings*, ed. Philip Davis (Boston: Ginn and Company, 1920), 611–24. On Wilson and his understanding of Americanization, see Hans Vought, "Division and Reunion: Woodrow Wilson, Immigration and the Myth of American Unity," *Journal of American Ethnic History* 13, no. 3 (1994): 24–50. On Wilson and American national identity more broadly, see Stuckey, *Defining Americans*, 151–97.
35. Theodore Roosevelt, Address to the Knights of Columbus, New York, NY, October 12, 1915. See "Roosevelt Bars the Hyphenated," *New York Times*,

October 13, 1915. An excellent study of American national identity in Teddy Roosevelt's public rhetoric can be found in Leroy Dorsey, *We Are All Americans, Pure and Simple: Theodore Roosevelt and the Myth of Americanism* (Tuscaloosa: University of Alabama Press, 2007).

36. Cited in Vanessa Beasley, *You, the People: American National Identity in Presidential Rhetoric* (College Station: Texas A&M University Press, 2004), 70.

37. On FDR and national identity, see Stuckey, *Defining Americans*, 211–17.

38. Eric Foner, *The Story of American Freedom* (New York: W. W. Norton, 1998), 165. In this exceptional study, Foner traced the changing meaning of freedom over the centuries from colonial times to the present. He focused in particular on the question of who among Americans deserved that freedom, the answer to which served as a proxy for whom was included in the definition of the American nation at various points in our history.

39. See Kaufmann, *The Rise and Fall of Anglo-America*, 214–18, for a brief but thorough analysis of public school U.S. history textbooks and the evolving presentation of the American national narrative from the nineteenth century through the 1960s. For a much more detailed treatment of the teaching of American history in public schools from the country's founding through the 1990s, see Nash et al., *History on Trial*. A concise account of these developments from the 1960s through the end of the century appears in Diane Ravitch, *The Language Police: How Pressure Groups Restrict What Students Learn* (New York: Knopf, 2003), 133–38.

40. Stuckey, *Defining Americans*, 283.

Chapter 2. Since the 1960s: Radical Multiculturalism, Its Critics, and How Obama Fits In

1. For a more detailed discussion of the development of multiculturalism and its various forms, see Gary Gerstle, *American Crucible: Race and Nation in the Twentieth Century* (Princeton, NJ: Princeton University Press, 2002), 347–57.

2. Stokely Carmichael and Charles Hamilton, *Black Power* (New York: Vintage Books, 1967), xi; Frantz Fanon, *Wretched of the Earth* (New York: Grove Press, 1965). See also Gerstle, *American Crucible*, 302.

3. Kazin and McCartin, "Introduction," in *Americanism*, eds. Kazin and McCartin, 6.

4. Kwame Anthony Appiah, "Identity against Culture: Understandings of Multiculturalism," *Occasional Papers of the Doreen B. Townsend Center for the Humanities*, no. 1 (1994): 12.

5. Ibid., note 13. In this paper, Appiah offers a singularly trenchant critical analysis of radical multiculturalism.

6. Richard Thompson Ford, *Racial Culture: A Critique* (Princeton, NJ: Princeton University Press, 2005), 5.

7. See, for example, Molefi K. Asante, *Afrocentricity* (Trenton, NJ: Africa World Press, 1988). See Nash et al., *History on Trial*, 117–22 for a summary of the impact Afrocentrism had on history and social studies curricula in the late 1980s and early 1990s.

8. See Jim Sleeper, "Blacks and Jews," *The Nation*, September 9, 1991, 252. See also Massimo Calabresi, "Dispatches Skin Deep 101," *Time*, February 14, 1994.

9. Cornel West, *Race Matters* (New York: Vintage Books, 1994), 7–8 and 142.

10. West, *Race Matters*, 98.

11. Ibid., 8.

12. See Catherine B. Cody, Arthur Woodward, and David Elliott, "Race, Ideology, and the Battle over Curriculum," in *The New Politics of Race and Gender: The 1992 Yearbook of the Politics of Education Association*, ed. Catherine Marshall (London: Routledge, 1994), 51–53 for the quotations and a summary of the affair. See also Robert K. Fullinwider, *Public Education in a Multicultural Society: Policy, Theory, Critique* (Cambridge: Cambridge University Press, 1996), 54–55. Diane Ravitch criticized the radical multicultural approach taken by the authors of the two New York State reports. See her *Left Back: A Century of Battles over School Reform* (New York: Simon & Schuster, 2000), 423–25. Certainly it is open to question whether Jeffries's views on the differences between racial groups are truly a part of multicultural thought, or whether they reflect any recognizable ideology at all considering their content. Nevertheless, the language quoted from the report does reflect a view of the United States and its history that coheres with that of the proponents of the most extreme form of multiculturalism.

13. See New York State Social Studies Development and Review Committee, *One Nation, Many Peoples: A Declaration of Cultural Interdependence* (Albany, NY: State Education Department, 1991), dissent by Arthur Schlesinger Jr. Cited also in Ravitch, *Left Back*, 424.

14. Nash et al., *History on Trial*, 99.

15. Ford, *Racial Culture*, 5.

16. Kwame Anthony Appiah, *The Ethics of Identity* (Princeton, NJ: Princeton University Press, 2005), 145–46. Appiah also clarified the difference between criticizing the prejudices of historical Enlightenment figures and rejecting the Enlightenment as a project (pp. 249–50).

17. Martin Luther King Jr., "Letter from a Birmingham Jail," April 16, 1963, in M.L. King Jr., *Why We Can't Wait* (New York: Penguin, 2000), 108.

18. Martin Luther King Jr., *I Have a Dream: Writings and Speeches That Changed the World* (San Francisco: Harper San Francisco, 1992), 104.

19. Orlando Patterson, *The Ordeal of Integration: Progress and Resentment in America's "Racial" Crisis* (Washington, DC: Civitas/Counterpoint, 1997), 102.

20. The Southern Poverty Law Center described Samuel Francis in 2005 as "a white

nationalist . . . one of the most important voices of the racist right." See "Sam Francis, Voice of the Radical Right, Dies Unexpectedly," *Intelligence Report*, no. 117 (Spring 2005), http://www.splcenter.org/intel/intelreport/article.jsp ?aid=532.

21. Todd Gitlin, *The Twilight of Common Dreams: Why America Is Wracked by Culture Wars* (New York: Metropolitan Books, 1995), 32.

22. Arthur Schlesinger, *The Disuniting of America: Reflections on a Multicultural Society* (New York: W. W. Norton, 1992).

23. See Patterson, *The Ordeal of Integration*.

24. For more on the parallels between multiculturalism and the so-called Christian Right, see Ian Reifowitz, "Same Difference: Radical Multiculturalists, the Christian Right, and American Pluralism," *The New Republic Online*, May 4, 2005; and Ian Reifowitz, "Majority Rules: What the Religious Right and Radical Multiculturalists Have in Common," *The New Republic Online*, August 10, 2005. See also Stephen Macedo, *Diversity and Distrust: Civic Education in a Multicultural Democracy* (Cambridge, MA: Harvard University Press, 2000), 162–65, and Stephen Macedo, "Multiculturalism for the Religious Right? Defending Liberal Civic Education," *Journal of the Philosophy of Education* 29 (1995), 223–38.

25. Reagan Hackleman, "Did Abortion Views Lead to Firing?" KXAN, Austin, TX, July 16, 2010, http://www.kxan.com/dpp/news/local/did-abortion-views-lead -to-firing%3F. The lawsuit itself is available at: http://media2.kxan.com/PDF /CivilRightsLawsuit.pdf.

26. See Michelle Goldberg, *Kingdom Coming: The Rise of Christian Nationalism* (New York: W. W. Norton, 2006).

27. Reifowitz, "Majority Rules."

28. For a broad discussion of this right-wing effort in recent years as well as its roots in prior decades, see Jill Lepore, *The Whites of Their Eyes: The Tea Party's Revolution and the Battle over American History* (Princeton, NJ: Princeton University Press, 2010).

29. Frances FitzGerald, *America Revised: History Schoolbooks in the Twentieth Century* (Boston: Little, Brown, 1979), 58.

30. Mariah Blake, "Revisionaries: How a Group of Texas Conservatives Is Rewriting Your Kids' Textbooks," *Washington Monthly*, January/February 2010.

31. James C. McKinley Jr., "Texas Conservatives Win Curriculum Change," *New York Times*, March 12, 2010. See also "Blogging the Texas Social Studies Debate IV," *Texas Freedom Network* (blog), March 11, 2010, http://tfninsider .org/2010/03/11/blogging-the-social-studies-debate-iv/. The text of the initial document and the changed version appear at the Texas Freedom Network site cited above, and these were picked up (without correction) by numerous other media sources. Jefferson penned the phrase "wall of separation between church

and state" in an 1802 letter to members of a committee of the Danbury Baptist association in the state of Connecticut. The text is available at the Library of Congress website: http://www.loc.gov/loc/lcib/9806/danpre.html.

32. Blake, "Revisionaries."

33. Richard Locker, "Tea Parties Issue Demands to Tennessee Legislators," *The Commercial Appeal* (Memphis, TN), January 13, 2011.

34. For a more detailed discussion of another event that explores the extreme positions taken by some radical multiculturalists, the 1992 battle in Oakland over social studies textbooks, see Gitlin, *The Twilight of Common Dreams*, chapter 1.

35. Obama, *The Audacity of Hope*, 45.

36. Alan Wolfe, *One Nation after All: What Middle-Class Americans Really Think about: God, Country, Family, Racism, Welfare, Immigration, Homosexuality, Work, the Right, the Left, and Each Other* (New York: Viking, 1998), 154.

37. Ibid., 158.

38. Ibid., 161.

39. Fifteen years prior Philip Gleason offered an early formulation of this position that perhaps served as a harbinger of things to come. See pp. 55–57 of his "American Identity and Americanization."

40. Pickus, *True Faith and Allegiance*, 147.

41. Lind, *The Next American Nation*, 351–52. For more on this in early American history, see Jennifer R. Mercieca, *Founding Fictions* (Tuscaloosa: University of Alabama Press, 2010), 34. Mercieca stated, "Political communities are invented and sustained through political fictions."

42. Tamar Jacoby, ed. *Reinventing the Melting Pot: The New Immigrants and What It Means to Be American* (New York: Basic Books, 2004), 14.

43. David Hollinger, *Postethnic America: Beyond Multiculturalism,* rev. ed. (New York: Basic Books, 2006).

44. David Hollinger, "National Solidarity at the End of the Twentieth Century: Reflections on the United States and Liberal Nationalism," *Journal of American History* 84, no. 2 (September 1997): 565. Likewise, see Lind's review of Hollinger's *Postethnic America*, "Review: Mongrel America," *Transition* 69 (1996): 200.

45. David Hollinger, "The Historian's Use of the United States and Vice Versa," in *Rethinking American History in a Global Age*, ed. Bender, 392.

46. Desmond King, *The Liberty of Strangers: Making the American Nation* (Oxford: Oxford University Press, 2005), 167–73.

47. See King, *Making Americans*, 283–86. See also Rogers Smith, *Civic Ideals: Conflicting Visions of Citizenship in U.S. History* (New Haven, CT: Yale University Press, 1997); Gerstle, *American Crucible*; and Gary Gerstle, "Liberty, Coercion, and the Making of Americans," *Journal of American History* 84 (1997): 524–58. Hollinger's "National Solidarity at the End of the Twentieth Century," which

appeared as part of a forum with Gerstle's article in that issue of the *Journal of American History*, challenged Gerstle's conclusion about the future as well as Gerstle's criticisms of his *Postethnic America*.

48. King, *Making Americans*, 291–92. Literally dozens of other books on the topic of unity, diversity, multiculturalism, and American identity have appeared in the past decade-plus. In addition to those discussed in this book, see J. W. Ceaser, *Reconstructing America: The Symbol of America in Modern Thought* (New Haven, CT: Yale University Press, 1997); Ronald Fernandez, *America Beyond Black and White: How Immigrants and Fusions Are Helping Us Overcome the Racial Divide* (Ann Arbor: University of Michigan Press, 2007); Nathan Glazer, *We Are All Multiculturalists Now* (Cambridge, MA: Harvard University Press, 1997); John Higham, *Hanging Together: Unity and Diversity in American Culture* (New Haven, CT: Yale University Press, 2001); Seymour Martin Lipset, *American Exceptionalism: A Double-Edged Sword* (New York: W. W. Norton & Co., 1996); Peter D. Salins, *Assimilation American Style* (New York: Basic Books, 1997).

49. Gary Gerstle, "The Power of Nations," *Journal of American History* 84, no. 2 (1997): 576.

50. Gerstle, *American Crucible*, 373.

51. Gerstle, "Power of Nations," 577. For another take on these debates, see Pickus, *True Faith and Allegiance*, 3–4.

52. King, *Making Americans*, 288, citing Rogers Smith, "Beyond Tocqueville, Myrdal, and Hartz: The Multiple Traditions in America," *American Political Science Review* 87 (1993): 558.

53. Hollinger, *Postethnic America*, 14.

54. Jacoby, *Reinventing the Melting Pot*, 310.

55. Macedo, *Diversity and Distrust*, part III. See also Michael Walzer, *What It Means to Be an American* (New York: Marsilio, 1992), 17–18, and Pickus, *True Faith and Allegiance*, epilogue.

56. Wolffe, *Renegade*, 167.

57. Beasley, *You, the People*, offers close readings of inaugural and State of the Union addresses from 1885 through 2000. She examined how these presidents have discussed issues such as the definition of the American people, the shared beliefs of Americans, immigration, race, and gender.

58. Bill Clinton, "Second Inaugural Address," January 20, 1997, http://www.washingtonpost.com/wp-srv/national/longterm/inaug/mon/speech.htm.

59. George W. Bush, "National Security Strategy," September 17, 2002, http://georgewbush-whitehouse.archives.gov/nsc/nss/2002/index.html. See also King, *The Liberty of Strangers*, 167–68. King also notes that the two most recent former presidents displayed a greater appreciation than their predecessors of the truly multiethnic (in the post-1960s understanding of that concept) nature of American society.

60. Beasley found that in their inaugural and State of the Union addresses, presidents from 1885 to 2000 "dedicated relatively little time" to racial issues other than during specific times of crisis, with Bill Clinton, and, interestingly, Calvin Coolidge, as clear exceptions. See Beasley, *You, the People*, 96, 118–20. See 161–69 on Clinton specifically.

61. Ibid., 119.

62. Toni Morrison, *Playing in the Dark: Whiteness and the Literary Imagination* (New York: Vintage Books, 1993), 47.

63. Danille Taylor-Guthrie, ed., *Conversations with Toni Morrison* (Jackson: University Press of Mississippi, 1994), 10. Morrison did in fact endorse Obama for president on January 28, 2008. The endorsement letter is available at: http://my.barackobama.com/page/community/post/samgrahamfelsen/CGVRG.

64. Theiss-Morse, *Who Counts as an American?*, 49 and 83–84.

65. Melissa Harris-Perry, "I'm Dreaming of a Black Santa," December 13, 2009, The Notion (the blog of *The Nation*), http://www.thenation.com/blog/im-dreaming-black-christmas. See also Stuckey, *Defining Americans*, 7.

66. Ellis Cose, *The End of Anger: A New Generation's Take and Race and Rage* (New York: Ecco, 2011), 7.

67. James T. Kloppenberg, *Reading Obama: Dreams, Hope, and the American Political Tradition* (Princeton, NJ: Princeton University Press, 2010), 151. Kloppenberg's book offers a detailed analysis of American political thought and shows how Obama draws from it in crafting his own approach, one that relies heavily on American pragmatism.

68. Remnick, *The Bridge*, 76. The references are to Dee Brown's *Bury My Heart at Wounded Knee*, and *Farewell to Manzanar*, by Jeanne Wakatsuki Houston and James D. Houston.

69. Ibid., 242.

70. Lind, *The Next American Nation*, 288.

71. See Cose, *The End of Anger*, 9–11.

72. Orlando Patterson, "The New Mainstream," *Newsweek*, November 10, 2008.

73. Patterson, *The Ordeal of Integration*, 157.

74. Patterson, "New Mainstream." See also Orlando Patterson, "Race and Diversity in the Age of Obama," *New York Times*, August 16, 2009.

75. Cose, *End of Anger*, 11.

76. Touré, *Who's Afraid of Post-Blackness? What It Means to Be Black Now* (New York: Free Press, 2011), 172.

77. Sarah Palin, "The Charge of Racism: It's Time to Bury the Divisive Politics of the Past," July 13, 2010, http://www.facebook.com/note.php?note_id=408166998434.

78. For more on Berlin's views on this topic, see Arie M. Dubnov, "Anti-Cosmopolitan

Liberalism: Isaiah Berlin, Jacob Talmon and the Dilemma of National Identity," *Nations and Nationalism* 16, no. 4 (2010): 570–75.

79. Todd Gitlin, "Varieties of Patriotic Experience," in *The Fight Is for Democracy,* ed. George Packer (New York: Perennial, 2003), 138.

80. Richard Rorty, *Achieving Our Country* (Cambridge, MA: Harvard University Press, 1998), 3–4.

Chapter 3. Obama's Search for His Own Identity

1. See Hillel Atalie, "Writers Welcome a Literary U.S. President-Elect," *Associated Press,* November 6, 2008; Michiko Kakutani, "From Books, New President Found Voice," *New York Times,* January 18, 2009; Joe Klein, "The Fresh Face," *Time*, October 15, 2006; Janny Scott, "The Long Run; The Story of Obama, Written by Obama," *New York Times*, May 18, 2008.

2. Kloppenberg, *Reading Obama*, 250–51.

3. Barack Obama, *Dreams from My Father* (New York: Three Rivers Press, 1995, 2004), xiv.

4. Klein, "The Fresh Face."

5. Obama, *Dreams*, xvi.

6. Ibid., 76.

7. Ibid., vii.

8. For much more on the life of Ann Dunham, see Janny Scott, *A Singular Woman: The Untold Story of Barack Obama's Mother* (New York: Riverhead Books, 2011).

9. Obama, *Dreams*, 27.

10. Ibid., 10.

11. Ibid., 30.

12. Ibid., 29–30. A search through the archives of *Life* did not turn up any article that resembled what Obama described. When asked about this, he offered that perhaps the article had appeared in *Ebony* or somewhere else, although no such article seems to have been printed in *Ebony* either. See Kirsten Scharnberg and Kim Barker, "The Not-So-Simple Story of Barack Obama's Youth," *Chicago Tribune*, March 25, 2007. See also Remnick, *The Bridge*, 238–39. Nevertheless, for the purposes of this book where or even whether this article ever ran is largely irrelevant. What matters is that he chose to present this incident as part of his public rhetoric. My book, because it offers an analysis of his rhetoric and is not a biography, operates from that premise regarding any and all statements Obama has made.

13. Obama, *Dreams*, 51.

14. Ibid., 51.

15. Ibid., 51–52.

16. Ibid., 52.

17. Ibid., 49.

18. Ibid., 47.

19. Ibid., 48.

20. Ibid., 60.

21. See Beverly Daniel Tatum, "Talking about Race, Learning about Racism: An Application of Racial Identity Development Theory in the Classroom," *Harvard Educational Review* 62, no. 1 (Spring 1992): 1–24. See also W. E. Cross Jr., *Shades of Black: Diversity in African American Identity* (Philadelphia: Temple University Press, 1991) for more on the five stages of black identity development. See also Beverly Daniel Tatum, *"Why Are All the Black Kids Sitting Together in the Cafeteria?": And Other Conversations about Race* (New York: Basic Books, 1997).

22. Daniel Tatum, "Talking," 10.

23. Obama, *Dreams*, 51.

24. Daniel Tatum, "Talking," 10-11.

25. Ibid., 11.

26. Ibid., 13.

27. Obama, *Dreams*, 25.

28. Ibid., 25–26.

29. Kloppenberg, *Reading Obama*, 88.

30. B.J. Reyes, "Punahou Left Lasting Impression on Obama," *Honolulu Star-Bulletin*, February 8, 2007, http://archives.starbulletin.com/2007/02/08/news/story02.html. The Reyes article quoted Obama's *Punahou Bulletin* piece. See also Michael Haas, *Barack Obama, The Aloha Zen President: How a Son of the 50th State May Revitalize America Based on 12 Multicultual Principles* (Santa Barbara, CA: Praeger, 2011).

31. Obama, *Dreams*, 60.

32. Ibid., 64.

33. Ibid., xv.

34. Ibid., 85.

35. Ibid., 81.

36. Ibid., 85–86.

37. Ibid., 85. Obama reiterated this point in an interview as president with David Remnick. See *The Bridge*, 233–34.

38. Obama, *Dreams*, 88.

39. Ibid., 89.

40. Ibid., 90–91. "Frank" was a pseudonym for Frank Marshall Davis (1905–1987), a black journalist and poet who expressed a radical left political ideology. For more on Davis and Obama, see Remnick, *The Bridge*, 94–97. The Obama campaign confirmed that "Frank" was Davis in a document produced to counteract falsehoods that appeared in Jerome Corsi's *Obama Nation*. The

document, called "Unfit for Publication," can be found at: http://obama.3cdn .net/a74586f9067028c40a_5km6vrqwa.pdf. Corsi also authored *Unfit for Command*, published during the previous presidential campaign, which took aim at then nominee John Kerry. Other than the names of historical figures and his own family members that he mentioned in *Dreams from My Father*, Obama provided pseudonyms for the characters in his memoir. Some of the individuals he discussed were actually composites of more than one person. See Obama, *Dreams*, xvii.

41. Obama, *Dreams*, 91.
42. Wolffe, *Renegade*, 178.
43. Ibid., 149–50.
44. William Finnegan, "The Candidate," *The New Yorker*, May 31, 2004.
45. Obama, *Dreams*, 98.
46. Ibid., 96.
47. Ibid., 97.
48. Wolffe, *Renegade*, 150.
49. Tim Jones, "Barack Obama: Mother Not Just a Girl from Kansas," *Chicago Tribune*, March 27, 2007.
50. Obama, *Dreams*, 98.
51. Ibid., 98–99.
52. Ibid., 99.
53. Ibid., 99–100.
54. Ibid., 100.
55. Ibid., 100.
56. Ibid., 101–2.
57. Ibid., 103.
58. Ibid., 104.
59. Ibid., 104.
60. Ibid., 109.
61. Ibid., 110.
62. Ibid., 111.
63. Ibid., 111.
64. Monica Davey, "As Quickly as Overnight, A Democratic Star Is Born," *New York Times*, March 18, 2004. For more on that campaign, see Remnick, *The Bridge*, 355–83.
65. Don Terry, "The Skin Game: Do White Voters Like Obama Because 'He's Not Really Black'?" *Chicago Tribune*, October 24, 2004.
66. Obama, *The Audacity of Hope*, 274.
67. Martin Luther King Jr., *Where Do We Go from Here: Chaos or Community?* (New York: Harper & Row, 1967), 53.

68. Obama, *Dreams*, 12.

69. Ibid., 120–21.

70. Ibid., 124.

71. Ibid., 127.

72. Monice Mitchell, "Son Finds Inspiration in the Dreams of His Father," *Hyde Park Herald*, August 23, 1995.

73. Obama, *Dreams*, 134–35.

74. Marty Kaufman is a pseudonym for Jerry Kellman. For more on Kellman's life and career, please see Phil Davidson, "Obama's Mentor," *Illinois Issues*, March 2009, http://illinoisissues.uis.edu/archives/2009/03/kellman.html. See also Remnick, *The Bridge*, 131–35.

75. Obama, *Dreams*, 152.

76. Ibid., 190.

77. Ibid., 194.

78. Ibid., 195.

79. Ibid., 197.

80. Ibid., 198.

81. Ibid., 199.

82. Ibid., 199–200.

83. Ibid., 202.

84. Ibid., 203–4.

85. Ibid., 278.

86. Ibid., 204.

87. Ibid., 261.

88. Amanda Ripley, "The Story of Barack Obama's Mother," *Time*, April 9, 2008.

89. Obama, *The Audacity of Hope*, 242. He discussed his parents' and grandparents' religious and spiritual views in some detail, focusing especially on his mother. See pp. 240–44. See also Charles Babington and Darlene Superville, "Obama 'Christian By Choice': President Responds to Questioner," *Associated Press*, September 28, 2010.

90. Obama, *The Audacity of Hope*, 242.

91. Obama, *Dreams*, 284.

92. Ibid., 286.

93. Ibid., 294.

94. Ibid., 437. For more on Martin Delany, see Molefi Kete Asante, *100 Greatest African Americans: A Biographical Encyclopedia* (Amherst, NY: Prometheus Books, 2002), 103–5.

95. Obama, *Dreams*, 437–38.

96. Ibid., 438.

97. Derrick Bell, *Faces at the Bottom of the Well: The Permanence of Racism* (New

York: Basic Books, 1992), ix. Obama was Bell's student at Harvard Law School and a supporter of Bell's protests against the law faculty's lack of tenured non-white women. For more on their relationship, see Remnick, *The Bridge*, 213–14 and 263–64. In August 2008 Bell predicted that Obama could prove to be this country's "salvation." See Jonathan Tilove, "For Scholars of Race, an Obama Dilemma," *Seattle Times*, August 13, 2008. Nevertheless, Bell remained deeply pessimistic, recently telling Ellis Cose that racism remains "permanent." (Cose, *The End of Anger*, 115).

98. Wolffe, *Renegade*, 152.
99. Obama, *Dreams*, x.
100. Wolffe, *Renegade*, 152.
101. Obama, *Dreams*, xi.
102. Wolffe, *Renegade*, 152.
103. Obama, *Dreams*, 438.
104. Ibid., 438–39.

Chapter 4. Obama on Racial Discrimination: Causes, Effects, and Policies to Combat It

1. Melissa Harris-Lacewell (now Harris-Perry), *Barbershops, Bibles, and BET: Everyday Talk and Black Political Thought* (Princeton, NJ: Princeton University Press, 2004), xxii.
2. Harris-Lacewell, *Barbershops, Bibles, and BET*, 26–27.
3. For example, on January 16, 2010, the Republican Party of Los Angeles held an event called "The Dr. Martin Luther King Jr. Legacy Awards." The event's invitation referred to King as "a Republican who stood for individual responsibility." The invitation was posted at: http://www.facebook.com/event.php?eid=211295545094, but is no longer there.
4. King Jr., *Where Do We Go*, 123.
5. Ibid., 44.
6. Ibid., 50.
7. Ibid., 17.
8. Ibid., 132.
9. Ibid., 50–52.
10. Martin Luther King Jr., *Why We Can't Wait* (New York: Penguin, 2000, originally published in 1964), 29.
11. Obama, *Dreams*, 141.
12. Hank DeZutter, "What Makes Obama Run," *Chicago Reader*, December 8, 1995.
13. Ted Kleine (aka Edward McClellan), "Is Bobby Rush in Trouble?," *Chicago Reader*, March 17, 2000.
14. Barack Obama, "Keep Church and State Separate," *Hyde Park Herald*, April 7, 1999.

15. Barack Obama, "Rethinking Approach to Juvenile Crime," *Hyde Park Herald*, April 16, 1997.

16. See, for example, remarks by Barack Obama, Howard University Convocation, September 28, 2007; Barack Obama, "Commentary: Senator Barack Obama," *Los Angeles Sentinel*, November 22, 2007.

17. Barack Obama, "Getting the Lead out of Our Children," *Hyde Park Herald*, March 25, 1998.

18. Barack Obama, "Ideologues Frustrate Gun Law," *Hyde Park Herald*, December 29, 1999.

19. Barack Obama, "Obama Sets Legislative Sights on Metra Neglect," *Hyde Park Herald*, November 5, 2003.

20. Barack Obama, "Laws Help Ex-Offenders Re-enter Society," *Hyde Park Herald*, April 3, 2002.

21. Barack Obama, "Special Session Brings Some Hard Choices," *Hyde Park Herald*, July 3, 2002.

22. King Jr., "Letter from Birmingham Jail," April 16, 1963.

23. King Jr., *Why We Can't Wait*, 80.

24. Ibid., 84.

25. Ibid., 83.

26. Ibid., 148–51.

27. Remarks by Martin Luther King Jr., Constitutional Convention of the American Federation of Labor and Congress of Industrial Organizations (AFL-CIO), December 11, 1961. Reprinted in *A Testament of Hope: The Essential Writings and Speeches of Martin Luther King Jr.*, ed. James Melvin Washington (San Francisco: Harper San Francisco, 1991), 206.

28. Fox Butterfield, "First Black Elected to Head Harvard's Law Review," *New York Times*, February 6, 1990.

29. Wolffe, *Renegade*, 324.

30. Obama, *The Audacity of Hope*, 277.

31. Ibid., 282–83.

32. Ibid., 276–77.

33. Ibid., 279.

34. Ibid., 282.

35. Ibid., 278.

36. Ibid., 279.

37. Cose, *The End of Anger*, 231.

38. Patterson, *The Ordeal of Integration*, 201. See also Paul M. Sniderman and Thomas Piazza, *The Scar of Race* (Cambridge, MA: Harvard University Press, 1993), 136.

39. Obama, *The Audacity of Hope*, 280.

40. Ibid., 288–89.

41. Ibid., 292.
42. Ibid., 291.
43. Ibid., 292.
44. Ibid., 295.
45. Ibid., 300.
46. Ibid., 301. For a recent discussion of urban black poverty that carefully presents all sides of the debate over its causes, see William Julius Wilson, *More Than Just Race: Being Black and Poor in the Inner City* (New York: W.W. Norton, 2009). Wilson, like Obama, avoids traditionally liberal and conservative approaches to this matter.
47. Obama, *The Audacity of Hope*, 301.
48. Ibid., 302.
49. Ibid., 302–3.
50. Ibid., 303.
51. Wolffe, *Renegade*, 152.
52. Ibid., 158.
53. Ibid., 153.
54. Jeff Zeleny, "When It Comes to Race Obama Makes His Point—With Subtlety," *Chicago Tribune*, June 26, 2005.
55. Jeff Zeleny, "Obama Grills Nominee on '87 Racial Remarks," *Chicago Tribune*, June 10, 2005.
56. Zeleny, "When It Comes to Race."
57. Lisa De Moraes, "Kanye West's Torrent of Criticism, Live on NBC," *Washington Post*, September 3, 2005.
58. Jeff Zeleny, "A Judicious Obama Turns up the Heat," *Chicago Tribune*, September 12, 2005.
59. Mike Dorning, "Obama Rips U.S. Effort after Katrina," *Chicago Tribune*, January 30, 2007.
60. See john powell, "Post-racialism or Targeted Universalism?" *Denver University Law Review* 86 (2009): 785–806. powell does not capitalize his name.
61. Obama, *The Audacity of Hope*, 293. john powell cited the paragraph that includes this quotation from Obama in his *Denver University Law Review* article when claiming that the latter supported targeted universalism. See powell, "Post-racialism or Targeted Universalism?," 804. In a more recent article, powell contended that the Obama administration has leaned too heavily on universal approaches that are not targeted enough. See john powell, "Obama's Universal Approach Leaves Many Excluded," *Huffington Post*, December 11, 2009, http://www.huffingtonpost.com/john-a-powell/obamas-universal-approach_b_389147.html.
62. Obama, *The Audacity of Hope*, 294.

63. For more on this, see Martin Gilens, *Why Americans Hate Welfare: Race, Media, and the Politics of Antipoverty Policy* (Chicago: University of Chicago Press, 2000), and on Tea Party supporters specifically (and the Tea Party phenomenon more broadly), see Vanessa Williamson, Theda Skocpol, and John Coggin, "The Tea Party and the Remaking of Republican Conservatism," *Perspectives on Politics* 9, no. 1, 25–43. The paper has been expanded into Theda Skocpol and Vanessa Williamson, *The Tea Party and the Remaking of Republican Conservatism* (Oxford: Oxford University Press, 2012).

64. Jon Ward, "Romney: Obama Will Keep Us From Being 'Nation Under God,'" *Huffington Post*, January 2, 2012. Available at: http://www.huffingtonpost.com /2011/12/27/iowa-caucus-2012-live_n_1170077.html#172_romney-obama -will-keep-us-from-being-nation-under-god-.

65. Maureen Dowd, "Oedipus Rex Complex," *New York Times*, January 4, 2012.

66. These comments received widespread media coverage, see for example Charles M. Blow, "The G.O.P.'s 'Black People' Platform," *New York Times*, January 7, 2012. Blow catalogued numerous examples of racially inflammatory rhetoric attributed to Republican presidential candidates. He also discussed another major presidential candidate, Representative Ron Paul of Texas, who published numerous newsletters in the early 1990s under his name that were rife with all kinds of bigotry, including relating to black recipients of entitlements. No bigoted public statements, however, have been attributed to Paul during the 2012 campaign or in recent years.

67. The video is widely available on the Internet.

68. Blow, "The G.O.P.'s 'Black People' Platform."

69. The video is available at: http://www.mediaite.com/tv/newt-gingrich-targets-elite -media-again-in-sc-victory-speech/.

70. Philip Rucker, "Gingrich Promises To Slash Taxes, Calls Obama 'Food Stamp President'," *Washington Post*, May 14, 2011. Charles Blow also included Gingrich's use of this phrase in the above-cited January 7, 2012, column, presumably written just before Gingrich repeated it on the evening of January 6.

71. *New York Times* Editorial, "Mr. Gingrich's Deceptions," January 23, 2012.

72. Obama, *The Audacity of Hope*, 66–67.

Chapter 5. Candidate and President Obama's Broader Rhetoric on Race

1. For a discussion of the varied responses from black Americans to the way Obama has approached race, see Randall Kennedy, *The Persistence of the Color Line: Racial Politics and the Obama Presidency* (New York: Pantheon Books, 2011), 66–105. Kennedy explores the matter of race and Obama from numerous angles in this profoundly insightful collection of essays.

2. Stanley Crouch, "What Obama Isn't: Black Like Me on Race," *New York Daily News*, November 2, 2006; Debra J. Dickerson, "Colorblind: Barack Obama

Would Be the Great Black Hope in the Next Presidential Race—If He Were Actually Black," December 22, 2006, *Salon.com*, http://www.salon.com/opinion /feature/2007/01/22/obama/index_np.html.

3. William Douglas, "Blacks Urged to Vote on Issues," *Seattle Times,* February 11, 2007. It is worth noting that ultimately Reverend Sharpton announced that he was "absolutely supportive" of Obama over Clinton for the Democratic nomination for president, although he chose for strategic reasons not to officially endorse one over the other. See Adam Serwer and Michael Saul, "During Rally, Al Sharpton Says He's Keeping Support for Obama Quiet," *New York Daily News*, March 19, 2008.

4. Leonard Pitts Jr., "Concentrate on Obama's Record, Not His Color," *Miami Herald*, August 15, 2007.

5. Remnick, *The Bridge*, 18.

6. Recording available at: http://www.npr.org/templates/story/story.php?storyId =12669366.

7. Zeleny, "When It Comes to Race."

8. Barack Obama, *The Audacity of Hope*, 15.

9. Don Terry, "The Skin Game."

10. Recording available at: http://www.npr.org/templates/story/story.php?storyId =7630250.

11. Barack Obama, "Commentary: Senator Barack Obama," *Los Angeles Sentinel*, November 22, 2007. A very similar article also appeared on December 5, 2007, in the *Chicago Defender* and the *Austin Weekly News*. While all three of these are publications aimed at a black audience, it is worth noting that the article was also posted on the campaign's website at: http://my.barackobama.com/page /community/post/samgrahamfelsen/Cxms. He also mentioned the Wilson case in the aforementioned statement on the Jena Six of September 13. Obama's thoughts on these cases were thus widely available in the mainstream media and to all voters.

12. "Wilson Released after Two Years behind Bars for Teen Sex Conviction," CNN, October 27, 2007, http://www.cnn.com/2007/US/law/10/26/wilson.freed/index .html.

13. Jim Farber, "Geraldine Ferraro Lets Her Emotions Do the Talking," *Daily Breeze* (Torrance, CA), March 7, 2008.

14. Rebecca Sinderbrand, "Ferraro: They're Attacking Me Because I'm White," CNN, March 11, 2008, http://www.cnn.com/2008/POLITICS/03/11/ferraro .comments/index.html.

15. Gene Maddaus, "Ferraro Defends Controversial Remarks on Barack Obama," *Daily Breeze*, March 11, 2008.

16. John McCormick and Mark Silva, "Obama: Stop 'Slicing and Dicing' Voters by Race," *The Swamp* (the blog of the *Chicago Tribune*), March 12, 2008, http://www.swamppolitics.com/news/politics/blog/2008/03/obama_stop_slicing_and_dicing.html.

17. Brian Ross and Rehab El-Buri, "Obama's Pastor: God Damn America, U.S. to Blame for 9/11," *ABC News*, March 13, 2008, http://abcnews.go.com/Blotter/story?id=4443788. For a discussion of the context surrounding this quotation, see Roland Martin, "The Full Story behind Wright's "God Damn America" Sermon," March 21, 2008, *CNN: AC 360* (blog), http://ac360.blogs.cnn.com/2008/03/21/the-full-story-behind-wright's-"god-damn-america"-sermon/.

18. Pew Research Center, *Obama Speech on Race Arguably Biggest Event of Campaign* (Washington, DC, March 27, 2008), http://pewresearch.org/pubs/777/obama-wright-news-interest.

19. Obama, *The Audacity of Hope*, 51.

20. Wise, *Between Barack and a Hard Place*, 41.

21. Ibid., 91

22. Ibid., 91–92.

23. Ibid., 40.

24. Ibid., 41.

25. On a number of other occasions, Obama employed similar language about recognizing children of all ethnic backgrounds as "our kids." See Barack Obama, All-American President Forum, Democratic Candidates, June 28, 2007; remarks by Barack Obama, National Education Association Annual Meeting, July 5, 2007.

26. "Reverend Wright at the National Press Club," April 28, 2008. *New York Times* transcript, http://www.nytimes.com/2008/04/28/us/politics/28text-wright.html?pagewanted=1&_r=1.

27. Jonathan Martin and Amie Parnes, "McCain: Obama Not an Arab, Crowd Boos," *Politico.com*, October 10, 2008, http://www.politico.com/news/stories/1008/14479.html.

28. Gwen Ifill, *The Breakthrough: Politics and Race in the Age of Obama* (New York, Doubleday, 2009), 30–31.

29. Ifill, *The Breakthrough*, 53–54.

30. Marc Ambinder, "Race Over?," *The Atlantic*, January/February 2009.

31. There exist hundreds if not thousands of articles on this affair, the details of which I will not go into here. For my take, please see Ian Reifowitz, "When Speaking about Race, Choose Words Carefully," *Post Star*, July 5, 2009.

32. Barack Obama, interview on *NBC Nightly News with Brian Williams*, May 29, 2009. Available at: http://www.huffingtonpost.com/2009/05/29/white-house-sotomayor-use_n_209262.html.

Chapter 6. Obama's Vision of National Identity and National Unity

1. Theiss-Morse, *Who Counts as an American?*, 172.
2. Andrea Stone, "Obama's Children's Book Ignites Controversy," *AOL News*, November 16, 2010, http://www.aolnews.com/2010/11/16/fox-headline-on-obama-kids-book-ignites-sitting-bull-controvers/. Cheney placed a rendering, without any explanatory text, of "Sitting Bull's Grave" on a page that contains drawings of other sites or monuments, including the Tomb of the Unknown Soldier; Mount Rushmore; the Alamo; the Portrait Monument of Lucretia Mott, Elizabeth Cady Stanton, and Susan B. Anthony; and the Vietnam Veterans Memorial. The page is called "'I' Is for Ideals." Her book consists of twenty-six pages, one for each letter of the alphabet, with each depicting something about America.
3. Stone, "Obama's Children's Book Ignites Controversy."
4. Lynne Cheney, *America: A Patriotic Primer* (New York: Simon & Schuster, 2002), 9.
5. Cheney, *America*, 1.
6. Barack Obama, *Of Thee I Sing: A Letter to My Daughters* (New York: Alfred A. Knopf, 2010), 15, 29.
7. Ibid., 23.
8. Ibid., 9.
9. Cheney, *America*, 17.
10. Obama, *Of Thee I Sing*, 24, 25.
11. Ibid., 29.
12. Ibid., 30.
13. Wolffe, *Renegade*, 237.
14. Obama, *The Audacity of Hope*, 62–63. In a toast he made at a summit of the leaders of the APEC (Asia-Pacific Economic Cooperation) countries on November 13, 2011, Obama did praise Hawaii as coming "about as close as you'll come to a true melting pot of cultures."
15. Obama spoke broadly about American unity on dozens of other occasions as well. For a few representative examples beyond the ones discussed in the following pages, see his speeches of: April 6, 2005, October 20, 2007, December 24, 2008, January 19, 2009, February 5, 2009, May 17, 2009, and May 22, 2009.
16. Obama, *The Audacity of Hope*, 4.
17. Ibid., 13.
18. Ibid., 67.
19. Ibid., 80.
20. Ibid., 258.
21. Ibid., 259.
22. Cathy Lynn Grossman, "An Inaugural First: Obama Acknowledges 'Non-Believers,'" *USA Today*, January 22, 2009.

23. "'Welfare Queen' Becomes Issue in Reagan Campaign," *New York Times*, February 15, 1976. For a trenchant analysis of how political campaigns have used implicit race-based appeals to increase their support among white voters, see Tali Mendenberg, *The Race Card: Campaign Strategy, Implicit Messages, and the Norm of Equality* (Princeton, NJ: Princeton University Press, 2001).

24. The remarks appear in Juliet Eilperin, "Palin's 'Pro-America Areas' Remark: Extended Version," *The Trail* (Campaign blog at the *Washington Post*), October 17, 2008, http://voices.washingtopost.com/44/2008/10/17/palin_clarifies_her _pro-americ.html. I will discuss them in more detail in chapter 8.

25. Michael Jonas, "The Downside of Diversity," *Boston Globe*, August 5, 2007.

26. Alberto Alesina and Edward Glaeser, *Fighting Poverty in the US and Europe: A World of Difference* (Oxford: Oxford University Press, 2005), 11. See also Eduarto Porter, "Race and the Social Contract," *New York Times*, March 31, 2008, who cites a number of other studies that make similar points. There is certainly a question about how the growing ethnic diversity in Europe will affect support for social spending there.

27. Erzo F.P. Luttmer, "Group Loyalty and the Taste for Redistribution," *Journal of Political Economy* 109, no. 3 (2001): 501.

28. Alberto Alesina, Reza Baqir, William Easterly, "Public Goods and Ethnic Divisions," *Quarterly Journal of Economics* 114, no. 4 (November 1999): 1243.

29. Appiah, *The Ethics of Identity*, 24.

30. Obama, *The Audacity of Hope*, 39.

31. Richard Alba and Victor Nee, *Remaking the American Mainstream: Assimilation and Contemporary Immigration* (Cambridge, MA: Harvard University Press, 2003), 11.

32. Alba and Nee, *Remaking the American Mainstream*, 13.

33. Samuel Huntington, "The Hispanic Challenge," *Foreign Policy*, no. 141 (March/April 2004): 30. See also Samuel Huntington, *Who Are We? The Challenge to America's National Identity* (New York: Simon & Schuster, 2004).

34. Jack Citrin, Amy Lerman, Michael Murakami, and Kathryn Pearson, "Testing Huntington: Is Hispanic Immigration a Threat to American Identity?" *Perspectives in Politics* 5, no. 1 (March 2007): 31.

35. Pew Research Center, *Muslim Americans: Middle Class and Mostly Mainstream* (Washington, DC, May 22, 2007), http://pewresearch.org/pubs/483/muslim -americans.

36. Paul Gallis et al., *Muslims in Europe: Integration Policies in Selected Countries* (Washington, DC: Report for Congress produced by the Congressional Research Service, November 18, 2005), http://www.fas.org/sgp/crs/row/RL33166.pdf. The report examines the U.K., France, Germany, and Spain.

37. The quotation from Husain appears in Johann Hari, "Renouncing Islamism: To

the Brink and Back Again," *The Independent,* November 16, 2009, http://www
.independent.co.uk/opinion/commentators/johann-hari/renouncing-islamism
-to-the-brink-and-back-again-1821215.html. For a brief, cogent analysis of the
failure to integrate Muslim immigrants in Britain and Germany, see also Kenan
Malik, "Assimilation's Failure, Terrorism's Rise," *New York Times,* July 7, 2011.

38. Remarks of Denis McDonough, March 6, 2011, http://www.whitehouse.gov
/the-press-office/2011/03/06/remarks-denis-mcdonough-deputy-national
-security-advisor-president-prepa.

39. Obama, *The Audacity of Hope,* 309.

40. Ibid., 310.

41. Ibid., 318.

42. Ibid., 274.

43. Ibid., 312.

44. Ibid., 312.

45. Ibid., 313.

46. Ibid., 313.

47. Ibid., 315–16.

48. Ibid., 317–18.

49. See Andrea Nill, "Angle and Vitter Use the Same Photo of 'Illegal Aliens' in
Racially-Tinged Attack Ad," *ThinkProgress,* October 6, 2010, http://think
progress.org/2010/10/06/vitter-angle-immigration/.

50. Morris Workman, "Angle Finds Receptive Audience in Mesquite," *Mesquite
Local News,* October 1, 2010. Frankford was annexed by Dallas in 1975. See
Jeff Simon, "Angle: Two American Cities under Sharia Law," CNN, October
9, 2010, http://politicalticker.blogs.cnn.com/2010/10/09/angle-two-american
-cities-under-sharia-law/.

51. Matthew Yglesias, "Anchor Babies, the Ground Zero Mosque, and Other
Scapegoats," *Washington Post,* August 8, 2010.

52. This language was changed in the revised bill, HB 2162. The original language in SB 1070 mandated that officers do so whenever they are engaged in
"lawful contact" with a suspect. See House Bill 2162, http://www.azleg.gov
/FormatDocument.asp?inDoc=/legtext/49leg/2r/bills/hb2162c.htm. On the
original bill, see Senate Bill 1070, http://www.azleg.gov/FormatDocument
.asp?inDoc=/legtext/49leg/2r/bills/sb1070s.htm.

53. Jay Reeves, "Alabama Immigration Law Spurs Exodus from Schools," *Associated
Press,* October 1, 2011.

54. Antonieta Cádiz, "Obama asegura que ley de Alabama es anti inmigrante," *La
Opinión,* November 9, 2011.

55. Julia Preston and John H. Cushman Jr., "Obama to Permit Young Migrants to
Remain in the U.S.," *New York Times,* June 16, 2012.

Chapter 7. Obama's Narrative of American History and Our Place in the World

1. Remarks as delivered by Barack Obama, Madison, WI, February 12, 2008.
2. Nash et al., *History on Trial*, 7.
3. Ibid., 15.
4. See Kazin and McCartin, "Introduction," in *Americanism*, ed. Kazin and McCartin, 6–9.
5. Transcript of Obama's remarks and crowd response is available at: http://archives.cnn.com/TRANSCRIPTS/0801/03/se.04.html.
6. Katha Pollitt, "Put Out No Flags," *The Nation*, September 20, 2001.
7. Obama, *The Audacity of Hope*, 115.
8. Ibid., 274–75.
9. See also Sheryl Gay Stolberg, "And Now, the Cheerleader in Chief," *New York Times*, January 30, 2011. Stolberg cited Obama's consistent record of praising "American greatness."
10. Obama, *Dreams*, 198.
11. Jillian Rayfield, "Bachmann: America Was Founded on Diversity (Video)," Iowans for Tax Relief, January 21, 2011, http://tpmdc.talkingpointsmemo.com/2011/01/bachmann-america-was-founded-on-diversity-video.php.
12. Proclamation issued April 2, 2010, Virginia Governor Bob McDonnell, "Confederate History Month," http://www.governor.virginia.gov/OurCommonwealth/Proclamations/2010/ConfederateHistoryMonth.cfm.
13. Anita Kumar and Rosalind S. Helderman, "McDonnell's Confederate History Month Proclamation Irks Civil Rights Leaders," *Washington Post*, April 7, 2010.
14. Quoted in "Gov. McDonnell's Airbrushing of Virginia History," *Washington Post*, April 7, 2010.
15. Statement of Governor Bob McDonnell, April 7, 2010, http://www.governor.virginia.gov/news/viewRelease.cfm?id=111.
16. Kumar and Helderman, "McDonnell's Confederate History Proclamation Irks."
17. Obama, *The Audacity of Hope*, 332.
18. Ibid., 333.
19. On World War I through the Cold War, see Ibid., 334–42.
20. See Karen Tumulty, "American Exceptionalism: An Old Idea and a New Political Battle," *Washington Post*, November 29, 2010.
21. For a summary of conservative commentators accusing Obama of having "apologized" for America during various foreign appearances in the spring of 2009 (including the Strasbourg speech), see "Fox Hosts Revive Fox-Manufactured Obama 'Apology Tour,'" *Media Matters for America*, June 3, 2009, http://mediamatters.org/research/200906030039.
22. "Race to the Bottom," *New York Times*, December 9, 2011.

23. Sarah Palin, *America by Heart: Reflections on Family, Faith, and Flag* (New York: Harper Collins, 2010), 69.

24. Obama made similar remarks about common humanity and building bridges aimed at international audiences many times. See, for example, remarks by Barack Obama, March 20, 2009; remarks by Barack Obama, April 7, 2009; remarks by Barack Obama, April 23, 2009; remarks by Barack Obama, July 11, 2009.

25. Joe Jackson and Bill Hutchinson, "Plan for Mosque near World Trade Center Site Moves Ahead," *Daily News*, May 6, 2010.

26. Mail Foreign Service, "'We Don't Want to Upset 9/11 Families But We Have to Balance Diversity': Mosque near Ground Zero Gets Go-Ahead," *Daily Mail* (U.K.), May 26, 2010.

27. It is worth noting that George W. Bush also spoke in similar terms, making clear that the United States was at war not with Islam but with groups who had falsely interpreted Islam to justify mass murder. Bush consistently spoke warmly about Islam as a religion and emphasized the positive contributions of Muslims to American life. Michael Gerson, Bush's chief speechwriter from 2001 to 2006, praised Obama's iftar speech and noted the similarities on that front between the two presidents' public rhetoric. See Michael Gerson, "Obama's Mosque Duty," *Washington Post*, August 16, 2010.

28. Ronald Reagan, "Farewell Address," January 11, 1989, http://www.washington post.com/wp-srv/national/longterm/inaug/mon/speech.htm.

29. David Brooks, "Obama, Gospel and Verse," *New York Times*, April 26, 2007. For more on Obama and Niebuhr, see Johann Hari, "Scribbled in the Margins: The Character of the Next President," *The Independent* (U.K.), October 16, 2008.

30. Remarks as delivered by Barack Obama, Madison, WI, February 12, 2008.

31. For an example of Obama offering a detailed chronology of events specifically relating to gender equality throughout American history, see his speech at the National Women's Law Center of November 10, 2005.

32. Remarks by Barack Obama, March 21, 2007; remarks by Barack Obama, May 2, 2007; remarks by Barack Obama, May 17, 2007.

33. Remnick, *The Bridge*, 585.

34. Sheryl Gay Stolberg, "Marking King Day, From Oval Office to Soup Kitchen," *New York Times*, January 18, 2010.

35. Kathy Keely and Judy Keen, "Nation Salutes Its War Dead on Memorial Day," *USA Today*, May 25, 2009.

36. Jake Tapper, "Bust of MLK Joins Obama in Oval Office," *Political Punch* (ABC News blog), March 18, 2009, http://blogs.abcnews.com/political punch/2009/03/bust-of-mlk-joi.html.

37. Barack Obama, interview on "The Tom Joyner Morning Show," August 30, 2011. Transcript available at: http://www.blackamericaweb.com/?q=print/news /moving_america_news/31939.

38. Josh Gerstein, "Norman Rockwell Painting Sends Rare White House Message on Race," *Politico.com*, August 24, 2011, http://www.politico.com/news/stories /0811/61677.html.

39. Obama's language closely echoed widely publicized remarks made a few weeks earlier by Elizabeth Warren, who was running as a Democratic candidate for the U.S. Senate from Massachusetts. Warren had previously served in the Obama administration, helping to set up the Consumer Financial Protection Bureau.

40. Charles Riley, "Obama Unveils $3.8 Trillion Budget," *CNNMoney*, February 13, 2012, http://money.cnn.com/2012/02/13/news/economy/obama_budget /index.htm?hpt=hp_t1.

Chapter 8. Rejecting Obama's America: Right-Wing Exclusionists and Left-Wing Race Critics

1. See *New York Times*/CBS Poll, *Obama's 100th Day in Office*, April 27, 2009, http://documents.nytimes.com/new-york-times-cbs-news-poll-obama-s-100th -day-in-office#p=1. The poll was followed up by a series of interviews that found strong optimism among both blacks and whites. See Susan Saulny, "Voices Reflect Rising Sense of Racial Optimism," *New York Times*, May 2, 2009; Pew Research Center, *Blacks Upbeat about Black Progress, Prospects* (Washington, DC, January 12, 2010), http://pewsocialtrends.org/pubs/749/blacks-upbeat-about -black-progress-obama-election; Gallup, *U.S. Waiting for Race Relations to Improve under Obama*, October 16-19, 2009, http://www.gallup.com/poll/124181/U.S. -Waiting-Race-Relations-Improve-Obama.aspx; ABC/*Washington Post* Poll, January 12–15, 2010, http://www.washingtonpost.com/wp-srv/politics/polls /postpoll_011610.html; CNN/Opinion Research Poll, July 16–21, 2010, http://i2.cdn.turner.com/cnn/2010/images/07/22/rel10a9b.pdf. See question 12, which found similar optimism among Hispanics as well.

2. See Sarah Kershaw, "Talk about Race? Relax, It's O.K." *New York Times*, January 15, 2009.

3. Marx, D. M., S. J. Ko, and R. A. Friedman, "The 'Obama Effect': How a Salient Role Model Reduces Race-Based Performance Differences," *Journal of Experimental Social Psychology* 45, no. 4 (2009): 953-56. See also Sam Dillon, "Study Sees an Obama Effect as Lifting Black Test-Takers," *New York Times*, January 22, 2009.

4. Cose, *The End of Anger*, 33.

5. Ibid., 35.

6. Eugene Robinson, "What We're Not Talking About," *Washington Post*, April 3, 2009.

7. Unless otherwise noted, Limbaugh's remarks are from *The Rush Limbaugh Show*. For a collection of Limbaugh's most divisive remarks on racial issues during the first nine months of the Obama administration, see Jonathan Chait, "Color Commentator: Rush Limbaugh's Race Obsession," *The New Republic*, November 2, 2009. For a collection of remarks by other right-wing media figures, some more prominent than others, where they called Obama, Attorney General Eric Holder, or the administration's policies "racist" either directly or indirectly during the administration's first eighteen months, see "One Year Later: Right-Wing Media Routinely Call Obama Racist," *Media Matters for America*, July 28, 2010, http://mediamatters.org/research/201007280007. See also Joan Walsh, "Right-Wing Racism on the Rise," *Salon.com*, July 29, 2009, http://www.salon.com/news/opinion/joan_walsh/politics/2009/07/29/beck/.

8. Sarah Palin, "Statement on the Current Health Care Debate," August 7, 2009, http://www.facebook.com/note.php?note_id=113851103434.

9. Michael Scherer, "'You Lie!': Representative Joe Wilson's Outburst," *Time*, September 10, 2009.

10. Maureen Dowd, "Boy, Oh Boy," *New York Times*, September 12, 2009.

11. "Carter Sees Racism in Wilson's Outburst," *Associated Press*, September 15, 2009.

12. E.J. Dionne Jr., "What Fuels the Grass Roots Rage," *Washington Post*, February 11, 2010.

13. David Neiwert, *The Eliminationists: How Hate Talk Radicalized the American Right* (Sausalito, CA: Polipoint Press, 2009), 12.

14. Ibid., 100.

15. Ibid., 24.

16. Ibid., 116.

17. Juliet Eilperin, "Palin's 'Pro-America Areas' Remark: Extended Version."

18. Chuck Norris, "Don't Tread on Me," *Human Events*, September 22, 2009, http://www.humanevents.com/article.php?id=33648&page=1#c1.

19. Kelley Shannon, "Perry Fires Up Anti-Tax Crowd," *Dallas Morning News*, April 15, 2009. One representative group within the secessionist movement is the Texas Nationalist Movement. Their website is at: http://www.texasnationalist.com/.

20. Chuck Norris, "I May Run for President of Texas," *World Net Daily*, March 9, 2009.

21. Dan Roem, "Health Care Law Has Wamp Hoping against Secession," *Hotline on Call* (blog of *The National Journal*), July 23, 2010, http://hotlineoncall.nationaljournal.com/archives/2010/07/health_care_law.php.

22. "Republican Zach Wamp Avows 'We Will Not Secede from the Union' if He's Elected Tenn. Governor," *Associated Press*, July 24, 2010.

23. Arizona Senate Bill 1069, June 11, 2009, http://www.azleg.gov/legtext/49leg/1r/adopted/s.1069jud.pdf.

24. Pat Kossan, "Arizona Schools Superintendent Pushes Ban on Ethnic Studies," *Arizona Republic*, June 12, 2010, http://www.azcentral.com/news/articles/2009 /06/12/20090612ethnicbanON0612.html.

25. Michael Martinez, "Tucson School Board Suspends Mexican-American Studies Program," CNN, January 12, 2012, http://www.cnn.com/2012/01/11/us /arizona-mexican-american-studies.

26. Remarks by Rick Perry, Liberty University, September 14, 2011. Video available at: http://www.c-span.org/Campaign2012/Events/Rick-Perry-Remarks-at -Liberty-September-14-2011/10737430651-2/.

27. Herman Cain, interview with Rick Persaud, *Christianity Today*, March 21, 2011. Transcript available at: http://www.christianitytoday.com/ct/2011/marchweb -only/qahermancain.html?start=3.

28. Scott Keyes, "Exclusive: Herman Cain Tells ThinkProgress 'I Will Not' Appoint a Muslim in My Administration," March 26, 2011, *ThinkProgress*, http://think progress.org/politics/2011/03/26/153625/herman-cain-muslims/.

29. Christopher Willis, "Obama Rejects Offering Slavery Reparations," *Boston Globe*, August 3, 2008. See also Barack Obama, interview on CBS News, May 17, 2000, http://web.archive.org/web/20010908173835/cbsnews.com/now /story/0,1597,196617-412,00.shtml. In this interview he noted the likelihood that even if a reparations law were passed, the courts would likely strike it down. Obama also told his University of Chicago law school class that, although he was sympathetic to the theory behind reparations, he found them to be "unworkable" as a policy and would not support them. See Remnick, *The Bridge*, 265.

30. Andrew Breitbart, "Video Proof: The NAACP Awards Racism—2010," http:// biggovernment.com/abreitbart/2010/07/19/video-proof-the-naacp-awards -racism2010/. On the website, the following correction appeared at some point after the public had learned the truth about the video: "While Ms. Sherrod made the remarks captured in the first video featured in this post while she held a federally appointed position, the story she tells refers to actions she took before she held that federal position."

31. See "Video Shows USDA Official Saying She Didn't Give 'Full Force' of Help to White Farmer," *FoxNews.Com*, July 20, 2010, http://www.foxnews.com /politics/2010/07/19/clip-shows-usda-official-admitting-withheld-help-white -farmer/Video/.

32. Sheryl Gay Stolberg, Shaila Dawan, and Brian Stelter, "With Apology, Fired Official Is Offered New Job," *New York Times*, July 21, 2010.

33. Joseph Williams, "Shirley Sherrod Returns to the USDA," May 14, 2011, *Politico.com*, http://www.politico.com/news/stories/0511/54970.html.

34. Joan Walsh, "Fox News' 50-State Southern Strategy," *Salon.com*, July 25, 2010, http://www.salon.com/news/opinion/joan_walsh/politics/2010/07/25/fox _news_southern_strategy.

35. Heidi Beirich and Bob Moser, "Defending Dixie: The *Washington Times* Has Always Been Conservative and Error-Prone—Now It's Helping to Popularize Extremist Ideas," *Intelligence Report* (Southern Poverty Law Center), no. 110 (Summer 2003), http://www.splcenter.org/intel/intelreport/article.jsp?aid =57&printable=1.

36. Wesley Pruden, "Obama Bows, The Nation Cringes," *Washington Times*, November 17, 2009.

37. For the text of the remark, see *Top of the Ticket* (blog of the *Los Angeles Times*), May 9, 2008, http://latimesblogs.latimes.com/washington/2008/05/barack -obama-wa.html.

38. For more on this email message on the fifty-seven states and the broader context, see http://urbanlegends.about.com/od/barackobama/a/57_states.htm. It is worth noting that in late 2007 two staff members of the Clinton campaign in Iowa forwarded emails that falsely accused Obama of being a Muslim. The campaign demanded (and received) the resignation of both individuals. See Nedra Pickler, "Clinton Volunteer Asked to Resign," *USA Today*, December 9, 2007.

39. The reference is to the 1962 film (remade in 2004). The original is a classic in every sense of the word, and I must give credit to my father, Jerry Reifowitz, for introducing it to me.

40. Pew Research Center, *Growing Number of Americans Say Obama Is a Muslim* (Washington, DC, August 19, 2009), http://pewresearch.org/pubs/1701/poll -obama-muslim-christian-church-out-of-politics-political-leaders-religious.

41. Newsweek Poll, *Obama/Muslims*, August 27, 2010, http://nw-assets.s3.amazon aws.com/pdf/1004-ftop.pdf.

42. Jason Hancock, "Santorum: Obama Is Detached from the American Experience," *Iowa Independent*, June 25, 2010.

43. Matt Bai, "Ethnic Distinctions, No Longer So Distinctive," *New York Times*, June 30, 2010.

44. Jeremy W. Peters, "Santorum Seeks to Broaden His Appeal Beyond Evangelicals," *New York Times*, January 1, 2012.

45. Adam Aigner-Treworgy, "Santorum Ignores Charge Obama Is a Muslim," CNN, January 23, 2012, http://politicalticker.blogs.cnn.com/2012/01/23/santorum -ignores-charge-obama-is-a-muslim/.

46. Robert Costa, "Gingrich: Obama's 'Kenyan, Anti-Colonial' Worldview," *The Corner: National Review Online*, September 11, 2010, http://www.national review.com/corner/246302/gingrich-obama-s-kenyan-anti-colonial-worldview -robert-costa. Gingrich cited Dinesh D'Souza as the source of this insight about Obama's behavior. D'Souza's views appeared in his article, "How Obama Thinks," *Forbes Magazine*, September 27, 2010, which appeared online on September 9, 2010 (http://www.forbes.com/forbes/2010/0927/politics-socialism-capitalism

-private-enterprises-obama-business-problem.html). See also, Tim Arango, "Magazine's Obama Critique Spurs Fact Checking and Media Soul Searching," *New York Times*, September 25, 2010. Arango characterized D'Souza's writings as "discrediting Mr. Obama's American-ness." D'Souza's views on Obama appear in detail in *The Roots of Obama's Rage* (Washington, DC: Regnery Press, 2010).

47. Chris McGreal, "Newt Gingrich Fires Up Supporters With Promise of Conservative Revolution," *Guardian* (U.K.), January 25, 2012, *Guardian.co.uk*, http://www.guardian.co.uk/world/2012/jan/25/newt-gingrich-conservative-revolution?newsfeed=true.

48. "Race to the Bottom."

49. Susan Moeller, "Jumping on the US Bandwagon for a 'War on Terror,'" *Yale Global Online* (a publication of the Yale Center for the Study of Globalization), June 21, 2007, http://yaleglobal.yale.edu/content/jumping-us-bandwagon-%E2%80%9Cwar-terror%E2%80%9D.

50. John McCain, "After the Shootings, Obama Reminds the Nation of the Golden Rule," *Washington Post*, January 16, 2011.

51. Jim Rutenberg, "Huntsman Enters Race with Promise of Civility," *New York Times*, June 22, 2011.

52. The killer's fifteen-hundred page "manifesto" reflects the influence of a number of well-known American far-right writers who have expressed similar sentiments. For more, see Scott Shane, "Killings Spotlight Anti-Muslim Thought in U.S.," *New York Times*, July 25, 2011.

53. Letter from J. Richard Cohen to Jonathan Klein, CNN president, July 24, 2009, http://www.splcenter.org/get-informed/news/splc-president-calls-on-cnn-to-remove-lou-dobbs-from-air-cites-newsmans-support-fo. For a brief summary of just some of the most extreme "birther" statements made on the right, as well as other related conspiracy theories, see John H. Richardson, "When Did Americans Turn into a Bunch of Raving Lunatics?" *Esquire*, August 4, 2009, http://www.esquire.com/the-side/richardson-report/obama-birthers-movement-part-one-080409#ixzz0VvOyPtKg; and "What Really Happens When You Demand the President Produce His Birth Certificate," *Esquire*, August 11, 2009, http://www.esquire.com/the-side/richardson-report/obama-birth-certificate-update-081109.

54. Public Policy Polling, *Huckabee Tops GOP Field, 51% Are Birthers and Love Palin*, February 15, 2011, http://www.publicpolicypolling.com/pdf/PPP_Release_US_0215.pdf.

55. David Weigel, "N-Word Sign Dogs Would-Be Tea Party Leader," *Washington Independent*, January 4, 2010, http://washingtonindependent.com/73036/n-word-sign-dogs-would-be-tea-party-leader.

56. S.A. Miller, "Tea Party Head Warns GOP of Fla. Repeat," *Washington Times*, January 6, 2010.

57. Zachary Roth, "Tea Party Fundraising Email Shows Obama as Pimp," January 28, 2010, *TPM Muckraker,* http://tpmmuckraker.talkingpointsmemo.com /2010/01/tea_party_fundraising_email_shows_obama_as_pimp.php.

58. Felicia Cravens, "A Note on Dale Robertson, Self-Described 'Tea Party Leader,'" *Houston Tea Party Society,* January 6, 2010, http://houstontps.org/?p=1050.

59. Photo by Jesse Russell in Madison, WI, http://www.huffingtonpost.com /2009/04/16/10-most-offensive-tea-par_n_187554.html.

60. Jim Spellman, "Tea Party Movement Has Anger, No Dominant Leaders," CNN, September 12, 2009, http://www.cnn.com/2009/POLITICS/09/12/tea.party .express/index.html.

61. Remarks by Tom Tancredo, Tea Party Convention, February 4, 2010. Video (originally from CNN) and transcript available at: http://mediamatters.org /blog/201002050021.

62. Dionne Jr., "What Fuels Roots Rage."

63. Judson Phillips, Press Conference, February 5, 2009, http://mediamatters.org /mmtv/201002050041.

64. William Douglass, "Tea Party Protesters Scream 'Nigger' at Black Congressman," *McClatchy Newspapers,* March 21, 2010, http://www.mcclatchydc.com /2010/03/20/90772/rep-john-lewis-charges-protesters.html#storylink=omni _popular.

65. Greg Sargent, "Rep. Ciro Rodriguez Called 'Wetback' by Anti-Reform Protestor," *The Plum Line* (blog), September 21, 2010, http://theplumline.whorunsgov .com/health-care/rep-ciro-rodriguez-targeted-with-ethnic-slurs/.

66. Quoted in Ashley Fantz, "Obama as Witch Doctor: Racist or Satirical?" CNN, September 18, 2009, http://www.cnn.com/2009/POLITICS/09/17/obama .witchdoctor.teaparty/index.html.

67. William Douglas and Erika Bolstad, "GOP, Tea Party, Try to Distance Themselves from Racial Taunts," *McClatchy Newspapers,* March 21, 2010, http://www .mcclatchydc.com/2010/03/21/90777/gop-tea-party-organizers-decry.html.

68. CNN, "Anderson Cooper 360 Degrees," September 14, 2009. Transcript available at: http://transcripts.cnn.com/TRANSCRIPTS/0909/14/acd.02.html.

69. For a fuller listing (with links) of Williams's offensive and/or racist characterizations of Obama through mid-July 2010, see http://mediamatters.org /research/201007190040.

70. Chris Good, "Mark Williams Steps Aside as Chairman of Tea Party Express," *The Atlantic,* June 18, 2010. http://www.theatlantic.com/politics/archive/2010/06 /mark-williams-steps-aside-as-chairman-of-tea-party-express/58402/.

71. "NAACP Delegates Vote to Repudiate Racist Elements within Tea Party," NAACP, July 13, 2010, http://www.naacp.org/news/entry/naacp-delegates -vote-to-repudiate-racist-elements-within-the-tea-pary/ (sic). See also http://

www.naacp.org/press/entry/naacp-delegates-unanimously-pass-tea-party
-amendment/. E. J. Dionne also wrote a trenchant commentary on the NAACP
resolution and the reaction to it by Sarah Palin and by figures within the Tea
Party movement. See E. J. Dionne, "What the NAACP Is Really Asking on
Racism within the Tea Party," *Washington Post*, July 14, 2010.

72. Peter Nicholas, "'Tea Party' Federation Severs Ties with Commentator over
Lincoln Blog Post," *Los Angeles Times*, July 19, 2010.

73. Sean Cockerham, "Tea Party Express Leader Rejects Message, Not Messenger,"
Anchorage Daily News, July 20, 2010.

74. "Williams Resigns as Tea Party Express Spokesman," CNN, July 23, 2010,
http://politicalticker.blogs.cnn.com/2010/07/23/williams-resigns-as-tea-party
-express-spokesman/?hpt=T2&fbid=XPwAEAOrLSt.

75. Gabriella Schwartz, "Trump Again Questions Obama's Birthplace," CNN,
March 23, 2011, http://politicalticker.blogs.cnn.com/2011/03/23/trump
-again-questions-obamas-birthplace/#more-151367.

76. A collection of photos from the rally that includes a number of birther signs is
available at: http://mediamatters.org/blog/200909170027. The original larger
collection from which these are drawn is available at: http://www.flickr.com
/photos/42406957@N04/.

77. Mark DiCamillo and Mervyn Field, *California Field Poll*, January 26, 2010,
http://www.field.com/fieldpollonline/subscribers/Rls2325.pdf.

78. CBS/New York Times Poll, *Polling the Tea Party*, April 14, 2010, http://www.
nytimes.com/interactive/2010/04/14/us/politics/20100414-tea-party-poll
-graphic.html. See also Charles M. Blow, "A Mighty Pale Tea," *New York Times*,
April 17, 2010.

79. Christopher S. Parker, *2010 Multi-State Survey on Race & Politics*, University
of Washington Institute for the Study of Ethnicity, Race, and Sexuality, http://
depts.washington.edu/uwiser/racepolitics.html.

80. Stephanie Condon, "Steve King Says Obama "Favors the Black Person," *CBS
News*, June 15, 2010. Available at: http://www.cbsnews.com/8301-503544_162
-20007729-503544.html.

81. Quoted in Adam Liptak, "Tea-ing Up the Constitution," *New York Times*, March
14, 2010.

82. Dionne Jr., "What Fuels Roots Rage."

83. Quoted in Ashley Fantz, "Obama as Witch Doctor: Racist or Satirical?"

84. Quoted in Tony Pugh, "There's No Denying Obama's Race Plays a Role in
Protests," *McClatchy Newspapers*, September 18, 2009, http://www.mcclatchydc
.com/J2009/09/18/75694/theres-no-denying-obamas-race.html.

85. Krissah Thompson, "NAACP Backs Report That Ties Racist Groups to Tea
Party," *Washington Post*, October 20, 2010.

86. Cose, *The End of Anger*, 38–39. On race and the Tea Party more broadly, see 37–49.

87. Williamson, Skocpol, and Coggin, "The Tea Party and the Remaking of Republican Conservatism."

88. Williamson et al., "The Tea Party and the Remaking."

89. See John Amato and David Neiwert, *Over the Cliff: How Obama's Election Drove the American Right Insane* (Sausalito, CA: Polipoint Press, 2010), 1–4. Amato and Neiwert described a number of racist hate crimes committed by whites a day or two after Obama's election and inauguration, and in most cases the perpetrators stated directly that they were responding to Obama becoming president and/or targeted visible Obama supporters.

90. Patrick J. Buchanan, "Traditional Americans Are Losing Their Nation," *World Daily Net*, October 20, 2009, http://www.wnd.com/index.php?fa=PAGE.view &pageId=113463#. Buchanan explored these and similar themes in greater detail in *Suicide of a Superpower: Will America Survive to 2025?* (New York: Thomas Dunne Books, 2011). Chapter titles include: "The Death of Christian America" and "The End of White America."

91. Leonard Zeskind, *Blood and Politics: The History of the White Nationalist Movement from the Margins to the Mainstream* (New York: Farrar, Straus and Giroux, 2009), xvi.

92. Louis Beam, "The Second Half of World War II Is Coming," *The Seditionist* 11 (Fall 1991). For more on Beam, see Zeskind, *Blood and Politics*.

93. Zeskind, *Blood and Politics*, 430. On Buchanan in 1992, see 279–93, in 1996, see 429–36, and in 2000, see 494–505.

94. Ibid., 488.

95. Ibid., 542. For more on Zeskind's thoughts on Obama's election and the future of white nationalism, see Mark Potok, "Measuring the Movement: An Expert on White Nationalism Reflects," *Intelligence Report* (Southern Poverty Law Center), no. 135 (Fall 2009), http://www.splcenter.org/intel/intelreport/article .jsp?aid=1073.

96. *Rightwing Extremism: Current Economic and Political Climate Fueling Resurgence in Radicalization and Recruitment* (Washington, DC: Department of Homeland Security, April 7, 2009), http://www.fas.org/irp/eprint/rightwing.pdf.

97. Brian Levin, "Controversial '09 DHS Rightwing Report Author Responds to Critics," *Huffington Post*, July 26, 2011, http://www.huffingtonpost.com/brian -levin-jd/daryl-johnson-dhs-interview_b_909786.html.

98. Hua Hsu, "The End of Whiteness," *The Atlantic*, January/February 2009, http:// www.theatlantic.com/doc/200901/end-of-whiteness#.

99. Ibid.

100. Ibid.

101. Brian Tashman, "CPAC Immigration Panel: Readying the Fight to Save the GOP and White America," *Right Wing Watch* (blog of People for the American Way), February 11, 2011, http://www.rightwingwatch.org/content/cpac -immigration-panel-readying-fight-save-gop-and-white-america. See also Daniel Denvir, "The Republican Party's Nativist Shift," *Guardian* (U.K.), February 12, 2011, *Guardian.co.uk*, http://www.guardian.co.uk/commentisfree/cifamerica /2011/feb/12/usimmigration-republicans.

102. See "White Nationalists Converge on Day Two at CPAC," February 12, 2011, *Imagine 2050*, http://imagine2050.newcomm.org/2011/02/12/white-nationalists -converge-on-day-two-at-cpac/. I spoke to Jill Garvey, the website's managing editor, who explained that the identifications of the white nationalists in the audience were made based on first-hand reporting.

103. For more on William Johnson, see the Southern Poverty Law Center's profile on him: http://www.splcenter.org/get-informed/intelligence-files/profiles/william -daniel-johnson.

104. A copy of the CPAC agenda is available at: http://cpac2012.conservative.org /wp-content/uploads/2012/01/Schedule-Of-Events_Latest.pdf.

105. The SPLC's profile of VDARE.com is available at: http://www.splcenter.org /vdare-foundation.

106. Peter Brimelow, "Immigration, Innumeracy, and the Case for Impeaching Federal Judges," *VDARE.COM*, April 2, 2009, http://www.vdare.com/articles /immigration-innumeracy-and-the-case-for-impeaching-judges.

107. Brian Tashman, "Steve King and White Nationalist CPAC Warn That America's Greatest Threat Is Its Diversity," *Right Wing Watch* (blog of People for the American Way), February 9, 2012, http://www.rightwingwatch.org/content /steve-king-and-white-nationalist-cpac-panel-warn-americas-greatest-threat -its-diversity.

108. Wise, *Between Barack and a Hard Place*, 142. See also 133–34.

109. Ibid., 89.

110. For a fascinating discussion of the idea of the narrative story of black America, and a call for it to include not only the crimes of the past but also progress and hope for the future, see Charles Johnson, "The End of the Black American Narrative," *American Scholar* 77, no. 3 (Summer 2008): 32–42.

111. Wise, *Between Barack and a Hard Place*, 89.

112. Ibid., 100.

113. Barack Obama, interview on American Urban Radio Networks, December 22, 2009. Transcript available at: http://newsone.com/nation/news-one-staff /transcript-obama-reaches-out-to-black-community-through-radio/.

114. Reid's remarks appeared in Mark Halperin and John Heileman, *Game Change: Obama and the Clintons, McCain and Palin, and the Race of a Lifetime* (New York: HarperCollins, 2010), 36.

115. Jeff Zeleny and Joseph Berger, "G.O.P. Chairman Urges Reid to Step Down over Remarks," *New York Times*, January 10, 2010.

116. Jillian Rayfield, "Georgetown Professor: Obama 'Runs from Race Like a Black Man Runs from a Cop (Video)," *Talking Points Memo*, January 11, 2010, http://tpmlivewire.talkingpointsmemo.com/2010/01/georgetown-professor-obama-runs-from-race-like-a-black-man-runs-from-a-cop.php. For more on Dyson and Obama, see Kennedy, *The Persistence of the Color Line*, 260-61.

117. Kirwan Institute, "Editorial: Obama's Speech Addressed Several Categories of People and Communities Except Race and Ethnicity," January 28, 2010, http://www.race-talk.org/?p=2348.

118. Quoted in Cheryl Gay Stolberg, "For Obama, Nuance on Race Invites Questions," *New York Times*, February 9, 2010.

119. Johnny E. Williams et al., "Open Letter to Senator Barack Obama from Sociologists and Scholars Regarding Philadelphia Speech on Racism," March 26, 2008, http://www.zcommunications.org/open-letter-to-senator-barack-obama-from-sociologists-and-scholars-regarding-philadelphia-speech-on-racism-by-authors-many.

120. Wise, *Between Barack and a Hard Place*, 141.

Conclusion

1. The following helped me clarify my own thinking about these connections: Dana Houle, "My Country 'Tis of Thee," *Daily Kos*, January 21, 2009, http://www.dailykos.com/story/2009/1/21/11352/5640/738/686748.

Selected Bibliography

Alba, Richard, and Victor Nee. *Remaking the American Mainstream: Assimilation and Contemporary Immigration.* Cambridge, MA: Harvard University Press, 2003.

Appiah, Kwame Anthony. *The Ethics of Identity.* Princeton, NJ: Princeton University Press, 2005.

Beasley, Vanessa. *You, the People: American National Identity in Presidential Rhetoric.* College Station: Texas A&M University Press, 2004.

Brubaker, Rogers. "The Manichean Myth: Rethinking the Distinction Between 'Civic' and 'Ethnic' Nationalism." In *Nation and National Identity: The European Experience in Perspective,* edited by Hanspeter Kriesi et al., 55–71. Zurich: Ruegger, 1999.

Cose, Ellis. *The End of Anger: A New Generation's Take and Race and Rage.* New York: Ecco, 2011.

Daniel Tatum, Beverly. *"Why Are All the Black Kids Sitting Together in the Cafeteria?": And Other Conversations about Race.* New York: Basic Books, 1997.

Dorsey, Leroy. *We Are All Americans, Pure and Simple: Theodore Roosevelt and the Myth of Americanism.* Tuscaloosa: University of Alabama Press, 2007.

Foner, Eric. *The Story of American Freedom.* New York: W. W. Norton, 1998.

Ford, Richard Thompson. *Racial Culture: A Critique.* Princeton, NJ: Princeton University Press, 2005.

Gerstle, Gary. *American Crucible: Race and Nation in the Twentieth Century.* Princeton, NJ: Princeton University Press, 2002.

Gitlin, Todd. *The Twilight of Common Dreams: Why America Is Wracked by Culture Wars.* New York: Metropolitan Books, 1995.

Glazer, Nathan. *We Are All Multiculturalists Now.* Cambridge, MA: Harvard University Press, 1997.

Harris-Lacewell, Melissa. *Barbershops, Bibles, and BET: Everyday Talk and Black Political Thought.* Princeton, NJ: Princeton University Press, 2004.

Higham, John. *Hanging Together: Unity and Diversity in American Culture.* New Haven, CT: Yale University Press, 2001.

Hollinger, David. *Postethnic America: Beyond Multiculturalism.* 2nd ed. New York: Basic Books, 2006.

Hooker, Juliet. *Race and the Politics of Solidarity.* Oxford: Oxford University Press, 2009.

Ifill, Gwen. *The Breakthrough: Politics and Race in the Age of Obama.* New York: Doubleday, 2009.

Jacoby, Tamar, ed. *Reinventing the Melting Pot: The New Immigrants and What It Means to Be American.* New York: Basic Books, 2004.

Kaufmann, Eric P. *The Rise and Fall of Anglo-America.* Cambridge, MA: Harvard University Press, 2004.

Kazin, Michael and Joseph McCartin, eds. *Americanism: New Perspectives on the History of an Ideal.* Chapel Hill: University of North Carolina Press, 2006.

Kennedy, Randall. *The Persistence of the Color Line: Racial Politics and the Obama Presidency.* New York: Pantheon Books, 2011.

King, Desmond. *The Liberty of Strangers: Making the American Nation.* Oxford: Oxford University Press, 2005.

———. *Making Americans: Immigration, Race, and the Origins of the Diverse Democracy.* Cambridge, MA: Harvard University Press, 2000.

King Jr., Martin Luther. *Where Do We Go from Here: Chaos or Community?* New York: Harper & Row, 1967.

———. *Why We Can't Wait.* New York: Penguin, 2000.

Kloppenberg, James T. *Reading Obama: Dreams, Hope, and the American Political Tradition.* Princeton, NJ: Princeton University Press, 2010.

Lind, Michael. *The Next American Nation: The New Nationalism and the Fourth American Revolution.* New York: Free Press, 1995.

Macedo, Stephen. *Diversity and Distrust: Civic Education in a Multicultural Democracy.* Cambridge, MA: Harvard University Press, 2000.

Nash, Gary B., Charlotte Crabtree, and Ross E. Dunn. *History on Trial: Culture Wars and the Teaching of the Past.* New York: Vintage Books, 2000.

Patterson, Orlando. *The Ordeal of Integration: Progress and Resentment in America's "Racial Crisis."* Washington, DC: Civitas/Counterpoint, 1997.

Pickus, Noah. *True Faith and Allegiance: Immigration and American Civic Nationalism.* Princeton, NJ: Princeton University Press, 2005.

Putnam, Robert. "E Pluribus Unum: Diversity and Community in the Twenty-first Century. The 2006 Johan Skytte Prize Lecture." *Scandinavian Political Studies* 30, no. 2 (2007): 137–74.

Remnick, David. *The Bridge: The Life and Rise of Barack Obama*. New York: Knopf, 2010.

Robinson, Dean E. *Black Nationalism in American Politics and Thought*. Cambridge: Cambridge University Press, 2001.

Roshwald, Aviel. *The Endurance of Nationalism: Ancient Roots and Modern Dilemmas*. Cambridge: Cambridge University Press, 2006.

Salins, Peter D. *Assimilation American Style*. New York: Basic Books, 1997.

Schlesinger, Arthur. *The Disuniting of America: Reflections on a Multicultural Society*. New York: W. W. Norton, 1992.

Smith, Rogers. *Civic Ideals: Conflicting Visions of Citizenship in U.S. History*. New Haven, CT: Yale University Press, 1997.

Stuckey, Mary E. *Defining Americans: The Presidency and National Identity*. Lawrence: University Press of Kansas, 2004.

Tesler, Michael, and David O. Sears. *Obama's Race: The 2008 Election and the Dream of a Post-Racial America*. Chicago: University of Chicago Press, 2010.

Theiss-Morse, Elizabeth. *Who Counts as an American? The Boundaries of National Identity*. Cambridge: Cambridge University Press, 2009.

Touré. *Who's Afraid of Post-Blackness? What It Means to Be Black Now*. New York: Free Press, 2011.

Williamson, Vanessa, Theda Skocpol, and John Coggin. "The Tea Party and the Remaking of Republican Conservatism." *Perspectives on Politics* 9, no. 1 (2011): 25–43.

Zeskind, Leonard. *Blood and Politics: The History of the White Nationalist Movement from the Margins to the Mainstream*. New York: Farrar, Straus and Giroux, 2009.

Index

About the Author

Raised in Smithtown, Long Island, Ian Reifowitz graduated from Brown University with a BA in history and from Georgetown University with a PhD in history. Since 2002, he has taught history at Empire State College of the State University of New York, and in 2009 he received the college's Susan H. Turben Award for Excellence in Scholarship. His opinion pieces and articles on American politics have appeared in *Newsday*, *The New Republic*, *The Post-Star*, *Daily Kos*, and other publications. His first book, *Imagining an Austrian Nation: Joseph Samuel Bloch and the Search for a Supraethnic Austrian Identity, 1846–1919*, was published by East European Monographs and distributed by Columbia University Press in 2003. He has published a number of academic articles in the *Journal of Jewish Identities*, *Nationalities Papers*, and *East European Quarterly*, among other publications, as well as numerous book reviews. He lives in New York City with his wife and two daughters.